EXPERT TESTIMONIALS AND ENDORSEMENTS

There is only one person in the world who could write a book which roams from indigenous traditions to Christianity; from Jainism to Islam while at the same time dismantling the myths and legends that lie behind contemporary economics. In a fascinating journey through the riches that lie just below the surface in all the great faith and cultural traditions, Prof. Shah asks us to listen again to ancient wisdom which has more to say about who we are and why we need to invest in a sustainable world than any UN declaration or economist forecast. Read this and discover hidden treasures of wisdom and see a potentially radically realisable different world.

Martin Palmer, Founder, BBC broadcaster and CEO, Faith Invest and author of twenty books

Professor Atul K Shah is a powerful voice speaking truth to power within the financial sector. He articulates what needs to be said, and done, with courage, integrity, profound wisdom and compelling case studies. His exciting organic theory of ethical finance offers practical solutions to inspire leaders to embrace sustainability ideals and to revolutionise financial leadership. This book fills me with hope that sustainable and ethical business and finance practice will once more transform the world and make it a far better place for everyone.

Dr Lynne Sedgmore CBE, Former Chief Executive of The Centre for Excellence in Leadership UK. Debrett's 500 list 2015

Inclusive and Sustainable Finance is a paradigm-shifting and ground-breaking book that shows how and why global narrow reliance of Western utilitarian economic and finance models and thinking has resulted in excessive greed, corrupt leadership and selfishness that have consistently devastated lives and global economies. By contrast, Professor Atul K. Shah, an eminent global scholar, shows that the world of finance and investment can learn a lot by drawing from diverse and alternative cultures, religions, and economic systems, such as Catholics, Quakers, Parsees, Sikhs, the Yoruba, the Kikuyu, Parsis, Jains, Hindus, Ismailis, Jews, Christians, and many other diverse faiths and communities. Drawing insights directly from finance and investment experts from different fields around the globe, Prof. Shah illustrates and develops a new organic theory of finance which can be taught and shared all over the world, helping society to prepare for a sustainable and inclusive future. This book is ideal for finance and investment students, practitioners, academics, policymakers, and regulators. I fully endorse and recommend it for your reading.

Professor Collins Ntim, Department of Accounting, Southampton Business School, University of Southampton, UK

This is an amazing, timely and hopeful book which directly addresses the awful mess we have made of the world and its citizens. We are threatened with extinction. Climate change is wreaking havoc across the globe. 25,000 human beings including tiny babies and small children die of hunger every day. Our spiritualties have been quashed by empty promises of beauty, luxury goods, social media mythical "perfect lives", and so on. In the face of this, our daily newscasts report on markets; we are informed of stock price indices, interest rates and currency values. Finance is central to our lives. Atul's wonderful book, not only dispels some of the myths surrounding finance, but turns the world upside down by considering ways in which finance might be reconfigured to provide some solutions to the dire mess we are in.

Professor Christine Cooper, University of Edinburgh, Editor – **Critical Perspectives on Accounting**

In the struggle for a compassionate and just world, finance is a powerful tool. As currently practiced, however, it is largely missing in action, its extractivist obsession on profits at all costs devoid of care for the environment and the well-being of workers and communities. Prof. Atul Shah has a response, a blueprint for finance that supports human and planetary flourishing. For me, Atul's is beautiful language about a topic that is usually described with the most self-referential, destructive vocabulary. Do not consider this a call for a "kinder, gentler" finance. Recognize it as a direct and clear treatise on the kind of finance necessary for the future of life itself.

The Rev. Fletcher Harper, Executive Director, GreenFaith www. greenfaith.org

Inclusive and sustainable finance is a vital work in a world dominated by a fundamentally Western and unsustainable financial system. The book centers around interviews with diverse leaders who have set inspiring and encouraging examples in their respective professional fields, paving the way for systematic reform of finance and accounting as we know it.

"A silent duty", Prof. Atul K. Shah calls it, the work that lies ahead of educators and representatives of professional bodies; work that will intertwine culture and principle to create a different world.

A new world in which mathematics, materialism and standardized practice no longer obfuscate ethical deliberation and consideration. A world in which there is room for diverse and organic practices of finance, and for embracing sustainable ideals.

Prof. Atul K. Shah personifies this very message, pioneering an approach that leads to the creation of practices sustaining the world for generations to come.

Margreeth Kloppenburg, educational innovator, author on professional honor and business integrity and chair of the faculty of Ethics, Culture and Behaviour of the Royal Netherlands Institute of Chartered Accountants

Having a rogue, parasitic finance sector that has captured the state is clearly unhealthy for any society. Since this is what we have in Britain and indeed most developed countries, despite the sector's brush with self-extinction in 2008, this is a very timely book. Atul Shah authoritatively outlines the problems that beset modern finance — it has become largely self-serving, short-termist, exploitative, inequality-fuelling and environmentally disastrous — while being divorced from most people's cultural and religious roots. Shah calls for fundamental reform and examines a range of solutions, including the adoption of a number of benign and culturally diverse sustainable finance practices from around the world, some of which have been in existence for centuries, and most of which are hiding in plain sight. He also calls for an urgent overhaul of how finance is taught to ensure the next generation of students are less obsessed with personal self-enrichment and more focused on purpose. Shah is a fierce critic of the current drive for Environmental Social Governance (ESG) and Corporate Social Responsibility (CSR), describing these as "hypocritical spin machines" designed to allow financial firms to carry on with business as usual, while sidestepping the need for fundamental reform. If you are concerned about the future of the planet, and want to ensure the finance sector becomes fairer, more responsible, and more accountable, this is the book for you.

Ian Fraser – Bestselling Finance Author, **Shredded: Inside RBS: The Bank that Broke Britain**

Here is another stunning masterpiece from the celebrated author Prof. Shah. This book is a riveting account of the role of culture and faith in the modern world of finance. For me, it is a page-turner and one of the most fascinating reads of the year. Prof. Shah has brought us an ocean of ideas in the areas of ethical finance and sustainable finance, through narratives and examples which make his writing very accessible. Prof. Shah has taken the bull by the horn and convincingly exposed the profound changes in theory and ontology required to make this shift to a sustainable world.

Professor Dr. Devendra Jain, Flame University, India

Prof. Shah addresses one of the meta-stories of neoliberalism: how unfettered financialised rent-seeking is destroying both the global economy and our planet. Another model of finance is required which places community, sustainable production, and ethical behaviour ahead of all other considerations. Atul makes an eloquent contribution to this crucial debate by drawing upon timeless wisdom traditions, so spread the word.

John Christensen, Founder, Tax Justice Network

Prof. Atul Shah's highly anticipated new work is akin to a Festschrift dedicated to all those individuals worldwide who have taken to heart Immanuel Kant's 1795 treatise of *Perpetual Peace*, in which a monumental yearning for commercial non-violence gained incisive focus by equating biocultural values with the potential for fair trade and equitable, intergenerational economics. Prof. Shah's *Inclusive and Sustainable Finance* underscores the critical hour for recognizing disparity, engendering co-symbiotic mechanisms for lifting nearly 3 billion of our fellow citizens out of financial marginalization, and 800 million, mostly young people, back from the brink of hunger – through juridical choices that begin with every consumer, and within every boardroom. I have known Prof. Shah for nearly three decades and have had the privilege of seeing the evolution of his own enlightened thought as it tackled the values in finance necessary to redeem what has, admittedly, been a history – a human history – of greed, waste, and predatory marketplace techniques of exploitation. He has examined accounting denominated standards, and the ill-equipped lexicon of loss and gain throughout human cultures and arrived upon a portal into an ecological and ethical realm.

Throughout Prof. Shah's "diverse ethics" orientation to capital, like John Ruskin, and Mahatma Gandhi – who himself was so taken with Ruskin's call to alleviate poverty through a back-to-basics, locally sustainable approach – Shah has brought tremendous wisdom and weight to bear upon the intrinsically ecological nature of exchange. To demonstrate with clear prose and pragmatic idealism how it works, what it is, and what we can do, each of us, to contribute to a planet that is, by every forensic metric, hemorrhaging in this, the Anthropocene, or sixth extinction spasm in the annals of biology. These are the enormous stakes involved in Professor Shah's extraordinary new book. It should be inculcated into the agendas of every nation, territory, community, university and hamlet; enlivening all those discussions and negotiations that will either serve this and future generations, or condemn us all, and the biosphere upon which we all depend for our breath, our water, our sanity.

I commend Atul for a brilliant new in-depth overview of what is clearly one of the key tools – finance and ecological accountability – for saving the earth. It will add clarity and loft to an existing movement which urgently requires this precise kind of cross-disciplinary approach to every form of reciprocity. Otherwise, we shall all wake up and discover, as Henry David Thoreau once said, in words to the effect: I spent four years at college studying economics only to learn that by doing so I had plunged my parents into irretrievable debt.

Dr. Michael Charles Tobias, Ecologist, and author of over 50 pioneering books including **Environmental Meditation** *and* **Life Force: The World of Jainism,** *President, Dancing Star Foundation*

It's time for conversations about economics, politics and public life which incorporate kindness and altruism to be put into the core analysis. Prof. Shah is an innovator who completely shifts the terms of our debates.

Professor Corinne Fowler, University of Leicester, Bestselling author of **Green Unpleasant Land: Creative Responses to Rural England's Colonial Connections**

Dr Atul Shah has penned a brilliant critique of the culture of finance capitalism and its devastating effects on societies and peoples' lives. More than this, he has mined the rich resources, traditions, wisdom, and ethics of multiple faith communities from across the world and brought them back to life. His aim is ambitious, and necessary: nothing less than to force the powers that be to rethink their ideas, culture, practices, and join the effort 'to transform behaviour and heal the planet...' by placing 'harmonious living communities at the heart of sustainable society.' A must-read book based on a lifetime's thought and intellectual effort.

Professor Inderjeet Parmar FAcSS, Political Economist, City, University of London

Atul tackles taboo topics that interact with money and finance: race, community, culture, ethics, faith and even death. It is a finance book without any equations or numbers which is truly rare. By documenting discussions with diverse leaders, he confronts the classical view that money and finance are neutral, and instead highlights the economic power imbalances that economics creates. This book exposes the deep cracks and fissures in existing finance science and teaching. As inclusivity and the environment come to the fore, more educators should follow his example and teaching.

Professor Mark B. Shackleton, Professor of Finance, University of Lancaster

Inclusive and Sustainable Finance offers insights rarely uttered by those in the accountancy profession. The book turns a leaf beyond classical economic aspirations opening alternative possibilities for finance. It embeds the field into notions of ethical leadership drawing on the experiences of individuals who foreground traditions of community spirit. The book above all calls for change that prioritises human and social growth above narrow financial purpose. It will provide balance to any finance professional's book collection.

Professor Alnoor Bhimani, London School of Economics

Echoing the poignant indignity of Swedish teenager Greta Thunberg's scorching 2019 address to the United Nations, Professor Atul Shah demands a radical rethinking of arid and abstract accounting and finance practices that are causing unnecessary and unconscionable poverty, discrimination, death, and environmental degradation on a grand scale. Shah's solution: listen to diverse voices who will speak the truth on their own terms. Shah brings these voices to life through a thought-provoking series of interviews and case studies of businesses across the globe that flourish through an embrace of culture, morality, and tradition. We ignore these voices at our own peril.

Professor Daniel T. Ostas, JD, PhD, Chair of Business Ethics, University of Oklahoma

As the cracks in financial expertise are widening, Atul Shah is showing us a richer tradition of financial practice which has been hiding in plain sight. The decolonisation of finance is already here, and we better pay attention.

Professor Hendrik Vollmer, Warwick Business School, UK

Just like the re-discovery of Eastern meditation techniques and yoga have been game changing for the mental wellbeing of many worldwide, Prof. Shah's contribution to rediscovering the wisdom inherent in the teachings of various timeless belief systems can be positive for the wellbeing of Western finance. We just need to be prepared to engage and listen with an open heart and mind.

Amit Lodha, Chief Investment Officer, Artian & Ex Global Fund Manager – Fidelity International

There's no question that finance sectors are broken and are disconnected from the human suffering they can cause, and greed is central to that. It's refreshing therefore to read about the wisdoms and traditions that pull finance back towards serving all people, economies and nature in healthy ways. It is urgently necessary, and this timely book illustrates hopeful ways forward on reclaiming this space which for so long has been lacking the respect and compassion that is essential for nourishing all life on earth.

Naomi Fowler, Tax Justice Network and Taxcast

Professor Atul Shah's latest book continues his trenchant criticism of the financial establishment. He implores us to reimagine finance by drawing inspiration from global faiths and wisdom traditions. I genuinely believe there is a lot for us to learn from these traditions and welcome the call for a diverse multifaceted ethical foundation to ground a new envisioning of finance.

Dr. Shamil Chandaria, OBE, Finance Scholar and Serial Innovator

An outstanding must-read for everyone with an interest in quality, insightful, high value perceptive writing on finance, leadership and ethics and sustainability – i.e., all of us. Culture is central to Finance and Atul has not only proven this but also shown how it can be made sustainable rather than extractive. Professor Shah is a world authority in the field and has undertaken substantial first hand research as well as pioneering interviews and analysis into a topic wrought with muddled views. This book will help you clarify your own actions in what needs to be done for your organisation.

Alpesh Patel OBE, Global Finance Pioneer, Government Advisor and Investor

INCLUSIVE AND SUSTAINABLE FINANCE

Instead of being a means to an end, finance has become an end in itself and a master of economic actions and priorities. The role of ethics, culture and faith has been diminished by neoliberalism over the last forty years, such that we are living through a profound moral crisis, rising inequality and plutocracy. This practice is destroying the social and trust capital that already exists and is in need of replenishing. This pioneering book draws upon diverse wisdom traditions and their current living business practices to show that not only is another world possible, but it is actually hiding in plain sight.

The author argues that our obsession with technocratic economic science has disabled us from exposing the organic and culturally diverse practices of finance. The climate and inequality crises demand new institutional and cultural solutions to transform behaviour and heal the planet. Through real-life examples and case studies, this book illustrates and develops a new organic theory of finance which can be taught and shared all over the world, helping society to prepare for a sustainable and inclusive future. It provides valuable empowerment to experts and professionals from different cultures and traditions to write about their own finance practices and in turn encourage their students and communities to embrace sustainability ideals.

There is a global audience for this book, given its multicultural outlook and the diversity of narratives and case studies, from entrepreneurs to MBA students and leaders in accounting and finance. It also has huge relevance for policymakers and educators keen on embracing sustainable finance in their curriculum.

Atul K. Shah is a Professor (PhD LSE) and Fellow of the Institute of Chartered Accountants in England and Wales and is an award-winning writer and broadcaster. He has taught at the London School of Economics, University of Bristol, University of Maryland, City, University of London, Hult International Business School, Essex University, University of Suffolk and University of Kent.

Contemporary Issues in Finance

For more information about this series, please visit www.routledge.com/
Contemporary-Issues-in-Finance/book-series/CONTEMPFIN

Dear Collins,

INCLUSIVE AND SUSTAINABLE FINANCE

Leadership, Ethics and Culture

Thanks for such a generous testimonial

Atul K. Shah

Routledge
Taylor & Francis Group
LONDON AND NEW YORK

Cover image: DragonTiger/Getty Images

First published 2023
by Routledge
4 Park Square, Milton Park, Abingdon, Oxon OX14 4RN

and by Routledge
605 Third Avenue, New York, NY 10158

Routledge is an imprint of the Taylor & Francis Group, an informa business

© 2023 Atul K. Shah

Library of Congress Cataloging-in-Publication Data
Names: Shah, Atul K., 1973- author.
Title: Inclusive and sustainable finance : leadership, ethics and culture / Atul K. Shah.
Description: Abingdon, Oxon ; New York, NY : Routledge, 2023. | Series: Contemporary issues in finance | Includes bibliographical references and index.
Identifiers: LCCN 2022020805 (print) | LCCN 2022020806 (ebook) | ISBN 9780367759421 (hbk) | ISBN 9780367759407 (pbk) | ISBN 9781003164746 (ebk)
Subjects: LCSH: Finance--Environmental aspects. | Finance--Moral and ethical aspects. | Finance--Social aspects. | Sustainability.
Classification: LCC HG101 .S38 2023 (print) | LCC HG101 (ebook) | DDC 332--dc23/eng/20220718
LC record available at https://lccn.loc.gov/2022020805
LC ebook record available at https://lccn.loc.gov/2022020806

ISBN: 978-0-367-75942-1 (hbk)
ISBN: 978-0-367-75940-7 (pbk)
ISBN: 978-1-003-16474-6 (ebk)

DOI: 10.4324/9781003164746

Typeset in Bembo
by KnowledgeWorks Global Ltd.

Printed in the UK by Severn, Gloucester on responsibly sourced paper

This book is dedicated to my father, Keshavji Rupshi Shah, who overcame polio to become a pioneering community leader who bred several generations of leaders and visionaries through his selfless service and courageous dedication. He spread sustainable wisdom through lived example.

CONTENTS

AUTHOR BIOGRAPHY

Professor Atul K. Shah is a Fellow of the Institute of Chartered Accountants in England and Wales. He has a PhD from the London School of Economics and is the author of *Jainism and Ethical Finance: A Timeless Business Model* (with Aidan Rankin, Routledge, 2017); *The Politics of Financial Risk, Audit and Regulation: A Case Study of HBOS* (Routledge, 2018); *Reinventing Accounting and Finance Education: For a Caring, Inclusive and Sustainable Planet* (Routledge, 2018); *Celebrating Diversity: How to Enjoy, Respect and Benefit from Great Coloured Britain* (Kevin Mayhew, 2007); and *Boardroom Diversity – The Opportunity* (Mazars, 2011). Atul is passionate about Business Ethics, Education Reform and Diversity. He has a PhD from the London School of Economics. Professor Shah has published a number of papers in international academic journals such as *Accounting, Organisations and Society*; *Accounting, Auditing and Accountability Journal*; *European Accounting Review*; *Journal of Financial Regulation and Compliance*; *British Accounting Review*; and *Business Ethics: A European Review*. Between 1995 and 1998, he published a series of papers predicting the global financial crisis, focusing on derivatives, systemic risk and regulatory arbitrage. Professor Shah has taught at the London School of Economics, University of Bristol, University of Maryland, Hult International Business School, Essex University, University of Suffolk and University of Kent. He has broadcast experience, with credits including BBC Radio 4, BBC World Service, Channel 4, Five Live, BBC Radio 2, Guardian and BBC Asian Network. Professor Shah also writes and comments for the *Financial Times*. In 2010, Professor Shah embarked on a historic 1500-mile Masala Tour of Britain, to showcase the depth and breadth of the diversity in Britain and help the country improve its cultural intelligence – this was featured in *The Guardian*. The tour was also widely covered on BBC Radio nationally. He is a top Business Ethics writer for *The Conversation*. His research on global accounting won the Best Paper award in 2019. His lectures, student field trips, interviews and public speaking consistently receive positive feedback.

Personal website and blog – www.atulkshah.co.uk

Twitter @atulkshah

LinkedIn Professor Atul Keshavji Shah; Email: diverseethics@gmail.com

For follow-up discussion of this book, please visit the above website – here is the QR code:

PREFACE

Finance today is very powerful and broken at the same time. It has become a chainsaw on nature and a promoter of inequality. Its core institutions, the financial markets, financial institutions and multinational corporations, have become bloated and removed from any 'feeling' of the pain and injury they are causing to both society and the environment. Finance leaders have become robotised technocrats, who imbibe the culture of selfishness, materialism and greed as the only right way to live. The academy, through its theories and research bibles, has promoted this culture aggressively as an 'objective' universal science, whilst at the same time destroying human diversity and environmental bio-diversity. The 2008 Global Financial Crash was an example of extreme hubris, but this has grown since, as the bad culture was bailed out and continued to be encouraged intellectually.

This book offers an alternative way of theorising and practising finance leadership. It looks to the past, times when money did not flood society but was instead put in its place. In developing a sustainable finance, it looks at traditions and communities which have truly sustained themselves through thick and thin. The book does not pretend to be suddenly concerned about equality and climate change, but instead draws from the depth of past wisdom traditions that placed morality at the front and centre of life and purpose. It also shows that tacit skills, gained from tradition and lived experience and upbringing, are highly relevant to sustainable finance, even when they are completely ignored in the modern professionalised business school.

Reading the book, you will discover the batons of finance cultures, relayed over generations through narratives and true stories of leadership. Furthermore, there are examples of informal communities who act as clusters of social, trust and relationship capital and become innovation hubs for sustainable and responsible finance. Here, finance is not broken but an instrument for spreading equality and respecting the richness of nature and its vast bio-diversity. Humility among leaders is the norm rather than the exception. Success in finance often heightens responsibility and accountability rather than arrogance and recklessness. The personal experience of years of international teaching and research, and living as a bridge between the east and the west, has informed the analysis presented in this book. Belonging to a living community has really helped shape the thinking and story-telling, helping to make the research understandable and accessible.

The primary contribution of this book is in its encouragement of professionals and intellectuals from different cultures and traditions to liberate from the baggage of modern finance and write their own local narratives within the cultural contexts with which they are familiar. Culture has been severed from contemporary finance, and instead a selfish, materialist and expropriative mono-culture has been imposed in the name of science. Whilst the secular academy treats all religions as dogma, the reality is that faith and belief are very diverse and often deeply entwined with culture and living practices. This ignorance and misrepresentation of faith is fundamentally unsustainable. All over the world, there are outstanding examples of different, more grounded and rooted finance practices, where corporate social responsibility is not a spin factory, but a silent duty. These are the cultures and principles which will help shape a more ethical and moral finance, which ought to ripple out to the wider world. Professional bodies have a lot to learn from this book in terms of reforming their curricula to relate more to the living cultures and beliefs of their students and embrace the rich diversity of contexts. Their current technical approaches to ethics education are failing and will make things worse – unless trainees are forced to be reflexive and encouraged to bring their own souls, cultures and values into the narrative. Professional bodies have a duty to cultivate a public and environmental conscience among the leaders they certify. At present, they are doing the opposite.

The germination of this book has taken four decades and is born out of courage, risk, self-discipline and perseverance. I would like to encourage diverse readers to take such risks and help improve finance which has become morally bankrupt. My journey started with the personal experience of cultural conflict in the professional workplace, and slowly became sharpened as I went into teaching and then research in accounting and finance. Still, confidence was low, the canvas was white and, of course, I had to 'fit in' and make every effort to do so. Worse was the total absence of non-white culture and faith from the finance syllabus and curriculum. Still I persevered and experienced setbacks and rejections. People kept asking about my culture – how do you spell the word 'Jain'? It turns out to be one of the world's most profound sustainable finance traditions, with a philosophical depth and a pioneering global diaspora, living by such pristine values even in modernity.

Writing and researching was an uphill task, but something inside kept reminding me that this is a pioneering culture of compassion for all life. It has a living community of kindred spirits who are open-minded, tolerant and very successful and agile globally. Respect for diverse wisdoms and beliefs is in-grained in the tradition (*anekant*). But then, how can I articulate this to a strongly secular academy? And the techniques and calculations had no space for culture, so how was I going to open that space, especially in finance, which had severed culture altogether? And if I were to write an academic paper, would the editors understand my cultural nuances? The research book or monograph became my refuge, and I wrote (with Aidan Rankin) my first book for Routledge, *Jainism and Ethical Finance: A Timeless Business Model*. It took thirty years to germinate and develop the confidence to write about my own culture in this way. This research was against the tide, as promotion depended on refereed journal articles in branded global academic journals. My next book, *Reinventing Accounting and Finance Education: For a Caring, Inclusive and Sustainable Planet*, has also helped germinate the present thesis.

Fortunately, I persevered and discovered the inner confidence. Also, more recently, the Black Lives Matter movement and the Climate Crisis have given me additional impetus. We should be allowed to speak our own truths in our own languages. This book is the result of all that reading, thinking, experimentation and reflection. And I am not afraid to admit that I am proud of it. I am very grateful to all my pioneering interviewees for their time and cooperation and to my publishers, especially Kristina Abbotts, who has been a rock of support for my work. For her, diversity is to be encouraged and nurtured, rather than ignored or diminished. Christiana Mandizha was very helpful at the design stage. Lynne Sedgmore CBE and my mentor Jim Harding have been extremely supportive of my struggles to establish my professional career and were there for me throughout my setbacks. One voice that I kept hearing as I wrote this was that of my mentor and political economist, Professor Lord Prem Sikka, who has always been encouraging of my research and writings. The errors and mistakes are all mine. I hope you enjoy the journey of reading, as much as I enjoyed the journey of writing. More importantly, I hope it gives you the courage to share your own cultural finance story, or research and write your own experiences and bring them to your students in the classroom. Even if we have to write in the English language, we no longer need to fear a white canvas – it has in history been a cause of great pain and suffering. Everyone needs different wisdoms for a sustainable world, even when they don't agree with your analysis. Go forth, write, teach and share your stories of a caring and charitable finance which is hidden in plain sight.

Professor Atul K. Shah,
London, July 2022

BIOGRAPHIES OF INTERVIEWEES

I would like to thank these senior leaders for sharing their wisdom and experience with me to help shape and mould the analysis presented in this book. I am truly grateful for their vast experiential wisdom and honest cooperation. Their true stories were much deeper than those reported in the book, and any errors are my own responsibility.

Amish Tripathi is the Minister of Culture in the Indian High Commission in the UK. He is also a former finance professional and is a bestselling author on Indian culture and wisdom and an expert on Dharma and Indian tradition.

Anant M P Shah is a co-founder of Meghraj Bank in the UK, one of the first ethnic minority-owned banks with a significant reputation for relationship finance, helping start-up businesses grow and flourish when such finance was denied elsewhere by mainstream banks.

Andrew Pike was Manager of Handelsbanken in Ipswich, with 40 years of experience in relationship banking, and shares this to show how when banks make culture central to their operations, their business grows naturally through word of mouth.

Andrew Rhodes is a founding partner of Sobell Rhodes, an award-winning, medium-sized Jewish accounting firm in London. He trains similar firms in sustainable leadership and management, helping to place culture and longer term relationships at the centre of accounting and advisory work for family businesses.

Deepak Shah is co-founder (with Mukesh Shah) of Strategic Consulting, headquartered in Nairobi, Kenya. They provide governance and pioneering inter-generational advice to historic and diverse family businesses all over Africa, helping them manage their culture, professionalism and transition in a sustainable way.

Dominic Burke is an investment manager. He has worked for several fund management companies, focusing on the social and environmental impacts of businesses, as well as corporate governance and ethics. He currently manages a mission-driven philanthropic endowment.

Abhay Firodia is an industrialist based in India, and a pioneer of transport vehicle manufacturing. His father invented the auto-rickshaw. He is a highly respected leader and places ethics, purpose and responsibility at the centre of business enterprise. He explains that industry and investment are needed to provide important social and public services.

Eynour Boutia is an international banker with decades of experience in asset trading and structured finance, principally with J P Morgan. He is an active member of the Ismaili community, whose Imam is the Aga Khan, and recently co-founded a private bank in France.

Francine McKenna is an investigative journalist, Wharton Professor and blogger based in North America, with a distinguished record of exposing auditing and governance misdemeanours and the breakdown in corporate and professional ethics. She is critical of the tick-box culture of compliance in large institutions, which often leads to massive corporate failures.

Janette Rutterford is an emeritus Professor of Finance, with a distinguished record in research and education, pioneering financial literacy through her research at the Open University. She also brings a rare historical context to modern corporate finance, exposing flawed assumptions and analyses.

Jasvant Modi is a medical doctor, a businessman, a community leader and visionary, a financial investor and an active philanthropist living and practising in California, USA. He has donated millions of dollars to universities all over North America.

John Christensen is the founder of the global Tax Justice Network, one of the world's most pioneering think tanks on tax and inequality. The impact of his work has transformed the global debate and policy on tax avoidance and evasion by multinational corporations.

Lord Andrew Phillips is the former Chancellor of Essex University and BBC Radio 2's Legal Eagle, with a regular audience of millions. Lord Phillips is a solicitor who is passionate about the breakdown in ethical finance, and the need for local businesses and communities, and professionals with conscience and public interest to speak truth to power.

Lord Prem Sikka is a world-famous academic in accounting, having conducted pioneering research on professional fraud and hubris at the Big 4 global firms, which has proved to be prescient with time. He continues to ask difficult questions to elites and law-makers who have shaped a system of corruption and inequality and offers practical solutions to embrace equality and social justice.

Nitin Mehta is a businessman and entrepreneur and the founder of Sheargold, a global supply chain enterprise. Nitin shares his experience of being a customer of banks, and the difference relationship finance can make to sustainable growth.

Satish Kanabar is a Ugandan Asian refugee who rose to become a Corporate Director with Barclays Bank and, along the way, helped support a large variety of growing businesses through charismatic relationship building, cultural sensitivity and inclusion. He also introduced pioneering training in cultural diversity and community social capital to bank professionals.

Subhash Thakrar is a Chartered Accountant, Business Guru and Entrepreneur, with a track record of pioneering leadership in community and enterprise. He has travelled with the UK Prime Minister on various overseas trade missions.

Vallabh Bhansali is co-founder of one of India's most prestigious investment banks, Enam Securities, which has given birth to many world-famous Indian businesses (like Infosys). It is also one of the very few premier investment banks without a blemish on their financial record in the last forty years, something very unusual given the greed and hubris prevailing today.

1

MORALITY

In 2019, fifteen-year-old Greta Thunberg was given the rare opportunity to address the United Nations General Assembly in New York[1]. This is how she started her speech:

> This is all wrong. I shouldn't be up here. I should be back in school on the other side of the ocean. Yet you all come to us young people for hope. How dare you!
>
> You have stolen my dreams and my childhood with your empty words. And yet I'm one of the lucky ones. People are suffering. People are dying. Entire ecosystems are collapsing. We are in the beginning of a mass extinction, and all you can talk about is money and fairy tales of eternal economic growth. How dare you!

Finance science and education have played a major role in our current crises, and to reverse the gloom, we need to address and reform the core beliefs, customs, institutions and professional practices. The needs and aspirations of future generations must be protected. Nothing less will do. There is no complacency behind intellectual brands, publications and qualifications – we must get real about the challenge ahead. Experts who have been a part of the problem cannot change their colours overnight and are still holding on to their power. Thinking and techniques need to change radically. Not only have humans destroyed thousands of species, but we have also attacked our own cultures and traditions, in the names of empire and science. Racism has been deeply woven into our fabric of academic knowledge, disguised by the quest for objectivity. We need a rethink of the very paradigm of finance knowledge and its planetary responsibility. To help us do this, cultures and wisdom traditions which have a history of respect for nature and living beings, become a priceless resource of hope and transformation.

DOI: 10.4324/9781003164746-1

Let's remind ourselves about the facts[2]. According to Oxfam, in 2017 ten families controlled 50% of the world's wealth. The wealth of the world's ten richest men has doubled in two years since the pandemic began. The UK has among the highest inequality in Europe, despite its public education, public health and welfare state provisions, higher than many Eastern European countries. Oxfam estimates that inequality kills 21,000 people every day in the world – they speak of '*economic violence*' conducted by policies and practices. Could bankers and accountants be 'violent' in their professional practices or institutional cultures? Humans have only been on this planet for 300,000 years compared to the 4.5 billion years it has been in existence – a small dot in history, but a vast epoch of aggression and greed. In just 200 years, our population has increased to 7.9 billion – eight times. As a result, the species extinction we have caused is 1000 times faster than if humans were not on this planet. In that time, there has been a 67% decline in wild animal species on the planet. The resulting loss of biodiversity has led to what is called the sixth mass extinction on planet earth. We humans are committing planetary suicide.

Finance, instead of being a source of equality and sustainable growth, has become a cause of the environmental devastation, social chaos and economic inequality[3]. The disciplines and premiere institutions of accounting and finance are undergoing a crisis of legitimacy[4]. Our knowledge and beliefs are central to the current Anthropocene[5] – they have helped man to dominate nature, and in the process brought the whole irreversible downfall of the planet and its ecosystem. As an academic and cultural expert in these disciplines, I have taken on the bold challenge of overhauling the core foundational assumptions and thinking in this book. This thinking has had an adverse impact on culture and practice, with serious consequences for both society and nature. There is a need for a new ecologically sustainable leadership in the knowledge and teaching of these highly influential professions. This book charts a case for making culture, conscience, compassion and virtues central to this reform. Leaders have a central role in this transformation, so there is a strong focus on sustainable leadership. Despite there being thousands of books on business leadership, and on accounting and finance science, there is total silence on what good and fair accounting and finance **leadership** looks and feels like. All we know from the scandals at Enron or Lehman Brothers or RBS and HBOS is what BAD finance leadership looks like. In fact, the fields have become so utilitarian and instrumental that even the question of leadership and its power and influence is not discussed by the experts. This book will show that there are many examples of good and culturally diverse practices hiding in plain sight. The academy and the professions have been blind to these sustainable practices which have lasted many generations in different cultures and communities all over the planet. If you are concerned about the planet and want to make finance responsible, humble, fair and accountable, then this book will help you in this journey. It will also point to new directions for research which make the professions more responsible, ethical and truly accountable.

Humanity is at crossroads and has no other choice but to reform its thinking and behaviour. The true stories and examples cited in this book will really inspire you and encourage the reader that a different world is possible. There is ample evidence that leadership in finance matters. The largest fund manager in the world, Blackrock, was only born in 1988, founded by Larry Fink who is still its Chairman and CEO. Dick Fuld was both Chairman and CEO at Lehman Brothers for fourteen years and led it to its collapse, so did Fred Goodwin after eight years at RBS Bank. HBOS Bank, which faced one of the largest ever bankruptcies in British history[6], was founded by Sir James Crosby and then led by Andy Hornby destroying its 350-year-old collective history within seven years. Starling Bank in the UK was founded six years ago by Anne Boden and is now one of the top challenger fintech banks in the UK. Goldman Sachs was headed by Lloyd Blankfein (both Chairman and CEO) for twelve critical years (2006–2018). Lord Colin Sharman at KPMG developed a 2020 vision for the firm and transformed it from an audit practice to a giant multi-disciplinary firm in the 1990s, with a strong commercial focus – he became Chairman of KPMG International in 1997. Niche and highly reputed and ethical Indian investment bank Enam Securities was founded and led by Vallabh Bhansali and Nemish Shah for thirty-five years. It is therefore strange that the subject of leadership is not discussed in the finance curriculum or in finance journals, given its huge significance. In order to moralise finance, we need to first spend time on how we got here and understand the profound challenges of reshaping the science and curriculum. Given the significant power of intellectual ideas and theories in shaping our education and institutions, it is critical that we address this history and understand it, before we can transform it.

COLONISATION AND STANDARDISATION OF THE CURRICULUM

The business curriculum has been colonised by western world views and theories, with secular neo-liberal and materialist economics at its root[7]. Globalisation and standardisation have directly attacked the real diversity of cultures, beliefs and institutions across the planet. Complex mathematics and technical standards and terminology have served to hide profound unethical assumptions and priorities which have led us to 'eco-cide'[8] – planetary demolition by large multi-national corporations and their shareholder capitalism. International accounting standards are imposed on the world as if every country, business practice, institutional environment and culture are the same. In truth, they have been designed to serve the financial interests of elites and large corporate stakeholders[9]. The MBA, the most sought-after academic programme in recent human history, has sought to undermine ethics altogether and leave students confused about the personal beliefs and duty in professional business enterprise[10]. Professional bodies of accountants and bankers and the Big 4 global accounting firms are doing a roving trade all over the world, training and certifying experts thereby giving them technocratic power and influence. Examples like the AICPA, the CFA, the ICAEW and ACCA and the Institute of Bankers colonise a technical, acultural and pragmatic world of skills and jargon which is increasingly shown to be deeply flawed and part of the problem rather than the solution[11]. Globalisation and standardisation have exacerbated the export of these *fictional sciences* and ideologies, indoctrinating young people from all over the world.

The damage inflicted by rogue finance and accounting institutions, markets and leaders and practitioners is in the trillions and growing[12]. Over the last four decades, processes of financialisation have demonstrated that, compared to the overall economy, the relative earnings of financial institutions have grown consistently more than the real economy[13]. This means that the finance industry, which is supposed to serve business investment and real production, has instead become more dominant and extractive. Blue chip global banks and financial institutions like Goldman Sachs, J P Morgan Chase, HSBC, RBS or the Big 4 accounting firms KPMG, EY, PWC and Deloitte are rarely out of the scandal press[14]. Professionals of finance use their institutions to act in their own self-interest, rather than improving the performance of the wider economy. Even Nobel laureates like Joseph Stiglitz admit that the science of economics is dangerously broken and needs fixing[15]. Animals, plants and nature have been treated as a resource or externality, not worthy of care or protection simply because they are intrinsic to nature.

At root is a deeper scientific and cultural malaise which has led us to a very partial and broken technocratic way of thinking and practising finance. The globalisation and standardisation of accounting and finance teaching and professional training have meant that diversity and culture are deliberately and actively suppressed by the curricula[16]. Human cultural and religious diversity, and its vast influence on communities all over the world[17], is simply ignored by economists and business scholars. A recent literature review of the emerging field of 'Cultural Finance'[18] found that most of the papers are still biased by neo-liberal views of the world and do not deviate from secularism and bounded rationality in financial decision-making.

The same applies to the Nobel Prize winning field of 'Behavioural Finance'[19], which is dedicated to individual decision-making, disregarding deviations from a focus on returns or even cultural or social influences on investment decision making. In stark contrast, the approach adopted in this book is based on faith, tradition and community practices in finance, which are by nature qualitative and highly influential in transforming local institutions and practices. Most finance scholars are trained in quantitative research, so their approach is to use the tools they have to examine culture, which misses the nuances of history, belief and diversity at the very time when we need to understand these. As it's often said, to a hammer, everything looks like a nail. In contrast, the research method adopted in this book is qualitative and ethnographic, allowing the interviewees to speak their own truths on their own terms. The cultural root for millions and even billions of people in the world is morality, fairness and interdependence. They come from a variety of languages and customs, so can never be classified or structured into a generic model, and instead, need to be understood from within their contexts. Fundamentally, both accounting and finance are cultural and social practices, created by humans for humans[20]. Neo-liberalism has suppressed the possibility for these wisdom traditions to teach us about sustainable finance precisely when we urgently need time-tested solutions.

The impression given is that this is irrelevant to good finance practice, when this book will show that the opposite is true. Morality and sustainable practices emerge when we engage with diversity and difference, rather than suppress them. The abstraction that is common in both accounting and finance practice is deeply misleading, and even the modern fashion of ethics education avoids engaging with the deeper systemic and political structures which create inequalities and social and environmental damage in the first place[21]. It personalises ethics, when often it is globalisation or market triumphalism which is the core driver of corporate greed. What is urgently needed is a holistic approach to ethics education where students are empowered to be self-critical and also understand the structural and political assumptions which promote certain 'truths' through accounting.

At the same time, given the profound power of the discipline, it has given experts exaggerated influence to do damage. This is evidenced by four decades of financialisation – the rise of excessive returns for accountants and financiers in comparison to real returns from production or manufacturing[22]. The findings in this book have been developed from three decades of teaching and scholarship in these disciplines, and a holistic reflexivity on the causes of the planetary crisis. The author has lived and worked in three different continents, and originates from a fourth, giving him not just education, but lived experience of the richness of diverse thinking and practices. Belonging to one of the oldest living cultures on the planet, the Jain tradition, the author brings a very different and 'deeply ethical' and responsible perspective to the analysis, which is rare. This book builds on his earlier work on 'Jainism and Ethical Finance' (Shah and Rankin, 2017) and 'Reinventing Accounting and Finance Education' (Shah, 2018b) and four decades of international teaching and research experience. A deep culture of secularism and American individualism and materialism has become the fundamental basis for the modern 'science' of accounting and finance.

MONO-THEISM IN SCIENCE

Paradoxically, the social sciences have become increasingly universalist in their orientation, trying to find ONE theory of finance or asset pricing that would apply equally anywhere in the world[23]. At the same time, they have been critiquing the monotheism of the Abrahamic faiths! The biodiversity and human cultural diversity of the planet are deliberately denied by the way in which these sciences are founded and framed. Experts have shown that the economic enlightenment project has failed – there are many different capitalisms on the planet, and the attack on culture has led to chaos and rejection[24]. In fact, Gray (1998) calls modern capitalism 'delusional' because of its market fundamentalism and mono-cultural arrogance. The Anthropocene has revealed the profound fallacies of this extractive way of thinking about our planet – this book will show that western economic theories and institutions have been a core reason behind human violence and attack on other species and our air, soil and water systems. Hence in challenging and critiquing finance, we need to be very careful to separate when we are challenging the surface symptoms and when the core 'ontology' and belief system. Beliefs about 'market triumphalism' and perfectly competitive free markets continue to shape top academic journals and teaching in these fields, even when they have been proven to be deeply flawed.[25] We also need to acknowledge that people trained in technical analysis will often be unable to see the fallacies of their foundational assumptions about reality. In the process, they can and often do much more harm than good, maybe even unwittingly.

In 2016, the 'Journal of Corporate Finance' published a special issue on culture and finance[26], with a bold ambition of trying to integrate the two themes, something which is now being acknowledged as a misleading gap. As this book will show, this gap is a product of history, empire, racism and arrogance towards understanding the nature and limits of money. However, the approach adapted in the special issue is broadly secular and technocratic, trying to measure Hofstede's power distance and its impact on financial decision making and institutional structures. It is the same set of tools commonly used in finance, but now applied *to* culture – the core theoretic utilitarian assumptions of materialism and wealth maximisation are not critiqued by this method. It is also a macro approach to finance, rather than the micro approach adopted in this book. There is no single paper which looks qualitatively at finance practices and communities of faith and belief, and how they embrace morality. In fact, the phrase sustainability is hardly even mentioned in this special issue.

The challenge embraced in this book is to look at finance from the ground up, rather than the top down, which has been the conventional approach. For that one needs to be 'ethnographic' and listen to narratives about finance, trust and relationships, and translate them into cultural theories and practices. These give *context* to finance, something which has been completely stripped off by the mainstream techniques and mindsets. Once context is removed, it is easy to impose a particular theory or worldview on society, but this is fictitious and unsustainable. What this book will show is how much we can learn about the nuances of finance by examining living cultures and communities. This helps us develop a more inclusive, ethical and sustainable theory of finance, which is our urgent need for today.

When experts are involved in damaging our planet, and they are then also involved in resolving the harm, society is left in a serious bind. The same people have turned chameleons and are now solving the problems they created themselves. Society is unwittingly trapped in relying on the very same experts to dig them out of the mess, making the outcomes harmful. Not enough people are raising their voice against anthropocentric experts, resulting in the '**expert capture**' of sustainable finance solutions, which are often extractive and anthropocentric in themselves. In many cultures, there is no separate role for experts or specialists – they are a part of the larger whole, no higher or lower, and usually not driven by materialist goals, but instead the service of public interest. This is where the authenticity of timeless wisdom traditions and their practitioners becomes especially valuable. This book is focused on raising the importance of these voices and bringing their wisdoms to bear in reshaping finance. Most of the interviewees for this research are non-academic business leaders, but also highly intelligent and reflective about their judgements, behaviours and actions.

Given climate change, inequality, tax injustice and social breakdown, we urgently NEED a finance that is caring, sharing, respectful to nature and sustainable. We need a science that is both responsible and accountable, rather than expropriative, greedy and selfish. Instead of individualism and market fundamentalism, we need to have sustainable cultures and communities at the heart and soul of finance science and education. This book opens the window to a real world of cultural and communitarian finance which has long been 'hiding in plain sight'. Rather than denying diversity and biodiversity, this book embraces it to showcase a caring philosophy for society and nature. In this sense, it is extremely ambitious in its scope and analysis as it addresses both ontology and epistemology at the same time and does not separate research from teaching, constantly exploring the pedagogical implications of a compassionate finance. It covers a diverse range of cultures, from Hindu, Christian, Islamic or Jain. It does not recognise the separation between faith and living culture and exposes how often business actions are entwined with belief, even when leaders do not openly show their faith. In the process, it shows that not only is a new world of sustainable finance possible, but it has also been alive and well for hundreds and even thousands of years. Sadly, contemporary experts in finance have completely missed this fact, both in terms of research and teaching, damaging the good work of our past generations and their wisdom.

ANTHRO-VISION

In her forensic analysis of the 2008 Global Financial Crash, Tett (2010) blames the ignorance of a greedy and transactional banking culture, flawed technical assumptions, silo thinking and hubris by both analysts and regulators of the financial sector. There was a 'social silence' about the systemic nature and extent of the riskiness of derivatives. Experts were complicit in keeping calm and carrying on. When culture has been severed from finance science and training, it is never easy to stitch it back again by adding a few more variables to the equations.

Tett's pioneering analysis proved that culture and finance are deeply entwined, and the bankers' dealing room is also a community with its own jargon, values and relationships. Understanding context is critical to finance practice,[27] and anthropology can provide tools and methods for doing so. Given that trust, relationships and community have always been at the root of money creation and finance, to weave back culture into our knowledge systems, it helps to be less reductive and more holistic and open-minded. Tett calls this *Anthro-Vision*. We need to develop a mindset of *listening* to diverse leaders tell their own stories in their own unfiltered narratives. Tett shows how this can be done through greater reflexivity than simply relying on models or past historic data, and the value it can bring. In this way, we can start to have a better understanding of the plural dimensions of finance and how they influence social relations and human attitudes to animals and nature. This opens a creative process of unravelling and understanding the biodiversity of finance knowledge and practice.

The European Enlightenment and the obsession with secularism have meant that truth and its various dimensions have been subverted by the new faith in a platonic universal and secular science called economics, and the sister disciplines of finance and accounting[28]. Through a series of wide-ranging interviews with business leaders and visionaries, this book exposes the diversity of finance practice, and its ability to open a very timely and important new dimension for research and teaching in business, accounting and finance. These leaders have been carefully and selectively chosen for their cultural and national diversity and their roles in community building in different parts of the world in the present time. In this sense, even when they draw from tradition in describing their philosophies, they are actively living them in the present milieu of neo-liberal capitalism and globalisation. Although trust is central to finance, it is rarely discussed or elaborated in the classroom. The author has chosen these leaders because of the trusted relationships he has built with them over many years, over decades in many cases. In this way, trust is central to the writing of this book, and even the reader is asked to trust the analysis and author. The biographies of these leaders are at the beginning of the book. They comprise a mixture of bankers, fund managers, business executives, legislators (members of House of Lords), finance consultants, community leaders, academics, journalists and industrialists. They have vast experience, not just from business practice, but also from living and belonging to communities in different parts of the world, where they are active participants and often leaders. They understand the language of economics, but often transcend it by living with different rules and an active public conscience. In the process, they have negotiated the changes of the last fifty years and seen the damage and also the resilience that living communities can bring.

In his BBC Reith Lectures on the Climate Challenge, Bank of England Governor Sir Mark Carney[29] started with examining the profound flaws of market triumphalism and neo-classical economics in devaluing what is important to humanity, like water and rainforests, and misinterpreting Adam Smith's *invisible hand* metaphor. Carney questioned the tautology of value, where market value decides that diamonds are more valuable and important than water, when in reality, it ought to be the other way round. Smith's philosophy was rooted in morality and community, and he never advocated economics which would exploit nature and society to enrich its own technocrats. Carney decried the absence of culture and society in contemporary economic models and abstractions and explained that this is precisely why we have such a profound crisis in mental health, a breakdown of communities and rising economic inequality. Morality and social and environmental protection need to be central to a new sustainable economics, he explained. For nature to be an economic externality is plain fiction and deeply damaging.

In addition, real-world case studies of accounting firms and financial institutions and their culture and leadership are also referenced throughout the book. Evidence from 'trusted' sources is used to illuminate the analysis – something which is seen as 'unscientific' from a Popperian mindset. However, given how trust is central to finance, trusted sources provide unique insights which would be missed by conventional science. On the other hand, often the scale of financial damage done by a few 'untrustworthy' people is significant and exponential. The ways in which auditors, regulators, market participants, media and non-executive directors cooperate in the hubris are exposed in some of the examples. It is shown that the leaders who rise to positions of influence in such organisations are often politicians and selfish operators rather than people of commercial acumen, conscience and a civic sense of duty. Recent scandals are littered with fraud and corruption at the highest levels going unreported for years.

POSITIVISM AND TECHNOCRACY AS 'GRAND NARRATIVES'

Edward Said (1993, 1994) explains that narratives are critical to sustaining culture and practices, whether or not these are explicitly cited or discussed. The grand narrative of accounting and finance has been that of a calculative, measurable science, focused on profits and growth, wealth creation, tax minimisation, competition and market efficiency with market triumphalism reducing the need for regulation or control by public bodies. The corporation has been set apart from society and nature. Even phrases like cultural and ethical 'neutrality' have been used in the mainstream finance literature. The role of good culture in finance is diminished and negated in this analysis. Furthermore, the huge shift towards 'positive' economics in the 1980s and beyond created a climate of 'irresponsible' science – experts focused on explanations and analysis of empirical evidence, rather than normative approaches to improving society and nature[30]. Conscience was removed from the equations.

Globalisation and corporatisation have also been endemic forces which have transformed the university as an institution of higher learning[31]. This has made the business school in particular less critical and more pro-business. There is a resulting profound change in academic incentives and culture, making academics more production machines, with measurable outputs and targets, rather than as leaders and role models for the propagation of truth and social and environmental justice. We will see later that teaching has been increasingly given a low priority in the elite universities, and there is virtually no reflexivity about finance education whatsoever, and plenty of questions have been raised about the effectiveness of business education. Some even argue that the business school should be 'bulldozed' altogether[32].

In this utilitarian and technocratic narrative, there is no place for cultural diversity, the diversity of financial histories and institutions all over the world, or for social or environmental responsibility[33] – somehow, focus on profits, competition and wealth creation will solve the world's problems automatically. This is more akin to ideology than science. Slavery, empire and the history of expropriation of land and peoples have *nothing* to do with the science of finance. In fact, the very separation of cultural analysis from finance was itself a narrative implying that people are irrelevant – it is methods and techniques of growth that are of over-riding importance. Unfortunately, technocracy has a strong tendency to hide profound cultural and environmental assumptions and render them irrelevant[34]. *Its role in the shaping of the Anthropocene cannot be underestimated.* The politics of economics and finance knowledge have also led to its unquestioning power and authority, something which prevails to this day in the shaping of financial markets and institutions[35], including the global accounting firms and their practices. Technocracy has a way of disabling its critique – this is no longer sustainable.

The challenge addressed in this book is to introduce a new and different narrative of finance – one that is plural, includes faith, morality and belief, and also a narrative that is respectful of social and environmental responsibility and accountability. In this sense, it is from the ground up, rather than the platonic approach to social sciences which is often top down – theory first, and then method and evidence. This is an altogether different approach to finance, one which will be found rarely in contemporary textbooks of accounting and finance, except perhaps in discussions on ethics. Calculation and measurement are not seen as devoid of cultural assumptions and are often directly involved in dividing the economic cake in the interests of capital and management, as opposed to employees or other stakeholders.

Graduates of accounting and finance may find it difficult to see these subjects from a cultural perspective, so disabled have they become by the overwhelming technocracy and materialistic narratives. There are plenty of true stories in this book which help readers to see plural wisdoms and cultures of finance and the ways in which they contribute to a sustainable planet. The fact that there are no calculations or formulae in this finance book does not mean that it is irrelevant to the science. Instead, it exposes a new and different way of learning about finance and its diversity of practice, with a view to building a sustainable society and planet. There is an active avoidance of rule by technocracy, and an empowerment of ordinary people to share their own stories and experiences of finance outside the familiar jargons.

ACTION RESEARCH – THE WISDOM THAT COMES FROM LIVED EXPERIENCE

For the research for this book, I have adopted an action research method, which is acknowledged to be helpful when charting new horizons or paradigms in research. By its very design and orientation, this approach is very applicable to ethics research and can be developmental, both for the world of practice as well as the researcher[36]. In this sense, it is a very 'adventurous' and joyful approach to research, where the outcomes are unpredictable, and the journey is as important as the destination. Even the writing of the research is seen as a critical part of the developmental journey, an act of both narrative making and personal reflexivity. I recommend it highly to other researchers – I have really enjoyed this journey.

Practising leaders of finance are interviewed to explore their experiences and achievements, and understand what drives them, and the extent to which morality and inclusiveness are important. Their names and brief biographies are listed at the beginning of this book. These leaders were not chosen randomly – most of them have been personally known to me, some of them over decades, and I have even worked with some in my professional life. They have been chosen for their cultural and geographic diversity, but by no means are seen as representative, nor is the list exhaustive. It is impossible in one book to cover all cultures and beliefs. There has been a relationship of trust which has enabled the conversations to be longer and deeper. Given the plurality of the approach and cultural variety of the interviewees, it was felt that action research is the best method, to use practice to help theory building. For far too long, our knowledge has been undermined and captured by a technocracy which is often culturally bankrupt. The aim of this book is also to encourage researchers from diverse backgrounds all over the world to collate and write about their own stories and experiences.

I have spoken to leaders from a range of backgrounds and beliefs, working in different parts of the world, and making a difference through their words, actions and services. In India, the pioneer of a boutique investment bank, Mr Vallabh Bhansali of Enam Securities, with an unblemished record of ethical advice, explains that 'meditation gives one a competitive advantage in finance'. In Kenya, Chartered Accountant Mr Deepak Shah founded a consulting firm which helps business families manage their inter-generational conflicts and challenges and create professional structures and methods to ensure sustained growth and trust. This advice is given to families from all cultures and backgrounds, from Kikuyu, to Sikh, Somali or Arab, even English families. When he meets the family in their boardroom, he asks them to start the meeting by reciting a prayer from their own culture and discovered that the entire tone of the meeting changes as a result.

Growing up in the town of Sudbury in Suffolk, Andrew Phillips OBE set up his own law firm and became a renowned national broadcaster on BBC Radio 2 as a 'Legal Eagle' reaching a weekly audience of 2 million. Later, he was appointed to the House of Lords, but still remained rooted to his hometown and is proud of its Christian and moral history. When he needed a Bank Loan to finance his first business property in London, he made a phone call to his Bank Manager in Sudbury, and within a few days, a 100% Loan was approved! The era of relationship banking is long gone now, but students should be taught that they did exist once and can come back again, if finance is to be responsible and ethical.

Handelsbanken[37], a 150-year-old Swedish Bank, is growing very fast in Britain, precisely because it places culture and relationships at its very heart. And this starts from the way it treats and respects its own staff, such that trust is high and turnover is low. Customers know that the Branch is the Bank – when they apply for loans or services, the decision making is done locally, rather than in a remote central bureaucracy. Even during COVID-19, all their clients were solvent, shared Mr. Andrew Pike, their branch manager in Ipswich. They are prudent business managers and choose to back resilient businesses, by judging character, prudence and integrity before making the lending decision. As a result, Handelsbanken rarely needs to promote and market itself, and the business just comes to them organically, through word of mouth and reputation. Unlike most Banks, they prefer to choose their customers wisely and not chase any buccaneer, no matter how clever or smart.

A majority of their lending is to owner-managed businesses. And given the manager has significant autonomy and authority in making the lending decisions, there is trust placed on him to do the right thing. There are even limits to growth and scale – a branch is not allowed to have more than a dozen people, and if there is more work, a new branch is opened, rather than using 'economies of scale' to reduce the costs and make even more profit. What this shows is that the relationships and personal service are valued more than the bottom-line profits, and this scale and culture are part of the Bank's risk management of lending, customer service and retention. Furthermore, trust is easier to monitor in a small organisation, than in a large organisation where rules and processes replace personal relationships. In his interview, Andrew Pike confided that local presence and intimacy helped them really understand the business landscape and its challenges and opportunities, something which technocratic and remote algorithmic calculations may not always capture.

The above are just a handful of examples from my interviews and conversations, which will be elaborated throughout this book. What they show is that once we start looking at diverse cultural approaches to accounting and finance, a whole Pandora's box is opened, and there is so much excellent financial practice hiding in plain sight. There is a whole world of people out there who are determined to act responsibly and morally not because there are external rules and laws, but because for them it is the right way to live. They have a conscience and tune into it and try as best to live by it. Leaders of such businesses care about their suppliers and customers, their employees and lenders because they feel it is in the only sustainable way to build and grow a business. Some of them do not grow into very large businesses or make millions in profits, but that is OK – they would rather be happy than be rich and insecure. These true stories are rarely shared in the classroom, but they deserve to be. That is the purpose of this book. To motivate a whole new generation of students to think and learn differently, and untap their own experiences, wisdom and virtues, whilst learning about others.

BOOK OUTLINE

At RBS, the CEO Fred Goodwin genuinely believed that focusing on targets and outcomes would lead the Bank to lasting growth and success – there was no need to create a caring and responsible culture[38]. The Board was too fearful to critique him. RBS is an extreme example of technocratic leadership leading to destruction. The same applied to another large British bank – HBOS[39]. These cases prove what happens when finance ignores culture and ethics and leaders become hubristic and politically influential. Chapter 1 sets the scene highlighting how urgent and important it is that we **transform the paradigm** of business finance by transforming BOTH research and teaching materials and practices. It explains how we got here and shows how different methods of business have been ignored by this drive for a universal economic science. Whilst acknowledging the challenge ahead, it does not underestimate the difficulties of the transformation needed. Culture change needs to begin with the academy and academics at a personal level. Chapter 2 explores the importance and contribution of **tradition** to corporate finance and elaborates on the diversity of traditions, and the wisdoms that have been nurtured over generations. Chapter 3 elaborates on **living communities** and their finance practices. In direct contradiction to the increasing transactional nature of finance and business, this chapter shows how these communities build relationships and trust and help engender sustainable enterprise in an instinctive way, rather than as a dictat from the United Nations or the World Council of Responsible Business. Chapter 4 examines in detail the notion of **experience** and learning that gives people from these communities rare skills and talents which not only help business growth, but also replenish trust and relationships in society rather than depleting them. In the process, it shows how ignorance of these skills in the business classroom is deeply damaging to those who come from such communities and to wider society in the avoidance of such distinctive exemplars of sustainable business. Chapter 5 examines the urgency of **Purposeful Leadership**, for which faith communities, and people belonging to them, have a unique advantage. Stewardship, governance and trust in finance all rely hugely on the character, integrity, compassion and soul-regulation of our leaders.

Tradition, community, experience and purpose have no place in neo-liberal economics, accounting and finance. They are seen as 'Luddite' and regressive, taking society backward in time to a fundamentalism we have long run away from in our new 'enlightenment'. The stories, examples and narratives in this book show how flawed this perception is and how its damaging beliefs have played a significant role in the Anthropocene. The examples of contemporary finance leaders practising in different parts of the world, be it Africa, Asia, Europe or North America, a different sustainable finance, demonstrate that traditions and their stories and memories provide rich moral discipline and empowerment towards a responsible and compassionate finance. They make finance personal once again and show the richness of subjectivity, when it is drawn from faith, moral conscience and an understanding of the limits of materiality. The examples show how leadership is elevated and encouraged to act more humbly and in service to a larger ecology than purely a selfish, materialistic greed, even when science wishes to endorse and encourage it. The reader is taken on a journey into a morally driven finance which has long been hiding in plain sight and thrives even today in spite of the highly political and materialist financial markets and institutions. The true stories expose the flawed boundaries of religion and culture which modern intellectuals have drawn and instead shine a light on the diversity of practices and moral sources of inspiration and accountable leadership. Belonging to a community helps leaders to stay rooted, to value reputation and honour and build lasting relationships of hope and economic progress. Just as a rain forest is much more than a collection of individual trees, a community is living repository of memory and history which provides us with huge lessons for sustainable finance. Chopping it from our teaching and research is to ignore the vast ocean of wealth and wisdom that comes from faith communities. The reader is taken on an inner journey of self-reflection whilst learning from the lives of pioneering finance leaders. Often their stories are unknown precisely because they do not seek fame, prestige or publicity, and understand the responsibility that their status and position endow upon them.

FAKE SCIENCE AND ETHICS

Private good, public bad is the silent mantra of business education[40]. The most extreme example of this is seen in the discussions on tax, which propagate that all companies should do their best to minimise taxes through using various offshore structures or clever techniques of tax avoidance. It is identified as a cost, rather than a repayment to the government for providing public services like roads, law and order, education and healthcare, which corporations rely on to make their profits[41]. So many important truths are falsified or made sub-conscious to disable students from challenge or critique and even to encourage them to transform their culture and worldview to one of accumulation and greed. Even when we look at simple economic analyses like the importance of scale in reducing costs, we see a strong justification for public education and public healthcare. However, very often such basic discussions are off the professional or undergraduate curricula. Falsehoods and half-truths are disguised as science. Professor Lord Sikka in my interview went even further and explained that all accounting and finance are profoundly ideological[42] and should not even claim to be objective or scientific – the professional bodies have become trade associations rather than upholders of public interest.

Both in corporate finance and corporate accounting, focus has been placed on developing the objective 'science' of large corporations, their performance, governance and accountability. An unstated assumption is made that this science is applicable to all business sizes, ownership patterns, geographies and cultures, irrespective of their local norms and practices. Individualism has been celebrated and nourished by science, at the expense of culture and collective inheritance and socialisation experiences. In a similar way, economics has encouraged utilitarianism, consumerism, materialism and wealth creation as mass definitions of the ultimate goal of human 'happiness'.

Rather than encouraging people to seek purpose and meaning, corporatisation has exaggerated the importance of selfish profit and tangible or material pursuits. The result is the virus of 'Affluenza' – for the very few who amass vast wealth, they are constantly unhappy, distrustful and insecure[43]. History, politics, ethics, sociology and culture have been stripped off these subjects, subconsciously giving students the impression that they are irrelevant to professional practice. A global pioneer in social and environmental accounting, Rob Gray, argued that if society were to embrace these two important priorities, we should not even start with contemporary financial accounting as it is arbitrary, flawed and inconsistent[44]. For ethical-minded business academics, the rise of Corporate Social Responsibility since the 1990s provided a ray of hope that the corporation at last may change for the better and accept its social obligations. Far from it – it turned out to be another hypocritical spin machine, with little substance or long-term commitment, and Fleming and Jones comprehensively declared the 'End of Corporate Social Responsibility' in 2012 with deep frustration and anger[45].

A growing technical jargon has been developed which closes off the disciplines to external critique, and at the same time keeps enticing students to come and learn the magic formula of wealth and prosperity, which is only accessible to a select few. Tett (2010) exposes the breadth and depth of the uncertainties and ignorance prevailing in the financial markets. Calculation has the subconscious ability to objectify subjective realities and hide ethical and cultural variances and assumptions, she explains. One of the major causes of the 2008 crash was that traders were able to hide the underlying risks of their derivatives positions from even their own bosses[46]! Managements were blinded by their ignorance and paralysed by the hubris. Risk is one of the biggest factors in finance, as it's a principal fuel for wealth creation, and its technical measurement often gives the impression of its perfect manageability and controllability. This could not be further from the truth – there is so much uncertainty in the real world which no model of risk calculation can fully encompass – there are unknown unknowns[47]. Both financial sector regulators and bank management had cultivated a false belief in risk manageability and free-market resilience.

CORPORATE CAPTURE: IDEOLOGY AS POWER

Naïve young students are often unable to discern wisdom from ideology or fake science or evaluate good role models or training institutions. Brands and public relations are used to draw them in, both in terms of the university they attend and the firm they join after graduation. They are converted into a flawed science which they are incapacitated from critiquing,[48] and their personal insecurity is exploited. The organisational structures, posh office buildings, marketing images and priorities of elite financial and accounting institutions prevent a critical dialogue on morality and the social and environmental impact of the services provided by them. The glamour of an office building and location subconsciously conveys success and achievement. At the height of its hubris, the CEO of RBS Bank, Fred Goodwin, commissioned a giant headquarters' building and campus which became the precursor to its downfall[49]. Instead of humility, arrogance was on display, and employees were asked to forget that it was other peoples' money that was being used. Paradoxically, symbols and spaces are often used to convey trust in finance, even when they are not discussed in the theory. In large institutions, there is a subtle yet active process of diminishing and squashing critique and whistle-blowing[50]. Given the power of financial institutions, and the systemic implications of their failure, theses intellectual capture and hubris are deeply damaging.

In the wake of increasing scandals, ethics has re-emerged in the professional courses, but is taught in a secular acultural way and is highly individualistic, ignoring the influence of unethical organisational structures and norms or lived practices[51]. Often the politics and power which shape financial institutions and their aggressive conduct are outside ethical debate in the business curriculum. Codes of ethics, rules and principles may sound good and honourable for a teaching curriculum, but it's in their living application that they are really understood. Whilst in a classroom, the best one can do is share examples or case studies, in the real world, I find students come with a variety of moral or immoral experiences and a range of cultures and beliefs, which are never discussed in the curriculum. This creates a very distorted and functional view of ethics – they are something to be learnt for the sake of passing the exam, and then forgotten as quickly. The famous Financial Times columnist Lucy Kellaway brought a group of corporate executives into a room and gave them a whole batch of corporate ethics codes to read. She then asked them to identify which specific statement belonged to their own firm[52]. Most of them could NOT identify their own firm's ethics code, even when they were Board Directors. Just like the students, they too perceive ethics codes as statements of spin, without any need for living adherence. Ethical compliance is at best a box-ticking exercise, rather than a behaviour change, even amongst the leaders.

When caught for unethical behaviour, firms and leaders have openly shared answers to ethical tests, showing how little, they care about morality or conscience[53]. The more technocratic the world of accounting and finance has become, the more it has distanced itself from human history, culture and social responsibility and accountability. Ethics are seen as a technique to be mastered for passing exams and then forgotten as quickly. The notion that money is a social construct, and its value depends on relationships, trust and confidence has been dumped long ago by the sciences, just as animals and nature have been expropriated. We know from history that European empires have been built on the subjugation of native peoples, their forced slavery or extermination and the occupation of land and natural resources[54]. This has led to wealthy nations and states, and elites who would rather forget the history of how the wealth was made and replace it with their own versions of 'objective' science, which continue to exploit and expropriate the masses.

OBSESSION WITH MARKETS AND MULTINATIONAL CORPORATE FINANCE

What we really have in modern finance is a multiplier of fictions hiding as facts and even worse, science. Money is a legal fiction and so is the limited liability corporation. Bakan[55] calls the corporation a 'psychopath' – like a genie released from a lamp, it is devouring society by promoting greed, exploiting nature and destroying jobs, making society constantly unsatisfied and wanting more and more. If today one did a Masters in Finance or Accounting course, there will not even be a single lecture on these fictions – what are the nature and limits of money, and why is an 'impersonal corporation' given so much power without responsibility or accountability? The ignorance of these themes in a postgraduate course exposes the secret desire to lie and defraud society and build a profes-sionalised technocracy whose ethics are lying and cheating. The ramifications of all this have been the devastation of the human and ecological landscape in the last five decades. Markets are imperfect in balancing social and environmental impact, yet they are celebrated as efficient and ideal – a market triumphalism prevails in the curriculum[56].

Large corporations have increasingly become profiteers from everywhere, and autocratic citizens of nowhere[57]. A lot of research and evidence has proven this thesis. For us to build a sustainable society, we need organisations that are responsible citizens everywhere and providers of necessary goods and services at fair prices. Above all, they need to be real and human, and not legal fictions quoted in stock markets, without a single bone of care and conscience. Family-owned businesses are often different because there is a shared structure of own-ership, the shareholders are not remote from the managers of the business and long-termism is at the heart of the goals of enterprise. Often, they personally know their customers and suppliers, build and nurture key relationships and are ready to lose money to keep such relationships going. For them, interdependence is a lived experience, not a remote theory, and they take pride in the human scale of their organisation.

I know many family-owned firms who refuse to expand beyond their manage-able scale, even when such opportunities arise. One hugely successful businessman recently confided in me that his business generates enough cash so there is little need for external finance. If he were to take it, as Banks were constantly knock-ing on his door, he felt that he would most likely waste it. When I go back to my textbooks, there is *no concept of 'waste'* in finance – the more money one can raise at low interest, the better for the growth in business value, is the presumption.

It is therefore a big mistake and deliberate mental pollution to make large remotely owned corporations and their operations the central feature of business science and education. It breaks the diversity of finance practice that is observed in the real world. Most finance textbooks do not even discuss small businesses and their different needs and scale. Large corporations are often flooded by 'other people's money' (OPM)[58] and leaders learn not to value and respect the wider stakeholders. OPM has become an OPIUM rubber stamped by neo-liberal science which endorses its addiction and spread. Hired professional managers learn to extract wealth rather than create it. They lack personal experience of risk or even enterprise, having been groomed into an analytical way of thinking and commanding power and authority. A top-ranking finance postgraduate of Harvard Business School, Andy Hornby, became the Chief Executive of HBOS Group, Britain's fifth-largest bank, and led it to financial disaster – the largest corporate failure in the history of Britain, with losses estimated at fifty-two billion pounds[59]. Prior to directing the Bank, his only experience was in retail business, but was promoted due to his youthfulness and ambition. Education and qualifications can and often do fuel financial hubris accompanied by cultural ignorance.

CULTURAL BREAKDOWN

Accurate and reliable accountings are critical to sustainable finance but missing in the annual reports[60]. Many businesses with excellent reported profits have collapsed, ENRON being one of the biggest and most glaring examples[61]. In spite of the need for independent external audits, large corporations are able to misrepresent their true performance, often with the help of these very same auditors[62]. Professionals in charge of these investigations are often compromised by the fees and glamour and become afraid to challenge frauds, even when they discover them. Their education and training are highly technical, and a tick-box culture is encouraged and promoted – auditors focus their energies on putting an audit file together and following rules, rather than using their own brains and professional judgement powers[63]. Their scepticism is compromised by commercial motives.

Accounting firms who make such significant errors often get away unchallenged, or worse have to pay a fine, which they see as a cost of doing business, rather than a reprimand of their professionalism and integrity. There are rare examples of professionals who blow the whistle and call out the fraud, but often they end up being marginalised and persecuted, rather than being thanked or rewarded for their efforts[64]. The combination of big business and big finance can lead to poor accountability. The trust placed on the managers by shareholders and investors can be eroded by a culture of arrogance and hubris. Conflicts of interest between management and the Big 4 professional firms are rampant. Such behaviour cannot lead to sustainable growth or success. Leaders in finance must have a deep sense of responsibility and accountability before accepting the public role.

There is a profound cultural problem in large corporations – very few people are willing to take ownership of their actions and the consequences of these actions[65]. Often there is very little skin in the game due to the divorce between owners and managers. For four decades, agency theory in finance encouraged managers' enrichment to incentivise them to increase the value of the firm[66]. Not only was culture separated from finance teaching, but selfishness among elite managers was also actively encouraged by science. Even shareholders are inactive and divided – they would rather sell their shares than to challenge management. Many shareholders are there for short-term gains, rather than longer term loyalty. Awash with public money from lenders and shareholders, executives in positions of power rarely behave responsibly. Crudely speaking, they put their hand in the till as no one is watching.

One of the most famous bestselling writers of contemporary finance is Michael Lewis.[67] Most of his writings focus on the high finance trading cultures shaped by the growth of globalised financial markets, in New York, London or Hong Kong. He culturally analyses the vast opportunities they have created for speculators in making exponential returns for little sweat. Insider experts are able to shove risk to others and maximise their own gains, using the capital and wealth of others. Banks are centres of casino capitalism, where even the gambled money belongs to others and this speculation is licensed and protected by Bank regulators. Lewis's pioneering writings show how inefficient markets are and how captured they are by powerful elites, rather than free, open and competitive. He busts the contemporary narrative of corporate finance. Hardly any of this is ever discussed in finance or accounting textbooks, implying that this cultural hubris and expropriation is irrelevant to students.

An eminent writer and finance academic, Professor John Kay, explains that there is an IBGYBG culture prevailing in finance – 'I'll be Gone, You'll be Gone'[68]. This is a self-centred, greedy, short-termist mantra which pervades those in power, who are motivated by using that power for personal financial gain, irrespective of the longer-term consequences for the organisation, its employees, customers and other stakeholders. In recent years, a new Golden Handshake has emerged for Chief Executives and senior officers, whereby they are paid just to come to run the organisation. Senior managers belong to an elite union and are able to command their own terms, salaries and bonuses, irrespective of actual performance. In spite of this rampant greed, the word 'trade union' is never applied to corporate executives, even when there is ample evidence of the prevalence of such elites and their resilience to economic cycles of boom and bust[69]. In recent decades, the rise in share buy-backs has significantly enriched the remuneration of executives, without much impact on real long-term performance[70].

CASINO CAPITALISM AND ADDICTION

One of the outcomes of modern finance is a speculative, casino mentality, which plays havoc on global markets and economies, as evidenced by our boom and busts[71]. The concentration of power is decoupled from social and environmental responsibility, and there is no blame or responsibility for the havoc that is left behind. It also causes severe mental health, drug and alcohol problems which ripple out from financial institutions into wider society[72]. Finance leaders often become addicted to money and its frills, and get psychologically damaged as a result, becoming psychopathic and dragging their institutions into losses and fail-ure[73]. They are desensitised from the pollution, inequality, homelessness and loss of savings, jobs and pensions that result from their actions. Instead, the science of market triumphalism means that the wider problems are believed to be caused by lazy people or inefficient government. There is a social silence on this vast ocean of damage done by the finance academy, encouraging people that they can get rich quickly with little effort and plenty of science, that is also unsustainable. The cultural side-effects of modern finance are dangerous and should not be ignored or excluded. Lack of morality, combined with significant power gained from other people's money, is a lethal combination.

The need for sweat and effort in making a living from finance has been replaced by this technocratic view and related hubris and arrogance[74]. Unearned income is the driver of high finance. Speculation is covered up by the narratives of risk management and hedging and justified as critical to free markets and efficiency. Traders in financial institutions are able to gamble with other peo-ple's money, with little consequences for them on the downside, and significant bonuses on the upside. Why would they want to behave differently once they are in the casino – they just get sucked in. Once in a while, big multi-billion-dollar scandals emerge, like the UBS 'London Whale' Kweku Aduboli[75] or 1MDB[76] (Goldman Sachs) which are then blamed on the lone banker, covering up the wider culture which encouraged and exaggerated the behaviours. Blue-chip names are involved, yet the institutions often survive unscathed. The finance academy has also ignored for a long time the systemic risks generated by this poor culture, whose costs are spread on global society. Regulation and control have been anathema to free markets and efficiency – so bad behaviour will be rooted out by the 'clever' markets, it is preached.

FLAWED UNIVERSALISM, SPECIALISATION AND A BLAME CULTURE

A highly lauded recent reformative book on Corporate Finance by a world-famous professor at London Business School, Alex Edmans, is called *Grow the Pie*[77]. The book explains through a combination of case studies and empirical research that businesses which have a long-term, purposeful and socially respon-sible outlook also build their profits and wealth at the same time. Particular success stories are used to generalise about their model. Subconsciously, the book claims that there is no need for structural change in corporate political economy – a renewed purpose with shareholder long-termism will do the trick. It carefully avoids the vast litter of failure to society and the ecosystem by giant multinationals where shareholders are divorced from managers and neither care about the long term. It also avoids the political capture that is so normal for these giant corporations – when they grow the pie, they grow and abuse their power too. It is 'evidence-based' – in a selective way. The paradigm of mainstream finance has been tinkered rather than shifted.

The Edmans book argues that the two goals of profit and long-termism are not contradictory – one does not have to be sacrificed for the sake of the other, and instead, they are shown to be complimentary. In this book, you will see a large number of examples of small-medium family-owned businesses, where the growth has been inter-generational. For them, the connection between purpose and long termism is not rocket science at all and requires no external research or evidence – they just know it from their family history and experience. However, the Edmans book does not look at such businesses at all. Neither does it discuss cultural diversity or faith and belief. It also avoids devoting chapters to taxation, a primary way in which businesses *ought to* contribute to society – by paying their fair taxes. When it speaks about purpose, the approach is rational and instrumental, rather than emotive, personal and faith-oriented. Technocracy is enough to embrace purpose. Subconsciously, the book says that we have nothing to learn about business science from small-medium family-owned businesses. Nor is culture and tradition important. In a progress-driven new world, it posits that we must develop 'new' sciences for business strategy and longevity.

We therefore have a finance *ideology* which is desperately trying to be universal and platonic, and completely ignores a ground reality of a vast diversity of finance customs and practices within any one country and also all over the world. Technical science does not want to 'see' culture and diversity and instead explains everything by theories of performance, risk and valuation. A focus on 'market managerialism' combined with profit maximisation dominates the curriculum, with political economy virtually absent[78]. Even ethical diversity is a huge challenge and a problem for the technocrats – why should there be any influence on pricing or risk because of ethics, they may ask, within the confines of their free-market ideologies and calculations? The positivistic ahistorical, apolitical and acultural construction of these disciplines is deeply problematic for society. It stampedes on the different cultural experiences of students and forces them towards an uncaring and technocratic view of accounting and finance. It is no wonder that most of these scholars have no clue about what holistic education is or why it is important. Research shows that within business schools, there is often a fight about the teaching of business ethics – with many arguing that it should not be taught at all, as it is too soft and subjective[79]. Even when it is taught, it is often taught as a stand-alone subject rather than a moral conscience that should pervade each and every business subject.

Francine McKenna was a compliance leader and manager in North and Central America advising many large organisations during a period of significant regulatory change and crises. One thing she identified was what she called the 'Waterfall' problem – in a large corporation, every department develops a culture of ticking their own compliance boxes, with no one responsible for overall monitoring and oversight. When a problem emerges, blame is cascaded downwards, rather than accepted from the top. The Waterfall leads to a tick-box culture of oversight, and one which tries to blame others and protect the managers. Responsibility and accountability are avoided in precisely the department whose role is to monitor and control business operations. Instead of managing organisational and business risk responsibly, leaders and managers manage their own personal risk, by following selective rules and capturing documents so that in the event of a crisis they can shift blame.

This is exactly what happened in the recent crisis at one of America's oldest banks, Wells Fargo[80]. To boost reported profits and share price, the CEO embarked on a new push called 'Eight is Great'. This incentivised and forced low-paid branch staff to sell new products to existing customers, and this led them to open fake accounts just to meet their monthly targets. One reason was that their basic salaries were so low that the only way they could afford to pay their own bills was through earning bonuses and rewards. Paradoxically, the rewards of the Board Directors were several hundred *times* the salaries of the branch staff. Like the waterfall, risk and effort were pushed downwards, and rewards were sucked upwards. In the group's profit announcements, this growth in new accounts was emphasised and celebrated, leading to a significant growth in the share price and the related bonuses for senior executives. When the frauds were discovered, there was an initial cover-up saying that the cheating was done by a few rogue employees. The Board Directors said they knew nothing about this nor did they incentivise such rogue behaviour. Then as more evidence about the wide scale of the corruption was revealed, no one admitted fault or resigned. In fact, the Director in charge of the branch network was given a multi-million-dollar payout – suggesting that she was PAID for her silence in not implicating other Board members in the scam. While some local branch staff were arrested, no Board Director went to jail. This case shows how leaders can destroy trust in large organisations through their conduct and targets, even in a historic Bank where maintaining trust is critical to sustainable growth and reputation.

KNOWLEDGE AS POWER – CALCULATION HIDES PREJUDICES

When knowledge and power collude, and ethics & conscience subside, we have a lethal and damaging cocktail for our society and planet. If we add to this the raw force of money and profit, we should not be surprised by the present predicament of business and professional science and education. Even researchers lament that the top scientific journals in business are all pro-business and do not allow any fundamental critique of neo-liberal theories of materialism and profit maximisation[81]. Many would say that in today's technocratic society, knowledge IS power. This makes it even more important that professionals in accounting and finance act with the utmost humility and check the abuses of power by NOT helping corporations to minimise their taxes, or executives to pay themselves high bonuses through creative accounting and financial engineering. Instead, what we often see is the active enabling of practices of extraction, corruption and political capture by giant organisations like the Big 4 global accounting firms or global banks like HSBC or Lehman Brothers.

In the classroom, the teacher has authority and power to set the syllabus and decide the grades. There are few standard exams at university level, although at professional level, there is an increasing global standardisation. In accounting, pressures to standardise have increased of late due to the demands for professional accreditation of courses, which constrains student thinking and development.[82] Students are often innocent and do not know what is best to learn for their own future careers, so rely on the professors and their 'responsible' use of this power. However, in the elite business schools, who thrive on their global rankings, the emphasis for professors is on research and not teaching. So segregation emerges, and the competition for quality research means more and more effort and resources have to be dedicated to building one's own resume as an academic and gaining promotion. Just as there is a divorce between owners and managers inside the corporation, there is a divorce between teaching and research, which is unhealthy for the cultivation of discerning professionals with sound qualities of analysis, judgement and scepticism.

The standardisation of the professional examinations is also deeply problematic. Research shows that countries all over the world have different laws and institutional histories, and there are even varieties of capitalism[83]. Standardisation suits the examining body and their growth aspirations, rather than the quality of knowledge and training. It is the enemy of diversity and holistic education. For example, the Chief Executive of the CFA, a fast-growing global finance qualification, was in 2017 on a salary of $1.2 million a year, and other senior executives are earning several hundred thousand dollars a year even though it is a non-profit organisation[84]. This fact alone should reveal that in spite of all the rhetoric about ethics such organisations espouse, the ground reality is that they are businesses focused on profit and wealth. The model of a factory production line, in the context of professional training and education, should be immediately abhorrent for those who understand the real meaning and duties of professionals in society. We should not therefore be surprised when professionals constantly fail in their duties to provide timely warning and challenge in the face of management hubris and frauds.

A topic highly relevant to finance is risk. Experts who advise on risk measurement and management would like us to believe that this can be done through sophisticated calculation, and derivatives and insurance can help us to hedge and minimise risk and maximise return. However, the truth is that there is a big difference between risk and uncertainty; for example, no one predicted the huge economic devastation caused by the pandemic globally, where many businesses failed or had to be bailed out. In reality, risk is a cultural and social construct too[85]. Faith and belief continue to be used as methods of risk management by many cultures of the world but have no place in an accounting or finance textbook. Providing a sophisticated method of risk calculation can give the illusion that experts know what they are talking about and can be trusted to manage it. The reality is often otherwise, and the cost to society of fraudulent risk management is huge, as we discovered in the 2008 global financial crisis. Financial institution failure causes a systemic domino effect, which means the mismanagement of one institution has much more profound, even global, economic consequences. This does not happen for other businesses[86]. One of the smartest banks on the planet, Lehman Brothers, collapsed like a House of Cards. Everyone on Wall Street knew that its Chief Executive was egotistical and reclusive – he had his own private lift to the 32nd floor so that he can avoid meeting his workers on his way to the office. Why did society entrust its financial risk to such an insecure leader?

Similarly, there is an obsession in finance science with market prices and valuation – known in the jargon as asset pricing. However, many family-owned businesses are not built for sale – their purpose is to serve their customers well, and if possible, pass the firm to the next generation. It is NOT for sale or even valuation. Many small businesses like market stalls are there simply to feed the family of the stallholder and enjoy the act of service. There is no other ambition or aspiration. What happens then? The unwritten answer is that any firm should be concerned about its valuation – that is the raison d'être of its very creation and existence. So now finance science has turned into a religion! Whilst claiming to be secular and objective, the fundamental assumptions of modern finance are deeply ideological. This reminds me of a true story about a blind Samosa seller in India, who was visited by a celebrity. The actor asked him how much is a samosa and he was told ten rupees. The seller felt the note and realised it was a hundred rupees instead of ten. He gave him change, to which the celebrity said you can keep it – I want to help you. The Samosa seller responded by saying that he makes enough from ten rupees – so please use the remaining ninety rupees to help nine other people! Unfortunately, contentment is actively discouraged in finance.

MISLEADING ACCOUNTING EDUCATION

In practice, students get thrown into the larger corporate milieu and into detailed learning of rules and standards, without getting any feel for the diverse cultural dimensions of finance. The fact that the profit and loss account is a highly political statement is never discussed in the classroom, as a result of which students always ask did I get the right profit answer, Sir! In truth, this is dishonest accounting training. To disguise an ideology as a science, and to corrupt truth by mathematics and calculation, is an abrogation of a teacher's duty and responsibility. It disempowers students' ability to think, question, evaluate and analyse for themselves. It makes them think that the wrong accounting is the right accounting. How can such education ever be sustainable?

In calculating profits, employees are treated as costs rather than whole beings who bring their own knowledge, culture and skills to the organisation and help shape its image and reputation. Similarly, government is totally absent as a supplier of valuable infrastructures like roads, healthcare, policing and laws to protect contracts and enable employee welfare and goods transportation. The State becomes a major silent partner in business by maintaining law and order, providing an educated workforce and facilitating energy and communications. To reduce this stakeholder to a single 'cost' number called taxation, and even more to treat it as a burden on business, is to deceive students about the networks of support and cooperation which really enhance growth and success. In truth, government is a stakeholder in all businesses, and at the very least, students should be taught the limitation of treating it as a cost.

In a similar way, balance sheets always exclude the natural environment and its role in providing vital services like rainfall to the agriculture industry, or warm climates for the tourism sector. The fact that none of us can live without clean air and a regular supply of oxygen is overlooked by accounting. The addition of assets and liabilities often give young students the false belief that accounting is like mathematics, and if you get the numbers right, all will be OK. Even the role of good culture and relationships is excluded from the asset side of the balance sheet. Similarly, the wisdom and capital employees bring to the organisation is ignored, and instead, all attention is focused on the shareholders, who only provide one type of financial capital and are often absent from the running and management of the organisation. How can this be fair?

Peace is taken for granted, even though we know from history that human life has been very turbulent, and revolutions and wars have been central to our past. Health and happiness are not measured, even when they influence business performance. Ethics, trust and integrity are nice to have, but not relevant to accounting calculation or valuation. Inter-generational equity is never on a balance sheet, nor is the extent to which the livelihoods of future generations are compromised by present actions, products or services. Even when firms encourage unnecessary consumption, and grow waste in society, the costs of this are not treated as a liability. Social responsibility and accountability are treated more as a spin gimmick rather than a duty of corporate citizenship. Limited liability is a privilege given by society, but taken for granted by the corporation. It is often interpreted as a license to maximum irresponsibility, when all that matters is profit and returns to managers and shareholders.

When young people go to university with innocence and a thirst for wisdom and are taught that everyone is greedy and selfish, we have a problem. Teaching that the world is just a collection of individuals, and material wealth is the only route to lasting happiness, they can and do become indoctrinated. This can be viewed as a type of abuse of the trust they place on their teachers and an exploitation of their vulnerability. Often this is done subconsciously, hidden in the layers of formulae and equations, rules and techniques that they are forced to memorise. They start learning to behave in an irresponsible way, and to emphasise their individualism, without even realising that that is where the equations are leading them. In the process, students subconsciously learn to diminish their own cultural or shared identity, and even ethics become what one can do within the rules and law, rather than listening in silence to one's own conscience. They are disabled from introducing their own cultural perspectives in finance. There is an active diminishing of culture and personality in the guise of economic science. Wrong education can be much more damaging than NO education. It can put the wrong kinds of leaders into positions of power, helping them to extract large amounts of culture and wealth from society and leave governments to pick up the pieces of the mess they have created. The cost of this in turn falls on ordinary hard-working citizens.

We have so far examined the reasons why finance science and education are in such a mess. Trust, the very foundation of finance, has been abolished by the science, through a transactional approach. This analysis has helped us understand the challenges for a sustainable finance. Now we turn to some constructive suggestions for reform, and these are then built upon throughout the book. Phrases like tradition, community or experience are never found in a contemporary finance textbook. They simply do not exist or are considered backward or unimportant. Yet the book will show how important they are to building a sustainable future. And more importantly, these practices are hiding in plain sight – we have not chosen to look there for theoretical and pedagogical change.

CULTURE, COMMUNITY AND CHARACTER IN FINANCE – CULTIVATING GOOD HABITS

The climate crisis and rising greed and inequality lead only in one direction – a transformation of culture and habit, towards more respect, compassion and care for all living beings. Given that good culture has long been divorced from finance, its reform requires a substantive change in both thinking and habit, one student at a time. This is a big transformation, given how commercial business and professional science and education have become and impersonal too. Technology has even encouraged professional bodies to standardise teaching and examining, making the whole process even more impersonal. Its challenge can therefore not be underestimated. As a result, there are deep structural and institutional barriers to reform which cannot be denied.

Sustainable leadership requires good character to begin with, and this is often moulded through childhood and upbringing. No business school or professional education can transform the habits that are moulded in these developmental years. This is a major limitation which needs to be acknowledged. My core argument in this analysis is that when students come with good character and habits, and even a conscience and caring nature, the current science and education system betrays their good nature. It subconsciously tries to change its thinking and habits in an unsustainable direction. This is fatal and needs to be changed.

The history of the professions shows that they were set apart from society, with morality and the practice of selfless virtuous conduct, as norms which distinguished them from trades or business enterprises[87]. The leadership they were supposed to provide was transformational, and not transactional, which is what we see widely among the business professions today. Professional bodies today have become large global self-serving businesses, with multi-million-dollar revenues, and an education, training and certification business which is highly lucrative and profitable[88]. They were supposed to be 'moral communities' with specialist skills to serve the public interest and not enrich the private self at the expense of the public. Sadly, the description of professions as a 'community' has virtually disappeared from the sound bites – they act like expert advisors to business, without much moral regulation or reflexivity. The professional badge is used to serve self-interest. This book will showcase many examples of such purposeful leadership, often influenced by a sense of public service and a defence of community. We have the opportunity to renew professional purpose towards meaning and sustainability, enhancing their public trust and respect. This will help professionals to renew their moral roots and transform themselves from the commercial and transactional roles they occupy today.

I was born in the town of Mombasa in Kenya, to parents who had migrated from Gujarat in India. We belong to the Jain tradition, one of the oldest living cultures of the world. Mahatma Gandhi famously learned about the science of 'ahimsa' or non-violence from a Jain poet and entrepreneur, Shrimad Rajchandra, whom he called a Guru[89]. Yet when I went to university in Britain as an undergraduate, my professors could not even spell the word Jain nor were they interested in my cultural inheritance. Just like empire, the education was top-down – and black cultures did not matter so far as intellect was concerned. Many readers will be familiar with this experience. My own stories of business or family experiences were irrelevant to the subjects of economics, accounting and finance. Presently, there is a rising awareness of the wisdoms of different cultures and beliefs and the need for a plural education, which 'decolonises' the curriculum. These rebellions pose significant challenges to expert researchers and teachers, who have made their lives and careers on the basis of an acultural, secular and expropriative science. Changing the syllabus and materials to reflect diverse cultures and practices will require serious determination and quality research to show different wisdoms and world-views. This book has been written in this vein with this larger goal and purpose in mind.

Prem Sikka was born in Punjab in India, and the family migrated to the UK when he was 14. At his London school, he stood up when the teacher walked into the class, and everyone laughed at him. This was the culture of respect for the teacher he was brought up in. He left school without any O levels, but through hard work, strong public values and a culture of determination and resilience, he became a multi-award-winning Professor of Accounting. His large volume of research publications are widely discussed and cited today for their pioneering insights into accounting and financial frauds all over the world[90]. When as an academic he started questioning his professional accounting body, the ACCA, about their opacity and lack of democracy, the leaders wrote to his university questioning his appointment as a professor[91]. His courage or critique of hubris and political capture never diminished, and today he has been appointed to the House of Lords in the UK. His research and writings span the fields of politics, economics, taxation, finance and accounting, and he is a trenchant critic of the systemic corruption in corporate regulation and governance. Professor Lord Sikka's life example shows that the genuine pursuit of wisdom involves a lot of pain and sacrifice, especially in a field like business studies where there are lots of powerful organisations, professions and lobbyists. When done with integrity and an honest pursuit of truth, irrespective of the consequences to one's name or reputation, the outcomes can be beneficial for the whole of mankind. The moral courage he has displayed is common in Hindu-Punjabi culture, from which he draws inner strength and resilience. Critical leadership in finance is urgently needed to transform research and education and its origins are necessarily personal and subjective, rather than universal and formulaic.

When knowledge and education are respected, a degree of trust is placed on the teacher and their expertise. That trust needs to be taken responsibly and students respected for their thirst for knowledge. Despite the fact that business education has been one of the fastest growing fields of learning in the world today, the practice of teaching has increasingly become a production line, where profit is more important than the content of the knowledge[92]. Even in the elite universities, where there is an active encouragement of research, all too often the famous professors are inaccessible to the students, and research has become separated from teaching. Many elite professors disrespect their students and distance themselves from them. Sadly, they make bad role models for their students and practice a selfish, competitive culture which has led us to this sustainability crisis in the first place. Many experts do not feel they need to walk their talk and are hubristic. Why should we then expect their science to be much different from their moral character? We should not be surprised by the outcomes when education becomes commercialised – truth and wisdom get suffocated from view. The emerging science of holistic education explains that knowledge is not something given to a student by the teachers, but a shared experience, where the mind, body, soul and culture of the student are critical to the learning.

DIVERSE PEDAGOGIES

In Indian tradition, a Guru is someone who helps a student seek their own inner wisdom, igniting their lifelong thirst for truth and knowledge, which is never confined to a school or a university or a piece of paper given as a certificate. Even subjects and boundaries between disciplines are avoided, and the larger inter-connected whole of science, nature and society are given more importance. There is no separation of animals, plants or the environment in the wisdom that is called Dharma[93]. As a result, even when Indians have moved from villages to cities, they have carried their spirit of community with them and kept up their experience of a shared identity and values wherever they have migrated. The former President of India and a profound philosopher, Dr Radhakrishnan believed in the criticality of human experience to the learning journey, explaining that there are a range of experiences which include sensory, intuitive, aesthetic, psychic and religious, all of whom help students to learn and grow. Discursive reasoning, emphasised in the western university and exported to the world, is only one of the methods of learning.[94]

In the rush to make science secular and remove it from historical experiences of religious domination and suppression, the diverse world of culture and faith has unfortunately all been tarred with the same brush of dogmatism and fundamentalism. In reality, students may have varying experiences depending on their own personal and family histories. And yes, many students come from business cultures, communities and families – in this sense, they have commerce in their DNA and a significant amount of tacit skills which make them exceptional entrepreneurs.

For us to improve the knowledge and training in accounting and finance, we need to understand the cost of mass technical education, and the waste and inefficiency this can create, at a time when the planet is crying out for respect, prudence and sustainable use of its resources. Standardisation often is done in favour of the standard-setters or powerful interests, to subjugate cultures and communities and make them serve their own personal needs of extraction and inequality. Making a subject appear complex and technical can serve to defend the expert from challenge or critique by making people feel stupid or incompetent, even when they are wise and moral. Students need to be empowered not diminished and subjugated through examination and 'failure'.

In particular, we need to recognise that morality and character are at the *heart* of accounting and finance and NOT peripheral to it. People place their trust in bankers and accountants, and this trust needs to be understood and respected instead of being betrayed. The nature and limits of money should be understood by each and every student anywhere in the world before they can become good accountants and bankers. This understanding should be based on dialogue, stories and experiences rather than top-down scientific treatises. In this way, students would be able to make their own judgements and hear the variety of opinions about wealth and happiness.

THERE SHOULD EVEN BE A DISCUSSION ON DEATH AND LEGACY

By making its science impersonal, economics subtly denies the reality and experience of death, which can end all happiness, comfort and wealth. Narratives of 'successful' entrepreneurs like those of Facebook's founder Mark Zuckerberg, who became a billionaire overnight, are very misleading for young people and give them false aspirations and hopes. They hide the political economy of business, and the roles of public-funded science and research and stock market infrastructures which enable very few people to become very rich very quickly. Also there is little discussion of the misery of 'affluenza' often caused by surplus and excessive wealth[95]. Success in business can give one money and power, but that power needs to be handled responsibly and may not make everyone happy and healthy.

If we are to develop a holistic science of accounting and finance, we need to acknowledge the vast diversity of cultures and world views our students come from and the different ways in which they have been raised. Many of them may believe in religion and have different languages spoken at home. They may have been raised in a culture of hard work and volunteering, which gives them very different experiences from the selfishness that is the science of economics. They may come from homes where none of their parents went to university, but where they were brought up in a rich culture of morality and conscience, and a character of self-discipline and truthfulness. Their experience of growing up in extended families and socialised communities can give them a richness which can be encouraged and built upon. Given their experiences of poverty and hardship, they are likely to be exceptionally hungry to learn and progress through education and willing to work long and hard to achieve a better livelihood. To throw a partial and 'ideological' science at them in such circumstances would be a betrayal. It could potentially diminish their capacity to provide moral leadership precisely at a time when we need it the most.

TACIT SKILLS

Just as business education and science have become increasingly powerful and ideological, the whole concept of tacit learning and experience has been diminished in importance. Business schools derive their very existence from students NOT knowing about business and coming to them for some magic formulae of wealth and success. In this sense as institutions, they prefer not to acknowledge cultural skills and strengths in enterprise. If I look at my own upbringing, my father was a very creative and driven social entrepreneur and that has influenced my own career trajectory. From a young age, I remember hearing the language of business at community events, even when I could not understand it fully. I recall Diwali mornings when businessmen gathered to open new books of account, a ritual known as 'Chopda Pujan', whose cultural and scientific significance took me years to unravel. I grew up in a vibrant and cultured immigrant business community in Kenya, where enterprise was profoundly woven into my cultural fabric. I did not need to go to university or become a qualified professional to understand the basics of business and its purpose.

Similarly, when I reflect on the interviews that I have conducted for this book, I realise that there are people with vast oceans of lived experience in business and finance, but hardly any academic has taken an interest in listening to their stories. Even when I researched the collapse of HBOS Bank, the largest business failure ever in British history, the key whistle-blower Paul Moore said he had been waiting for academics to contact him so he could share his story[96]. No one had felt the need to hear his side of the story, even though he had a very senior role in the Bank and warned much earlier about the hidden dangers lurking within the high-growth mentality. It seems that in our desperation for an objective, rational science, and the desire to prove theory or add to the existing stock of scientific knowledge, the real world has become a nuisance to be kept at a distance. Routinely we hear practitioners saying that research has moved farther and farther away from their craft, such that they cannot even understand or relate to the research findings that experts discuss in their scientific papers.

To add insult to injury, accounting and finance have become increasingly separated as disciplines[97], such that the scholars do not talk to one another, and even if they did, they would not understand each other. Specialisation has taken over, and connection and inter-disciplinarily have withered in a structural way, making scientific collaboration more and more difficult, even when the subjects are so inter-related and feed off one another in their theories and frameworks. This cannot be healthy for a planet and society that is desperate to be understood through its interdependence and holistic problems and challenges. The expertise itself can become unsustainable. Many would argue that the science is actively making the world unsustainable, by emphasising the material at the expense of the cultural or environmental priorities. It therefore needs to be fundamentally overhauled.

In her TED Talk, the writer and activist Elif Shafak explained that cultural and personal complexity cannot be objectified or denied[98]. Individuals should not be simplified or aggregated, summarised or materialised to suit our need for power and control. Empathy, emotions, love, care and compassion are necessary for sustainable living and should not be turned into proxies or replaced by money and comforts. In his series of BBC Reith lectures, the Chief Rabbi Jonathan Sacks explains that in spite of the enlightenment's hope of the death of God, there has been a surprising persistence of belief[99]. People who belong to faith communities have a sense of history, a respect for the family and community, and self-discipline and conscience which often regulates their moral conduct and character, irrespective of the behaviour of other people. It is therefore important that in cultivating a moral science of accounting and finance, we engage with this diversity of belief and culture, rather than dismiss or ignore it.

When Indians from East Africa first migrated to the UK in the 1970s, many of them started with a corner shop – a local store where people can buy newspapers and basic groceries. These were open long hours and even on weekends, when most businesses were shut. Customers were treated as visitors to their own home – such was the respect and hospitality. One day, when a young person came into a friend's store in Clacton and put the batteries in his pocket, he saw it. Instead of admonishing the child and asking him to return the batteries, he spoke to him saying that next time if you want anything from this shop, ask for it and I will give it for free. He did not want him to grow up in a life of shop-lifting or thinking that stealing is the way to success. In these businesses, moral lessons were also imparted through lived example to customers and suppliers. This is a sustainable business in practice. It does not destroy trust and actively encourages kindness and empathy. My friend is a devoted Hindu by faith and even has a temple in his own house, which he opens and shares with the public, sometimes welcoming school trips and pilgrimages from far off towns. For him, business is an act of service to the community, not a method of extraction from it. Its purpose and meaning are not separate from his own beliefs and values. He lives and operates as a whole being.

Later in this book, through examples and case studies, you will see that when accounting and finance leaders are not greedy or selfish, they end up replenishing trust in society, rather than depleting it. Their very conduct and behaviour inspire and encourage others to be good and do good, and act unselfishly, especially when they become rich and wealthy. When the interdependence of society is understood and respected, the quality of the advice given by professionals, and the trust it generates, enhances social welfare and cohesion.

OUR COMMON FUTURE

Quality accounting and finance science and practice are critical to the sustainability of any society and economy. With ethical, fair and professional practice, these professions can play a valuable role in supporting and facilitating business growth and progress without compromising society or the environment. There is a crucial role for the creation of credit, sound evaluations of risk and for high quality accounting and accountability. Trust can be enhanced by good professionals, not depleted as we often see today. For this to happen, morality needs to be central to the training and science, and not peripheral or incidental to the teaching and research in these disciplines. Similarly, the diversity of faith and cultures cannot be ignored in the education and training – in fact in many cases, people raised in faith traditions are determined to operate fairly and ethically and afraid to betray their trust and reputation. The way young people are raised shapes their personal morality, and to completely ignore or suppress it in the professional journey is to betray the possible positive impacts on ethical professional practice. They have already been moulded to act morally, so it is better to build on this rather than suppress it and instead speak of ethics in a rule-based abstract and impersonal way, remote from any lived experience.

When it comes to authentic professional skills in accounting and finance, small can be beautiful, and big can be problematic. Niche firms or personal advisers develop a relationship with their clients and may want to retain their clients and grow their reputation through referrals rather than marketing or PR. They are keen to obtain clients who are honest and worthy, rather than those who are after a quick buck or a cheap professional service. It is possible that for good experts, clients are seen as partners and vice versa – they take personal responsibility of the consequences of their advice. I come from a community of accountants – the Jains are one of the largest per capita community of accountants in the world. Competency and professionalism seem to be part of their DNA, and they excel at their work and keep on growing their clients. One friend, Mr. Pravin Shah, passed away recently and once his clients heard about it, they were all in tears and at a loss. The clients came from all cultures and ethnicities, yet each of them saw him either as a brother, a family member, or a relative, someone who was fair, honest and reliable and very professional in the quality of his advice. For people with family businesses, a good accountant is not just an adviser but a colleague and mentor and someone with whom they can also discuss their personal problems as well as their business challenges. When accountants serve a variety of businesses at the same time, they build up knowledge and experience about the marketplace, and valuable contacts and networks with lawyers, bankers and other professionals which can be used to help their clients grow their businesses.

Techniques of measurement, risk calculation and valuation are not unimportant. However, their social and cultural context needs to be understood. Similarly, the limitations of the assumptions behind the calculations need to be explained and not forgotten in the pursuit of the holy grail method of valuation or profit maximisation. When this is not done, students are misled and betrayed into accepting subjective methods as objective truths. The moral dimensions also must be reinforced. Good character and conduct of the finance professional need to be demonstrated as a core quality, and something which should be maintained. Its nurturing is directly entwined with the calculations and NOT independent of it. The moral values can be taught through alternative methods – true stories, narratives and case studies can help students discuss and engage with moral dilemmas, and in the process, develop their own virtues and conscience. Even methods like meditation or visualisation can be put on the curriculum to help students understand the nature and limits of money and to see that success in finance need not compromise personal health and emotional satisfaction. A happy customer or client will tell five others, but an unhappy customer may tell the whole world – so it is so much better to satisfy the customers than to knowingly give them the wrong advice in pursuit of a higher commission or fees. The roles of culture and community in business and finance also need to be discussed – how trust can be nurtured and reinforced, or abused and depleted. Students need to be encouraged to have self-discipline to ensure that they do not betray the trust placed on them. Such training would also enhance their social and professional skills.

Small-scale personal narratives of advice and professionalism can then be extended towards larger corporate scale and even globalisation. Students are more likely to relate to intimate stories to understand the links between knowledge, morality and quality advice, and the effect this can have on both the clients and the professionals. Stories have a power to convey the depth and meaning of trust, something central to finance, in a very intimate way. The personal experience of risk and fraudulent advice can be discussed through real-life narratives and traumas caused by bad finance. The distance between the feeling and the calculation is bridged in this way, rather than abandoned or discarded as irrelevant. When clients come seeking short cuts or tax evasion advice, accountants and bankers could stand up and say no, we are not willing to do this or certify it.

This act of challenge and defence of personal standards could be discussed extensively in the classroom, to explore the consequences and implications. I do know many accountants in real life who have said no to their clients and are unwilling to bend the rules to enhance their fee income. These stories rarely come out or get told in the training curriculum, but they can be very inspirational.

We now turn to explore the vast wisdom and knowledge which are passed down through generations of tradition, customs, reflexivity, memory, stories and beliefs. Contrary to popular belief, sustainability is not a new idea or science. It has been lived for generations in many parts of the world. This bank of experience can help us find new direction with the challenges we face today. They are authentic and sincere.

Notes

1 Speech delivered by Greta Thunberg on September 23, 2019.
2 Various sources – www.populationmatters.org; Oxfam 'Inequality Kills' Report 2022.
3 Carney (2021) and Shaxson (2018).
4 Throughout this book, the term finance is used in a generic way to include BOTH accounting and finance science and practice.
5 Scientists have proven that in the last seventy years, one species has done irreversible damage to planet earth – in terms of rain forest destruction, thousands of whole species have become extinct, and air, sea and soil have been severely polluted – it is the human species who is directly responsible (Ellis, 2018).
6 See Shah A. (2018a), Fraser (2015) and McDonald and Robinson (2009).
7 Parker (2018) and Gray (1998).
8 Whyte (2020)
9 For example, see Arnold (2012), Arnold (2009), Sikka (2008) and Sikka and Willmott (1995).
10 See Huhn (2014) for a cogent and critical analysis of the MBA curriculum and its domination by technocratic economic thinking, which is utilitarian and completely impersonal.
11 See Shah A. (2018a,b), West (2003) and Zeff (2003).
12 See Shaxson (2018) which is a sophisticated critique of the curse that is modern finance.
13 See Zwan (2014) and Blakeley (2019).
14 See Brooks (2018) and Shaxson (2018).
15 Stiglitz is a prolific writer and critic – see e.g. Stiglitz (2019) for a critique of economic ideology and corporate abuse of power.
16 Komori (2015) shows how, in Japan, researchers have to suppress their cultural difference and identity to write for international accounting journals, suggesting that accounting research is unsustainable if this is how diversity is suppressed. Annisette (2003) writes about racism in the accounting profession. Lombardi (2016) finds discrimination for indigenous Australians entering the accounting profession.
17 See Sacks (2003).
18 See Nadler and Breuer (2019) which analyses over 100 published research papers and develops a structured framework for looking at 'Cultural Finance'. This book will show that such approaches are problematic as Culture is the framework around which finance needs to be analysed, and cultures differ in context and content, so there is no general framework we should be seeking.
19 See Thaler (2013).
20 Lehman (2005) and Hines (1988).

21 Boyce (2008) is an excellent critique of contemporary ethics education and Sikka (2015) shows how UK accounting firms and practices perpetuate inequality.

22 Zwan (2014) and Blakeley (2019).

23 See McGoun and Zielonka (2006). Daly and Cobb (1994) represent a prescient analysis of the flaws of materialist and utilitarian economics.

24 See Hall and Soskice (2001) and Gray (1998).

25 See Brooks et al (2019) and Brooks and Schopohl (2018).

26 See Aggarwal et al (2016).

27 Tett (2021) is a detailed account of the need for holistic 'anthro-vision' among finance leaders.

28 Daly and Cobb (1994).

29 Carney (2021). www.bbc.co.uk – Reith Lectures – Episode 1 – 'From Market to Moral Sentiments' is worth a listen.

30 Daly and Cobb (1994), Frankfurter and McGoun (2002), Soros (1998) and Sandel (2012).

31 Parker (2011) is an excellent analysis of this.

32 Parker (2018a, b).

33 Gray (1992) explains the flaws very well.

34 Daly and Cobb (1994) is an excellent analysis of the failure of economics to incorporate ethical and spiritual values and instead impose an ideological materialist worldview without any humility or reservations.

35 Erturk et al (2007) is a powerful critique of agency theory in finance. See also Engelen et al (2012) on the role of experts in the 2008 financial crisis.

36 Nielsen (2016) makes a bold case for the importance and relevance of action research in the field of business ethics.

37 Bukovinsky (2019) explains its radical banking model very well.

38 Fraser (2015) is a masterful account of this hubris and shows how Goodwin was a chartered accountant and technocrat who was feared by everyone. The role of culture in good banking was not even seen to be important – accounting professional training excludes culture and its links to fair accounting practice. He believed numbers are enough to run a Bank, and even built a 350-million-pound gigantic headquarters campus at Gogarburn in Scotland without fearing how much it would distance the Bank from its stakeholders and savers.

39 See Perman (2012).

40 See Parker (2018a,b) who recommends bulldozing of the business school altogether.

41 Tax Justice Network (2015) and Brooks (2014).

42 See Sikka (2015) for the role of accounting in producing inequality and injustice.

43 See James (2007) – the case studies in the book reveal the deep insecurities that come from wealth, something which finance education totally ignores to society's peril.

44 See Gray (2015).

45 See Fleming and Jones (2012).

46 See Tett (2010, Chapter 9).

47 See Kay (2015, Chapter 2). Das (2011) also exposes the deep uncertainties and risqué behaviour.

48 See Parker (2018) for an accessible critique.

49 See Fraser (2015, Chapter 16).

50 See Heffernan (2011).

51 Shah A. (2018b) elaborates much more on this.

52 Kellaway (2015).

53 McKenna (2019) shows how KPMG US partners did this repeatedly for several years – even accounting leaders have no regard for compliance with ethics rules.

54 See Harare (2015).

55 See Bakan (2004) and there is also an excellent documentary on YouTube called The Corporation made by Bakan.

56 See Sandel (2012) for an excellent critique of the moral limits of markets.

57 See Korten (1995), Bakan (2004), Hertz (2001), Goodman (2022) and Bakan (2021).
58 See Kay (2015).
59 See Perman (2012).
60 See Gray (1992).
61 See Elkind and McLean (2003).
62 See Sikka (2008; 2009), Mitchell and Sikka (2011) and Brooks (2018).
63 Sikka et al (2018) exposes the deep malaise that is the modern auditing industry in Britain.
64 Brooks (2018, Chapter 7) details how the Big 4 firm PWC chased their whistleblowers in the case of LuxLeaks.
65 Hertz (2001).
66 Erturk et al (2007). Shaxson (2018) and Kay (2015) critique conventional theories of finance and moral hazard as misleading and a misrepresentation of truth.
67 See Lewis (2008; 2011; 2014).
68 Kay (2015).
69 See Glattfelder and Battiston (2019).
70 Hillier et al (2016).
71 Strange (1986) predicted this a long time ago.
72 Ferguson (2010) depicts this very graphically in the film, which shows how drugs and prostitution were paid for by financial institutions, and used to attract client business, spreading the vice.
73 Stein (2011) found a culture of mania incubated the 2008 crash. This is echoed by Das (2011) who calls it a 'cult of risk'.
74 Sayer (2016) calls this legalized corruption and highly damaging – we simply cannot 'afford' the rich.
75 Fortado (2015) exposes the broken culture in the UBS trading floor and the huge pressure on Adoboli as the most senior trader (at the age of 31) to make large profits, which led to the risk and fake trades. Adoboli had a very good character and charisma, but the trading floor pressure turned his care for the team to faking the deals to make the team look good in front of the bosses.
76 See Palma (2022). Tim Leissner who perpetuated the fraud and has pleaded guilty, admitted that he had a risqué lifestyle and was very ambitious and greedy at the same time. Goldman Sachs promoted him to partner and celebrated the revenues he was bringing in, despite knowing his character. Leissner had to bribe to get some of the deals and this was overlooked.
77 Edmans (2020).
78 Parker (2018).
79 Seto-Pamies D and E. Papaoikonomou (2016).
80 See McLean (2017) for a forensic account of how even whistleblowers were ignored by management in their greed for higher profits and bonuses; also watch 'The Wagon Wheel' documentary, part of the Dirty Money (2020) series on Netflix for a visual account of how the fraud was perpetrated by the leadership.
81 Harney and Dunne (2013) and Brooks and Schopohl (2018) analyse decades of finance research to expose the profound lack of diversity in research methods, topics and theories.
82 See Shah (2018b) which examines in detail the reforms needed for accounting and finance education.
83 Hall and Soskice (2001).
84 Butcher (2018).
85 Beck (1992), Douglas and Wildavsky (1982), Douglas (1992) and Shah and Baker (2015).
86 Shah (1997a,b).
87 Sama and Shoaf (2007) explain how a moral community can be fostered among professions, and West (2003) focuses on the history of the accounting profession and how it has transformed itself in modern times to serve corporate interests rather than advance truth and fairness.

88 Hanlon (1994) charts the history of the commercialization of accountancy from profession to business.
89 Gandhi M. K. (1982) devotes a whole chapter to this relationship and the dialogues between the two.
90 There are several references in his name in the bibliography – these are a small part of his hundreds of articles and blogs.
91 Sikka et al (1995) discusses the perils of academic or critical accounting work, but also the importance of speaking truth to power.
92 See Parker (2018) a life-long academic, who argues that the business school is a production line which should actually be shut down as it does more harm than good.
93 Dr. Radhakrishnan, an eminent philosopher of India, established September 5 as Teachers Day, because he believed good teaching is critical to sparking the inner light of students. See Murty and Vohra (1990).
94 See Murty and Vohra (1990).
95 See James (2007).
96 Shah (2018a).
97 See Hopwood (2007; 2009).
98 Shafak (2017).
99 Sacks (1990).

2

TRADITION

We are living in the age of the Anthropocene. Mankind, one of the most intelligent species on the planet, has been found guilty of the most heinous of crimes – we have done irreversible damage to our own homes, destroying forests, rivers, oceans and even whole species have become extinct, as a result of our activities. All this has happened in the space of just a few hundred years. Our population growth, technologies of killing, chemicals in agriculture, oil extraction and pollution have poisoned and destroyed our very own home. In short, we have been suicidal to humanity, in many cases knowingly and deliberately. Business and its products and practices have been a significant part of the problem – they have exacerbated and amplified our self-destruction. Sixty percent of the largest economies in the world are 'undemocratic' multinational corporations NOT countries. Power without accountability is hard-wired into their DNA[1].

'In the era of the free-market, now fast slipping from memory, the past hardly existed. Only the present had any reality, and it was being constantly re-fashioned and made new. New industries, new careers, new lives were being continuously created, then discarded, according to market imperatives. Grandiose doctrines came up to support the belief that the free-market capitalism that had been adopted in a handful of countries would prevail over every other economic system.'

This is how the eminent political economist John Gray begins his prescient book 'False Dawn' with a revised preface after the 2008 crash (Gray, 1998). Sadly, even today, finance research and education continue on this flawed trajectory. This is a direct frontal attack on the vast cultural bio-diversity of homo economicus and is unsustainable. It denies the role of diverse cultures and traditions in influencing business and financial practice. In this chapter, we look at the role of traditions in shaping economic practice.

The world's oldest known corporation, Stora Kopparberg, was born in 1288 in Sweden as a mining company, and its environmental record has been

DOI: 10.4324/9781003164746-2

devastating – soil, sea and forests have been destroyed, and today it is the second-largest paper producer in the world. Yet it has never faced any fines or penalties for its *eco-cide*, demonstrating how corporations are an engine of planetary exploitation[2]. Accounting and finance, while appearing benign, have given fuel to the fire, by making inequality and environmental destruction appear profitable and ignoring the pollution or destruction of species in the calculation of costs[3]. Stock markets have channelled vital savings and investments to these damaging technologies, adding fuel to the fire and in the process burning our forests and animal habitats. Corporate conduct has been made invisible by the fiction of their glamorous offices, marketing spin and misleading profit calculations, which do not take account of social and environmental damage.

The contemporary perception of Africa as a 'dark continent' with poverty and economic underdevelopment is a far cry from its history and traditions. Here is what one eminent scholar noted about its economic history and traditions[4]:

> ...long before the arrival of Europeans, Africans maintained vibrant political and economic systems; developed writing systems; domesticated animals; used iron; traded in many major commodities, such as gold, silver, cloth, guns, horses, camels, fish, salt, cloves, wax, and agricultural produce; and even developed institutions of higher learning. Pottery, glass-making, basketry, and sculpture were widespread on the continent to the extent that, when the Europeans landed off their caravels and other wind-propelled ships during the fifteenth century and later, they encountered sophisticated societies and markets where they could immediately exchange their goods.

The arrival of the Europeans brought a culture of greed and expropriation, slavery being the most extreme, which spread globally, and destroyed native cultures and ways of life, including their finance and economic principles and ethics. Prior to the Anthropocene, there was a period of global cultural genocide between the seventeenth and twentieth centuries, which then created a culturally vacuous economic and finance theory, after sustainable and timeless traditions were destroyed. Secular neo-classical economics is built on a desert of its own creation – and then it has been used to ideologically conquer planetary economic cultures and systems. In this book, we are trying to rediscover these traditions and give them the respect they richly deserve. Lessons of history are important in understanding why we have come to be where we are.

PRACTICE AS CULTURE NOT SCIENCE

Many of you may know an accounting or a bank professional in your family or friend circle. However, it is unlikely you will see them as an eco-criminal – they wear smart suits, talk clever-clever, work in high-rise offices, are usually male, and earn a lot of money – so surely they must be doing something good? This is the paradox that is being analysed in this book – there is a direct connection between the accounting calculations, methods of working and the wider impact on both society and nature. However, it is always hidden from plain sight, and often very difficult to critique as the jargon is simply overwhelming and complex if you are not trained in those disciplines. Even if one is trained in those disciplines, one may fail to see the wider connections and impact, because of the narrow specialist way in which the training is conducted and the partial content of the knowledge and education. However, this educational fraud is unsustainable for our planet. Current and future generations of students need to know what they are signing up for. Behind the calculations, there are big decisions about politics, equality, society and the environment which are often adverse and deeply damaging.

The United Nations is making a strong push towards global sustainable development and in 2015 issued seventeen Sustainable Development Goals for all nations, which embrace principles like ending poverty and hunger, practising equality, respect for human rights, quality education for all, quality jobs and working conditions, good housing, care for land and forests, good health and social welfare, and the protection of rural communities[5]. Products and services provided by businesses should also be necessary and produced in a way that does not deplete human and environmental resources. In 2017, specific measures and targets were announced for countries to move towards achieving these goals. Although corporate activity, accounting measures and finance did not appear directly in these goals, there is an implication that the incentives and targets provided by accounting and finance should encourage corporations to behave responsibly and sustainably and not exploit or expropriate, as is so common with giant corporations.

In the wake of this crisis, humanity has awoken and is claiming to have found 'solutions', like carbon neutrality, making us believe that the same people responsible for the calamity have now switched sides and are protecting the environment. They have become smarter and savvier with science and technology, and we are led to assume that all will be better and safer now if these solutions are implemented. What about human cultures and behaviours? Have they all suddenly been reversed? How can we now trust the 'experts' to solve the problems which they profited from in the first place? A lot of the switch to a green economy is spearheaded by large commercially driven consultancies like the Big 4 global accounting firms – can we really trust[6] them given their history? Is sustainable policy and consulting just another giant spin machine (greenwashing), where new-fangled experts have found yet another opportunity to profit and cheat, because people are confused and desperate[7]? Are we re-acting because we need to show that we are doing something 'good' for the environment?

In contemporary accounting and finance theory and education, there is no place for tradition whatsoever. It is assumed that we have 'progressed' as a society so much that business has become a science. Tradition is like going back in time, backward in both knowledge and techniques. Instead, we are marching forward boldly into the future, with sophisticated financial markets and methods of calculation and valuation. We have a new 'enlightened' world view called 'science' which is going to liberate and save us. To incorporate concerns like social justice, inequality and the environment, all we need to do is adjust our equations and calculations. To bring back tradition is to be a Luddite, someone who is against technology and evolution. Without tradition and communities, however, it is very difficult to have a public and social conscience to transform society at a time when we need urgent action. Instrumental laws and policies are not enough on their own – they need living communities for their practical implementation. As we saw in Chapter 1, modernity and the enlightenment have not only severed forests, they have severed morality, culture and tradition and instead created a technocracy. Economics has taught us bad habits about selfishness and materialism and made them righteous and scientific through its own positivist, utilitarian and neo-liberal narratives.

ESG WITHOUT MORALITY

Dominic Burke has worked for many years in ESG funding and investment. ESG is one of the new mantras in finance – it is the mantra which says we are monitoring ethical and environmental performance by corporations and rating and ranking them. It stands for environmental, social and governance – the three big priorities now deemed critical to transforming the corporation to a sustainable entity. Sadly, after years of talking to companies and participating in meetings, he is disillusioned. No one speaks about virtues, morality or the right way to behave, Dominic complains. Instead, the jargon now is about climate risk or environmental and social risk – how these can be measured, evaluated and reported upon. Risk to investors has replaced the moral or eco-friendly way to do business.

The experts are sitting on a 'neutral' fence, appearing to be independent and objective, but in reality, completely missing the truth, the empathy and the humility needed for our species to reform and transform. The proxy measures have become the goals – honesty is not needed, nor do we need to admit the significant limitations of such analysis. Can new wine be sold in old, recycled bottles? Do we not need to revisit the fundamentals of economics, business and finance and make sure that the thinking which led to the devastation is repaired and rewired? The desire for sustainability can lead to the creation of a new cadre of experts who see an opportunity to profit from the crisis. In our modern history, there is plenty of evidence of experts colonising jargon and disciplines to suit the needs of power or profit[8]. We need to be aware that a technocratic society will constantly develop technocratic solutions as knee-jerk responses, because reforming the fundamentals of our markets and institutions is much more problematic. Furthermore, these solutions are likely to be self-interested to preserve their own professions and territories.

GOOD TRADITIONS HAVE SUSTAINED

Old cultures and traditions which are outside the theories and equations have sustained themselves over hundreds or even thousands of years and many generations. In the process, they have kept alive spirits of family and community, having respect for animals and nature and are not just theories but lived practices, still alive and vibrant today. Do we have something to learn from them to guide us through this crisis? Could it be that the reason they have survived and sustained themselves is precisely because they have not lived beyond their scale, learnt the importance of giving and sharing and not allowed money to take over their lives? Surely their very history and resilience should encourage us to make them role models and teachers for the kinds of transformations we need to make as a human society? I believe we have nothing to lose from trying to understand and learn from them. Often with older traditions, production and consumption are within limits and scale, and there are no grand plans to go global or expand to reduce costs of production. Profit is not the priority, but morality, wisdom and contentment are. Peaceful co-existence is more important than economic growth or monetary wealth and possessions. These are priorities which are very different from contemporary society, and for hundreds and even thousands of years, these traditions did not damage our ecosystem irreversibly, so there will be much to learn from their wisdom and experiences. Even consumption habits were simple and contented, rather than greedy and wasteful. Mahatma Gandhi used to say – there is enough in the world for our needs, but there will never be enough to fulfil our greed.

At a very basic level, our primary needs for survival are food, shelter and clothing. If we kept our needs at this level, surely there will never be a recession or poverty? The modern money economy instead uses jobs and mortgages as a way of keeping the wheels churning. It is also driven by speculation, booms and busts, fraud and corruption, all of which create insecurity and destroy people's jobs, savings and livelihoods. We lose our sense of basic needs and purpose and instead become overwhelmed by the need to earn and borrow, often trying to compete with others for toys and gadgets instead of practising kindness, friendship and charity. Materialism destroys our appreciation of history and tradition, and the importance of retaining culture and values and not allowing consumerism to overwhelm our habits.

As we have already seen in Chapter 1, the disciplines of accounting and finance have desperately tried to be 'objective', rational and scientific, even though in reality they are often deeply ideological. One element they have completely ignored is indigenous cultures and their practices. This chapter is about a grounded approach, whereby instead of trying to impose a platonic science, we seek to learn from lived experiences and draw upon these to develop frameworks for an organic and sustainable finance. There is a wisdom in generations of ancient cultures that we should not ignore. We forget that the depth and breadth of the importance of money in the local economy and society is a relatively new feature of human life[9]. For hundreds and thousands of years, societies managed without money and lived a life of cooperation and mutuality, where not everything was about worth or material well-being. Instead, the priorities were about the survival of the group, and the care for the land, animals and nature. Villages were local countries, economies and resources of knowledge, health and well-being, and outside money was not allowed to influence this peace and harmony or disrupt it. There was conflict, but also relatively more peace than we give it credit – people lived settled lives. Large anonymous corporations were nowhere to be seen, and technologies and markets in other parts of the world could not disrupt what was happening locally.

FAITH AND FINANCE

Most faith traditions have belief and value systems which prioritise peaceful co-existence. Many faiths have several thousand-year-old histories of birth and evolution, like Hinduism, Judaism, Islam, Christianity, Zoroastrianism, Taoism, Confucianism, Buddhism and Jainism. They are more than systems of philosophy and belief – they have large groups of followers and communities all over the world. Just as a rain forest is not simply a collection of anonymous trees, faith traditions are eco-systems which have grown across time and space and evolved from history, memory, rituals and lived experiences. It is also important to note that within themselves, there is considerable diversity of practice in each faith. Principles, practices and even beliefs can be diverse and multi-lingual, as faiths change across time and space. Given that economics is the science of wealth creation and distribution, and all communities need systems of trade and exchange, all faiths have economic practices and customs which adopt varying attitudes to wealth and equity. Contemporary accounting and finance education simply ignores this history, the varying philosophies and beliefs and the diversity of cultural practices around finance. This is deeply flawed.

More and more books are now emerging on different faiths and their approaches to finance[10]. The divorce between man, belief and nature in contemporary economics is one of the main sources of critique. Eisenstein (2021) pleads for a 'Sacred Economics' where money is a means to an end and respects laws of nature rather than defy them. Compound interest has the power to exponentially 'grow' money and wealth without effort, and this is a serious bone of contention. Islamic finance has very old roots and a complex series of beliefs and customs, which are well documented. Today, it is the most well-researched area of faith-based finance outside of contemporary economics. In terms of research and material, its coverage far outnumbers any other faith, underpinning the importance of morality in Muslim business and financial transactions.

Fairness, equality and justice are woven into the fabric of its 'Sharia' laws, and regular charity is strongly emphasised (Zakat). Economics and law in Islam have been designed for the service of a peaceful and harmonious society, with trade serving as a mechanism for providing useful products and services at a fair price.

The centrality of moral purpose to economics is hard-wired in Islam, a faith with over two billion followers in the world today, from all cultures and continents. Nowadays, investments and institutions need to be certified as Sharia compliant to attract customers and funding. There are also separate Islamic financial markets and institutions which have emerged from this. The Jewish community have a long history of engagement in finance, and they have also been persecuted in history for this. However, they are today one of the premiere global diasporas in finance and have clearly developed some niche knowledge and skills which have helped them succeed for millennia. Tzedekah[11], a key principle, combines charity and justice at the same time – success has to be shared AS justice, not kept to oneself. It is unjust to keep wealth to oneself.

For the very poor, money and credit can make a difference between starvation and survival. They have long been forgotten by society and removed from its property claims and economic markets. The depth of their struggles has often meant that their self-esteem and dignity come from faith. Micro-finance, whereby small loans at very affordable rates are given, combined with the tools and education to make their small enterprise work, has often been their lifeblood. Looft (2014), in an exhaustive global study, finds that faith is often the common denominator of the origins of microfinance and the care and compassion with which the ongoing support and dignity are given to the marginalised. The poor are not looking for charity, and charity often fails. However, micro-finance helps them to become small entrepreneurs by giving them valuable credit at the right time, which enables them to grow their business and feed the family. Hundreds of millions of lives are saved by micro-finance. In fact, in the so-called developed nations, the poor are often left to loan sharks and made to feel embarrassed by their poverty and 'perceived uselessness'. The reach of micro-finance and financial literacy is very low in these developed nations. In the accounting and finance academy, this problem rarely features in the textbooks and is simply ignored altogether, even though it affects hundreds of millions of people in developed nations. This is another example of a social silence which is unsustainable. Looft's research provides contemporary evidence of how the lives of millions of people are uplifted by faith-based, compassionate micro-finance.

It is therefore surprising that both accounting and finance education today make no reference to the Jewish community and its unique beliefs and skills. In fact, it is often through faith that business leaders develop a sense of meaning and purpose, which helps them to take risks, expand, trade and grow the economy[12]. Business success helps fund important community institutions like schools, hospitals, churches, temples, community meals and festivals. Society and modernity cannot forget that for a long time in human history, critical needs like education, health and social welfare were provided by faith communities, who in the process developed mutuality, social cohesion and trust. When we look at history, faiths have often given birth to financial practices and innovations and improved trust and relationships. Members of faiths have traded with one another, learnt and taught each other new skills, shared information and networks and even provided hospitality to traders as they travelled to different towns and cities.

In his path-breaking five-thousand-year history of finance, Graeber (2014) found that throughout human history, debt and faith have been inter-twined, and lending and borrowing have been driven by relationships, beliefs and needs between peoples. From the above, we can say that the ignorance of faith, even its denial, in contemporary accounting and finance, may be one of the central reasons why the current system is so corrupt, fraudulent and broken. There is little fear or conscience, and personal character, reputation and honour are not even discussed in the classroom, let alone feared. We will see later that even leadership, purpose and meaning are not discussed when it comes to doing a postgraduate degree in finance. The whole discipline has been deliberately made impersonal and 'objective'. Long-term ethical leadership in finance, like all leadership, can be tough and challenging, and having and belonging to faith can make a big difference in the strategies and policies. We will see later that the accumulation of wealth can also bring its own perils and dangers, and to keep wealth can be very difficult and challenging. Here again, faith traditions have solutions and practices, like charity, which help give wealth a flow and circulation, often leading to continuing success for the givers. The humility that is central to finance often comes from faith, and the corollary is also often true – lack of faith leads to egoism and extreme selfishness.

CULTURE IS CENTRAL TO FINANCE

Culture is a broad general term, which includes shared values, memories, stories, art, music, food, character, moral norms of conduct and behavior, language, tradition – many aspects of life contribute to human culture. Religion and belief have been central to culture for most of human existence on this planet – it is only in the last 500 years that we have sought to separate ourselves from it, believing that it can be dogmatic and irrational. Even then, religion has refused to go away. Many argue that neo-liberalism and free-market fundamentalism are also a religion by another name[13]. Even when our accounting and finance theories and textbooks profess to be secular by design, they are underpinned by ideological beliefs in materialism, free markets, primacy of capital providers, and conservatism. The challenge that culture poses is that it is difficult to define precisely and therefore it cannot be measured or valued. As result, it has hitherto been ignored to our peril. Precise definition can mean uniformity and boundary, something which is there to serve power and authority. The unique diversity of world cultures defies this, and in the process also shows the richness that we can all live and learn from.

Keith Darcy, one of the most senior global Ethics and Compliance professional leaders, examined a range of multi-billion-dollar corporate scandals, including big names like Toyota, WorldCom, Enron, and Lehman Brothers[14]. His professional work has brought him to understand in detail compliance and monitoring systems inside giant multinationals, and his findings are bleak. Darcy discovered that the most common denominator of failure was a broken culture, where lying and cheating is normalised and leaders do not have a sense of 'personal' responsibility and accountability. They lack conscience and forget the huge responsibility which comes with the power they command. No amount of systems, rules or processes would compensate for a bad culture.

Sadly, even when examining evidence of cheating from young American college students, Darcy found a similar pattern – they had normalised this in order to pass exams. Darcy claims that no amount of rules or regulations can reform culture – it has to begin from the inside, the soul and spirit of the leader, and leaders need to value good culture and give primary importance to role modelling it. This is where they fail, first in the corporate boardroom, and then in their social and environmental impact. This shows how important tradition and belief are to shaping the conscience and behaviour of leaders and to neglect this is to fail in our teaching and science.

Being a finance leader necessarily confers power and prestige and can have a magnetic effect on other people and organisations, who may clamour to be in your network. All the diverse finance leaders I have interviewed for this book never sought fame or power. In fact, they positively avoided it and instead operate humbly and live their values, rather than preach them. They understand the true meaning of the phrase 'fiduciary' – other people's money is not their own and needs to be handled with care and responsibility. When they did succeed and attain fame or influence, they did not take this to their head. Instead, the leaders sought to share it and help others grow and flourish, either through their enterprises and job creation, or through their charitable work, or both. This is an example of sustainable finance leadership – where the inner soul is not separated from the outer work. The stories and examples to follow will show how they achieved this.

Open virtually any contemporary textbook of accounting and finance and there will be little or no reference to faith or culture. This is true even in international editions of such textbooks. How paradoxical it is then to know that both accounting and finance are social and cultural creations – in communicating financial reality, we actively construct it[15]. By making the subjects mathematical and technical, we subconsciously give the impression that they are precise and accurate representations of financial performance and valuation. In a similar way, the professional examinations, many of which are also done globally, do not have any element of cultural reference or diversity. If we think from a globalisation and profit maximisation lens, cultural diversity is perceived as a *nuisance* and barrier to standardisation of knowledge and practices. However, the ground reality is that people do have culture, and these cultures are truly diverse, including the practices of accounting and finance.

TO TRANSFORM SOCIETY, WE MUST REFORM OUR BEHAVIOURS

As sustainable living and practice require us to reform our behaviours and practices, we have no choice but to engage with existing cultures and belief systems. This is antithetical to present-day theories and techniques, but the Anthropocene demands nothing less than such a revolution. We cannot change culture through technocracy, but we can transform awareness and understanding through culture. The reform of accounting and finance practice needs to engage with behaviours and customs, beliefs and relationships, including social networks of trust. Cultural transformation can only happen if we start by understanding what cultures students come from and what these behaviours and beliefs mean for society and nature. This means that a class in accounting and finance should start from student dialogue about culture, business meaning and purpose, enterprise and ecology. Students should be encouraged to discuss their personal beliefs and values – what is important to them and why. It[16] should not start with double-entry book-keeping as happens in many parts of the world today. Book-keeping straight-jackets the subject into a technical practice, free from moral meaning and purpose. It gives the false impression of an exact calculative method, rather than the truth that accounting and finance practices vary all over the world and between cultures and communities.

Even in the much more well-established field of economics, there is a growing rebellion against the North Atlantic domination, both in theory and expertise. There is firm control of science through the editorship of prestigious journals, all of which are Western, and there is little diversity of language or cultural theories of development and economic transformation[17]. In short, the science fails to reflect the diverse nature of the 'real' world[18]. In his critique of capitalism, global financier George Soros[19] argues very strongly that economic theory is deeply flawed and can never be a natural science. It is based on beliefs and perceptions, and these vary across time, cultures and space and are never constant.

For Soros, market fundamentalism is the biggest problem of contemporary economics. However, even when he explains that reflexivity is central to economics, he denies the influence of faith in modern society and argues for a new 'open society' which is based on reason and reflection – a liberal secular perspective, which is itself a belief. Faith for him is backward and dogmatic. The fact that reflexivity has for thousands of years been hard-wired into his own Jewish tradition is completely ignored. Sadly, many cultures and communities suffer this fate in their migration to the West – there is a phase of denial and suppression of one's own tradition and beliefs, and a rush to discard and assimilate.

In this sense, Soros misses the link between culture, religion and belief which is so prevalent in global economic practices today, by allying with Popper and modern scientific method. He denies his own Jewish history of success in finance as an outcome of tradition and belief. In addition, most of the research in behavioural finance is secular, mono-cultural and based on *personal* psychology rather than groups or cultures and social psychology and usually based on white subjects living in North America[20]. It is also uni-dimensional in its focus on materialism, risk and returns on investment rather than the wide variety of financial needs, cultures, communities and aspirations. Nobel Laureate Professor Thaler is Jewish by heritage, but paradoxically he does not see any need to connect his theories with his own cultural roots, even when he is a founder of behavioural economic science.

INTRA-FAITH DIVERSITY AND CULTURAL MIGRATION

From a secular finance perspective, all faiths are dogmas, unscientific and irrelevant for a progressive, rational future. However, from a real-world observational perspective, faiths are influential, enduring and hugely diverse, both between one another and within one another. Global faiths are practised in wildly different countries, from the East to the West, by people with different nationalities, languages and histories. As a result, even within a faith, there is a vast diversity of belief and practice. This makes them complex and difficult to classify or put into one textbook. However, they also help enrich life, purpose and meaning in a variety of ways, bringing 'dignity' to difference (Sacks, 2003). There are hundreds of books and articles on different faiths and their beliefs and practices, attracting research from not just theologists, but also sociologists, anthropologists and indologists. One global religion, Islam, has such a widely divergent character in different parts of the world, that to consider it a mono-culture is to completely misunderstand it[21].

Travel, migration and history also have huge influences on cultures and beliefs. For example, due to its particular geographic location in North-East India, the state of Gujarat, with its ports and coastline, has been very active in global trade for at least a thousand years and more[22]. This trading culture has brought with it pluralism, tolerance, new migrants to Gujarat, like the Parsees (Zoroastrians), with their own very old culture and history and enriched the local economy and customs in a significant way. Today it is one of the richest states of India, and one of its best exports are Gujarati merchants[23] and professionals, who are now spread out all over the world, boosting the economies they have chosen to migrate to. In the days before business schools and professions, experience, geography, merchant culture and community were the main methods of training.

The leadership, pluralism and assimilation qualities of Gujaratis are such that they have built some of the most important cultural and architectural monuments in the countries they have migrated to. The BAPS Swaminarayan Hindu Mandir in Neasden, North London, was built by Ugandan Asian Gujarati refugees and opened in 1995[24]. David Dimbleby of the BBC dubbed it one of the greatest additions to British architecture in the twentieth century. Its design was copied from the world-famous Jain temples at Delwara in Mt. Abu, Rajasthan. Royalty and Presidents have queued to visit this outstanding monument to wisdom and tradition.

Diaspora churches, temples and mosques, funded and built by migrants in various countries all over the world, are themselves monuments to the movement and respect for cultures and beliefs and their centrality to social and civic life. Often these are funded by merchants, who have the most wealth to donate, showing a recycling and reinvestment of financial success towards lasting communal progress and collective well-being. We can even say that for many finance leaders, philanthropy of this kind, combined with their faiths, gives them purpose and meaning, a type of 'servant' leadership which is inspirational and sustaining.

Some of the interviewees in this book are anonymous philanthropists for such critical cultural and educational institutions. In North America, the Jains have built over 50 temples and they comprise less than 100,000 in population[25].

Such misrepresentation and misunderstanding of faiths in contemporary finance are very common, primarily because the whole concept of culture and diversity is virtually excluded from it. Reason and rationality are deemed to be superior, and even when there are significant calls for reform of banking or accounting culture, all we get is discussion without any action. The reason for this is that no one is addressing the fundamental dislocation of culture from finance theory, science and institutions in the first place. As a result, any attempt to reform will at best be superficial. The thinking and training are profoundly ideological and impersonal, leaving no room for social norms and psychology.

As an example, the Chinese diaspora is well known to be very successful in business and enterprise. There is a close overlap of ownership, control and family, with a dominant executive and centralised decision-making[26]. Family is the core trusted network, and loyalty, hard work and discipline are the norms. Given that labour, resilience and skill are key business resources, to have these as a cultural resource is a priceless source of start-up capital. There are very strong cost and financial controls and a high degree of strategic adaptability. Just within Asia, there are over fifty million Chinese in countries like Singapore, Malaysia, Asia, Indonesia and Philippines, with significant economic power and influence. There is also growing population in Africa, North America and parts of Europe too. They do not operate in the western contractual and transactional model and value reciprocal business relationships.

In this book, we address such cultural complexity and diversity through our leadership interviews and some case study examples. However, by no means is this work exhaustive, and to consider it so would be to betray the vast wealth of diverse cultural practices that exist in the world. The beauty of stories and narratives is that they have the power to convey depth and breadth, but at the same time remain open and accessible to a variety of readers, without being blocked by opaque rules or jargon. I hope readers will be able to see from reading this book what is lost when we ignore culture and diversity and get some idea of the socio-economic costs and losses suffered by societies as a result of this naiveté.

JUDAISM AND JAINISM

Judaism is one of the world's oldest living cultures, and also Jewish intellectuals are some of the most talented in the social sciences. Many Nobel prizes in Economics have been given to Jewish academics in spite of the strong anti-semitism that prevailed in the nineteenth and twentieth centuries. As of 2012, twenty-nine of the first sixty-eight Nobel Laureates in Economics were Jewish[27]. Banks like Goldman Sachs and Lehman Brothers were founded by Jewish families. Because of their history of persecution, Jewish communities placed a lot of emphasis on knowledge and learning. Also the culture never saw money or trade as evil, and on the contrary encouraged it. However, wealth creation was tempered with distributive justice. Deeply woven in the Jewish faith is the concept of *Tzedakah* – social justice, compassion and charity as critical to work and enterprise[28]. Modern Jewish intellectuals in business and finance tend to be secular, perhaps as a reaction to their history of persecution. The late Chief Rabbi Lord Jonathan Sacks, a renowned author and philosopher, makes a prescient case for the importance of faith to modernity, especially in terms of moral progress and sustainable culture[29]. Furthermore, hard work and self-discipline are strongly encouraged in the faith, values which often lead to growth and success.

When I interviewed Andrew Rhodes, co-founder of the award-winning London firm of accountants, Sobell Rhodes[30], he explained that trust, relationships and culture were central to their founding principles, and they wanted to treat their people and clients with equal respect. Both founders are Jewish by origin, though not necessarily religious. In fact, Andrew also provides leadership and strategic advice to other firms of accountants, and organic, people-centred growth is more important to him than acquisitions and mergers. His past experience of inorganic fast-paced growth had bruised him and he did not want to go back there. The firm has built a quality brand name and client base, and new clients come naturally through networks and referrals. To me, their tradition gave them a sense of honesty and integrity which helped them to grow in professionalism, reputation and trust. My friend Satish Kanabar had introduced me to them, so it was a trusted introduction. Andrew's son Mark is now a senior employee at the firm, showing an inter-generational legacy which can come from businesses based on culture and relationships. There is a certain fluidity about our past which none of us can deny – it moulds our character.

In Jain Dharmic wisdom, each and every living being is worthy of respect and our thoughts and actions ought to be non-violent (*ahimsa*), for harmony with our inner selves as well as society, animals and the environment[31]. From a young age, a child is taught not to harm or kill an insect. In this practical teaching, there is a more subtle underlying message – we must not hurt others just because we are bigger and mightier, and if anything, that power should be used to protect and nurture, rather than to exploit and dominate. This makes self-control and self-discipline the heart of our character and leads to a community of kindness and tolerance. And when such a community decides to focus its actions in business enterprise, the same culture and character flow into their actions, such that harm is minimised and greed is avoided.

Like the Jewish tradition, trade and enterprise were actively encouraged among the Jains. In fact, when the first Jain students arrived in the UK in the 1970s the only firms which would give them professional apprenticeships in either accounting or law were Jewish-owned. There was a mutual respect for immigrants and faith. This is how the communities developed expertise, growth and success in business. To such a community, sustainable inter-generational equity becomes a natural act, a right way to live. To ignore such cultures in our theories and techniques of accounting and finance is unscientific in a world where we know so much about different traditions and beliefs. Similarly, when students from such cultures enter the business school class, they should not be 'culturally ignored' just because a neo-liberal platonic science wants to bulldoze its individualist beliefs onto them. Neither should they be 'white-washed' by white privilege. Racism and finance have a long history[32], and this needs to be brought into the classroom.

SIMPLICITY IS WISE

If the Anthropocene is a newly discovered phenomenon, are we surprised that thousands of years ago, cultures like the Jains or the Native Americans lived in harmony with the environment, not because human life on earth was threatened, but because it was seen as the scientific and responsible way to live? In fact, most cultures lived then within scale and means, and economics was a servant to society, keeping its power in its place. More broadly, the question I pose in this chapter is that for us to develop sustainable finance, we should be looking towards communities and cultures who foresaw the need to live in harmony with the planet and not through its exploitation and disruption. We have a huge opportunity to *trust* them more about what sustains in finance and to draw from their wealth of wisdom and experience. The starting point of distrust that has been given to us by modern secular science is false and misleading and a betrayal of truth and wisdom.

We can and ought to go back and learn from a time when this legal fiction called money was not so overwhelming in society, and there was a limited population, and cooperation and community were the norms in everyday life. Experimental science and behavioural research are too rooted in the present. In many traditions, there was more trust and integrity in the science and wisdom, because it is not borne out of malice, or power and authority, but simply out of a kinder, gentler way to live. Furthermore, looking at ancient cultures helps us to see beyond the highly monetised and materialistic world we inhabit today, which is now shown to be antithetical to planetary sustainability. What is more difficult however is to study cultures from the inside out and not outside in. This is very tricky, especially in a world where there is so much human arrogance and intolerance. The realities of global warming, inequality and climate change are forcing us to rethink our ways.

Most of the *new business experts* of sustainability in economics and finance make little or no reference to ancient wisdom traditions. That is unjust and inauthentic, given the huge possibilities of travel and technology today to unravel and engage with different cultural and philosophical systems. It continues the long history of ignorance, prejudice and racism, where non-European cultures were assumed to be inferior and incapable of intellectual wisdom or contributing to universal science and understanding. The colonial project relied on the conquest of foreign lands and the subjugation of foreign cultures and intellectuals gave credence and justification to this[33]. This racist fallacy is also inaccurate science, assuming away the role of culture and lived experience in sustainable living. To transform habits and culture, we must start with what we have, not ignore or superimpose a new technique or method onto it, without engaging with the present. The emerging literature on ethical finance tries to bridge this gap[34] and demonstrate for example that there is co-operative finance practised in developing countries, and such activities increase trust and community rather than deplete it. These methods also overcome the barriers of fund-raising which many start-up businesses without any credit history face. They often choose to avoid the anonymous commercial bank altogether.

HINDU BANKING AND RELATIONSHIP CULTURE

Satish Kanabar came to the UK as a young Hindu refugee from Uganda. In 1972, General Idi Amin who had taken over the country as a Dictator got angry about the significant Indian influence on business and the economy and overnight decided to expel them from the country. Being a former British colony, the UK had to accept its nationals, and most of them came here penniless and were housed in temporary homes and shelters across the country. There was at the time a significant British resistance to such migration, and old fears and prejudices were rekindled. However, fifty years later, it is now widely recognised that what these Indians did to the economy of Uganda, they replicated manifold in the UK. Though they arrived here penniless, they brought their culture and spirit of enterprise in their souls and spirits. In addition, they had priceless social capital and experience of relationship business and finance, which was to transform their new lives and the country where they landed. It is a riveting true story of organic finance and the sustainable migration of entrepreneurial skills and relationship networks.

As a young banker with Barclays in London, he understood this community very well. He had idyllic memories of growing up in Lughazi, Uganda, his hometown and how peaceful and beautiful it was, and how united the community was. Like the concept of Ubuntu, Satish claims that it was Lughazi which made him who he is today. From childhood, he had a strong sense of community spirit and desire to help his fellow Indians. This was a time of prejudice in commercial banks, and most managers and decision-makers were white and started most loan applications with a deep suspicion due to the distrust they had of minorities. Many minorities feared even to make a loan application, even though they needed this finance desperately to start up their businesses. This prejudice prevails to this day[35].

Over the years, through his patience, professionalism and diplomacy, Satish Kanabar became a significant bridge between a large high street bank and a highly skilled group of entrepreneurs who needed finance to expand and grow their businesses. Every year he met his lending targets or even exceeded them, and at the same time had a very low failure rate. He brought in good quality, trustworthy and reliable new business – In Indian culture, borrowing is treated with the highest responsibility, and prudence and thrift are deeply woven into the family life. Due to these cultural and tacit business skills, which were unrecognisable to the majority of bank managers, the community was able to expand and grow, helping boost the wider UK economy.

Culture played a hugely important role in this sustainable finance model. The culture of the borrower plus also the cultural understanding of the lender. There was an active risk management of business through previous skills and experience that this community brought to UK, but also the careful use of finance, and not growing beyond natural limits, or to a scale when the business could run out of management's control. Satish Kanabar confided in me that on the rare occasions when they rejected a loan application, he would go out of his way to explain to customers the rationale behind the decision. Instead of giving a cold rejection by letter, he personally went to the business and sat down with the applicant, giving them commercial advice about how else to grow the business and the risks to avoid. Here again was a novel approach to banking which was deeply respectful and honourable.

One of his clients, Mr Nitin Mehta, explained how unusual this method of banking was and how he misses Satish's relationship approach to banking. Most bank managers in his experience were looking after THEIR own interests and not of the client. During the recent 2020 pandemic, when they phoned to offer 'help', Nitin told them flatly on the phone that I do not trust your offer of help. He explained: 'When in future I will hit a hurdle, all you will care for is your money and not your client. I would rather not borrow from you and risk losing my family business.' In UK, this has been a widely documented and bitter experience of many family-owned businesses all over the country especially in the decade after the 2008 financial crisis. The Banks were bailed out during the crisis by the government, but these same managers decided then to bankrupt many of their clients whose businesses had temporary difficulties, the RBS-GRG case being the most egregious example[36]. Satish would often pop at short notice to Nitin Mehta's business, without any motive other than to see how his client is doing. There was no 'transactional agenda' to sell new products or services – merely to maintain a relationship and wish the client well. This is exactly how in Indian culture we keep in touch with friends and relatives – we pop in and visit them at their homes. And the welcome is always very warm and touching – in Indian wisdom, it is said that a guest is like a god who has come to grace your home. Welcome them with the best hospitality and generosity.

COMMUNITY BANKING

Mr Anant M P Shah comes from the Jain faith, one of the oldest living cultures of the world and one which has had a significant record of success in finance across generations. His father, Mr Meghji Pethraj Shah was a highly successful industrialist and pioneer in East Africa, and a major patron and philanthropist[37]. After he died, the two sons Anant and Vipin decided to open Meghraj Bank in the UK, one of the first ethnic-minority-owned licensed banks in UK. One of the motives for doing so was that they had found members of the community and diaspora who were part of their relationship network, constantly asking them for banking advice and contacts. They saw a business opportunity, and the rest is history. One of his early clients, a small businessman and Uncle of mine, Mr Bhikhu Shah, recalls how when he first applied for a modest loan after being rejected by other Banks, Anant asked him – is there any other way we can also help you? He could not believe this question, which was at once respectful and generous at the same time. Of course, this meant that Bhikhu never left the Bank and became a client for life. Some clients became 'disappointed' when they were labelled customers and not friends. They felt that Meghraj was their business friend and partner in times of success as well as difficulty. One of the rules in Banking is called 'Know Your Customer' or KYC. Today for large banks, this has become a paper exercise, but for Meghraj, their policy was not to take customers from the street, and instead obtain personal references, usually from the diaspora networks, before new accounts are opened. KYC to Meghraj really meant know the history and character of your customers, not just collect a distant application form. Here again, we see sustainable finance in practical action. Meghraj was clear that they were dealing with people and not simply distant anonymous businesses with financial track records.

A good banking relationship is a key to sustainability. It involves trust, information exchange, expert advice often given for free, understanding of new trends, competition, and awareness of new products and services. A relationship banker can be a very helpful advisor, given the wide variety of businesses they serve. They can help in improving trust and relationships, rather than depleting them, as is so often lamented today. In science, we play a significant importance to primary data – evidence gathered directly in the field. This is raw, unfiltered and can provide an original contribution to knowledge. When bankers visit their clients who have made loan applications, they get a first-hand understanding of the business and are able to see who is in charge and how organised and happy the employees are. This was Satish Kanabar's style of banking. He said that this helped him understand the challenges and complexities as well as the opportunities, much better than a loan application form or a set of cash flow forecasts. Once again, culture can trump sophisticated but distant technical analysis, done by professional managers who have little understanding of the nature of their client business.

Trust and relationships are also cost-efficient – they save money in the long term. Without trust, we need lawyers and contracts, who add another layer of fees and even then, may not help achieve the objectives. They are also central to a sustainable society. They cannot be taught as a formula in the classroom to be memorised and analysed. Stories and narratives like these can help give people some ideas about how trust operates and the advantages it can bring in the world of business. There would be different stories from different cultures and different ways of cultivating and maintaining business relationships. Religions can play a big part in these narratives as faith is often an important self-regulator of human behaviour. Given that trust is central to finance in any culture, collecting such stories from a variety of cultures would be very illuminating indeed. From my own experience, I have found that when we ask such questions to students in the classroom, they bring their own examples and stories from different parts of the world. Sometimes these stories are about corruption and betrayal of trust, but this also helps to illuminate the different dimensions of social networks and the varieties of laws and enforcement in different countries. It is better to engage with different cultures and learn than to ignore or over-ride existing cultures and patterns of behaviour which students are familiar with and values which they observe in everyday life. Sometimes such experiences give them an opportunity to reflect on their own culture and morality, something which is also not common in modernity.

The roots of Barclays are Quaker – it was founded by a Quaker family, which placed ethics and social responsibility, front and centre and that is also what helped it grow organically in the early years[38]. After the global financial crash of 2008, where Barclays was very badly bruised, and there were calls for a wholesale reform of culture, a new Chief Executive, Anthony Jenkins, who came from a retail banking background was hired to lead the global bank. Sadly, his tenure did not last long, and hard-nosed and aggressive investment banking took over and he was replaced within a few years. This episode exposes the huge market and short-term profit-driven structural and institutional restraints on global sustainable banking today. Modernity broke the back of tradition and helped to make finance unsustainable. The new CEO was also forced to leave due to untruths about his links with the disgraced paedophile, Jeffrey Epstein.

CULTURAL IGNORANCE AS 'CAUSE' OF BANK FAILURE

Modern corporate finance theory and education *ignores* culture and diversity at a huge cost to society. HBOS, Britain's fifth-largest bank, was formed out of a merger of two historically prudent organisations – Halifax Building Society and Bank of Scotland[39]. However, the new Board and especially the CEO, Sir James Crosby, were target driven from day one of the merger in 2001, and this eventually led to the largest ever corporate bankruptcy in Britain, at a cost of fifty-two billion pounds in 2008. Their strategy was highly instrumental and transactional, with little regard for the history and tradition of these two organisations which had together been around for three hundred and fifty years. In this short span of time, a growth and expansionist mindset began to ignore risk and culture, and then exploded. When in 2004 the Head of Risk and Compliance, Paul Moore, warned that the Sales Target culture was compromising risk, he was dismissed. The second CEO Andy Hornby was a top finance graduate of Harvard Business School, and he continued its break-neck growth. During the entire period, the Board, both Executive and Non-Executive had no cultural diversity and no Banking experience whatsoever. Not only culture, but experience was also not seen to be important. And as a result, the institution collapsed and ended its sustainability.

In my detailed research of this collapse, I discovered that in many ways it was a textbook example of contemporary irresponsible finance theory – focus on high leverage, mergers and acquisitions, earnings targets and dividends to boost the share price and maximise shareholder value. In the process, culture was damaged, risk was increased and the business was conducted in a highly transactional and bonus-driven mindset. Despite being a high street bank, the Board never really saw culture, in the sense of trusted long-term relationships, as important. Nor did faith take any priority in building an ethical culture. Not only does contemporary teaching of finance eschew culture, it dismisses and diminishes its relevance, deliberately making businesses less and less sustainable. One global corporate finance textbook even went so far as to say that to the extent that a business focuses on maximising shareholder value, we consider all its actions to be ethical[40]. So even ethics are compromised and misrepresented in finance education.

This case is in very stark contrast to the earlier examples. However, the stock market loved HBOS and welcomed its regular dividend bribery, without much probing or questioning. The share price kept on growing and growing in the first five years after the merger. The markets saw the growing dividends as confidence of the underlying strength of the business. They did not ask customers of the commercial bank how they were being treated or ponder into how easily the Bank gave home mortgages to its customers, breaking the rest of the market. They relied on management speak and audited accounts, which later turned out to be biased and subjective. In fact in the case of the sacking of the whistleblower Paul Moore, the auditors KPMG were called by the Board to independently investigate this, knowing that he had complained about the aggressive sales culture. Despite Paul Moore being a former partner in the firm, KPMG saw no conflict of interest in helping HBOS management endorse their sacking of Moore.[41] KPMG did not find anything untoward in the dismissal, and supported the Board in its technocratic growth strategy, even when their job was to independently audit and question the governance of the Bank.

Anthropologist Luyendijk (2015) conducted a series of interviews of UK Banking and Finance employees in various departments and a variety of managerial and clerical roles to unlock the culture. He gave his book the title 'Swimming with Sharks', exposing the backstabbing and highly insecure culture, often fuelled by drugs and addiction. Kindness, care and compassion were virtually absent from the vocabulary, and everyone seemed to be a competitor rather than a team player. When Parliament completed its series of enquiries into UK Banking after the 2008 crash[42], the critique was stark – at root was a seriously broken culture and poor management and leadership, and a failure of governance and regulation. This was seen as a systemic problem, one whose resolution is still distant, as the track record of the last fifteen years has shown. When tradition is replaced by a faith in modernity, science and technology, culture suffers and eventually paralyses the whole system.

FINANCIALISATION DESTROYS TRADITION

As Banks play a critical role in the financial and economic system, they are closely regulated and monitored. However, they are also very powerful and influential, and in the UK, there had been a policy of light-touch regulation where responsibility for the detailed monitoring prior to 2008 was delegated to the Board, and regulators chose not to interfere[43]. There was also a process of vetting senior officers like Directors before they joined Boards, but all HBOS Directors got this approval, even though none of them had any Banking experience. In the case of RBS, another large UK Bank which also went into trouble, there was a disastrous series of acquisitions made just before the 2008 crash.[44] Both these Banks required multi-billion-pound bailouts, something which is never available to failing family-owned businesses. To add insult to injury, as businesses suffered temporary challenges after the crash, instead of supporting them, these transactional Banks decided to pull the rug from under them, making very sound viable businesses insolvent in the process. Even though the big Banks were supported and bailed out by the UK government, this support was not extended to their client businesses. As a result, many owners lost everything they had built, and became distressed, with some even committing suicide.

On reflection, we can say that whilst HBOS ignored people's faiths and relationships in its business lending decisions, through pushing financial targets and bonuses, it incentivised them to behave in a very greedy and transactional way. This led to transforming the culture of Bankers who came from different beliefs, who were forced to work under those targets irrespective of their own personal values or restraints. There was even shaming and humiliation of bankers who did not achieve their monthly targets so that everyone was forced to toe the line[45]. Banks through their systems and processes can transform culture in the name of profits and growth, leading to high risk and ruination, precisely because the adverse impact on people's behaviours and prudence was not understood or ignored. Also my research has shown that institutions cushion conscience and restraint, and forget the systemic ramifications of their risk-taking altogether. Processes and systems end up replacing conscience, and when disaster strikes, everyone and no one is responsible, so leaders get away without any punishment whatsoever.

With large organisations, culture and relationships are difficult to maintain and police. We saw earlier when we were examining Handelsbanken (interview of Andrew Pike), that culture was made central to its strategy, and Branch managers were recruited after significant prior vetting and due diligence[46]. Each Branch had autonomy and a restricted team size, helping to create a team culture with local knowledge. They are given significant authority to take lending decisions based on their own experience and professional judgement. The Branch Managers are not incentivised to grow the loan book and expand for the sake of more fees and income. Even the size of the branch is controlled to maintain the team spirit and relationship culture. When it comes to sustainability, small is beautiful indeed. And large can easily become reckless, especially in profit-driven banking and finance. This damage is not just restricted to the Bank but can ripple into the customer businesses and their potential for survival and balanced growth. The power and status of the banker need to be handled with enormous care and responsibility, as it is other people's money that is lent, and this should not be frittered away recklessly.

PUBLIC VISION, RESPONSIBLE OWNERSHIP AND FAMILY VALUES

In India, Dr Abhay Firodia, whose late father Mr. Navalmal Firodia invented the three-wheeler auto-rickshaw (also known as tuk-tuk), explained that his father had gone to jail several times during the Indian independence movement. As a result, a strong spirit of public service was inculcated, and even though he had a thriving legal practice, he decided to go into industry after independence to serve the new and growing India. Lasting purpose and service to the country was his driving motto. One priority for the family was to serve the ordinary man, and the 'tuk-tuk' is now a common public taxi all over India and has become a global export – cheap, efficient and good at negotiating traffic jams. They were manufactured in a joint venture between the family and Bajaj. There are millions of tuk-tuk's in operation all over India providing public transport today. Each tuk-tuk is supporting a tiny family business – giving income to the driver and thereby supporting his family. Dr. Abhay Firodia later expanded the business into larger transport vehicles like vans and trucks and it is now known as Force Motors.

During my research interview, I probed into the philosophy of leadership, and Dr Firodia kept on citing his Jain culture and philosophy as a key driver behind the business. Products should be manufactured not to serve the elites, but the ordinary man or woman. There was a clear sense of purpose and mission. Similarly, prudence and growth within managerial scale are also critical, and the family are net lenders to Banks rather than borrowers from them, and they have always been like that. Their open-mindedness and relationship approach helped them to do joint ventures with some of the biggest blue-chip names in manufacturing – Rolls Royce and Daimler Benz. Workers were to be treated with dignity and respect, as they are seen as key stakeholders in the business, not simply resources.

Above all, charity and philanthropy are seen as a continuing duty for the family. In the Jain spirit of *Aparigraha*[47] (detachment from material wealth), when the founder Navalmal retired, he withdrew completely from the business, never signing a single piece of paper afterwards and went headlong into charitable works and projects relating to education, health and social welfare. *Aparigraha* helps business leaders understand the nature and limits of money, and through this understanding, it gives them a leadership philosophy which is selfless and not selfish. When Dr Firodia asked his father in his final days what phase of his life he enjoyed the most, he said without doubt it was the charity phase. Sustainable business leadership is about service to society, whatever form it may take, either through business in the creation of useful products and services, or through social enterprise, providing for the needs of the poor and marginalised in society.

REFLEXIVE LEADERSHIP WHICH DRAWS FROM TRADE AND TRADITION

To hear a business leader having such a sophisticated understanding of Jain philosophy, and its implications for leadership and management was not surprising for me. Jains have had a long tradition of reflexive leadership and enterprise and significant humility and charity[48]. Their upbringing and community networks have given them a profound understanding of shared living and ownership, and leadership which is purposeful and sustainable inter-generationally. Family name and reputation are given a high priority and never to be compromised for short-term gain or fame. Pride and ego which come from success were to be restrained. The fact that the founder of the Firodia businesses was a former freedom fighter shows how profound the understanding of public service is – business is a means to an end but should not compromise the duties of state citizenship and the responsibilities which come with it. Private enterprise is understood to be interdependent with the state and wider society, not independent from it. Belonging to a traditional culture and philosophy, and understanding and respecting this, is important in capturing the spirit and continuity that sustainable business demands from society. It involves duties and obligations, not just freedoms and choices. When in finance we ignore traditions and indigenous cultures, we are making a significant error. Solutions and strategies that have stood the test of time are being over-ridden, precisely at a time when the world needs them the most.

Few people are aware that Mahatma Gandhi's guru was a *Jain* merchant called Shrimad Rajchandra[49]. Yes, the person whom the world calls a 'mahatma' or great soul, had a teacher who was a businessman! Rajchandra used to trade in precious stones, and there are many stories about how fair and transparent he was in his dealings and would even accept returns without question if the customer changed his mind[50]. At the same time, Rajchandra was a poet and philosopher, and meditated regularly, having had significant experiences of the purity and immortality of the atman or soul. He also had extra-sensory perception and intelligence. Trade has the potential to be a teacher and an educator – to be successful, one needs to understand the customer, their needs and their culture, to be effective. Even Prophet Mohammed was a businessman and trader. Honesty and trustworthiness, when nurtured and regulated by the self, often bring repeat trade and business. Such aspects of trade are not easily taught through the textbook or the classroom, but learnt through experience, upbringing and mentoring in the field of the real world. The story goes that one day Shrimad Rajchandra was invited to the palatial home of the founder of Tata Group, Jamshedji Tata, in Mumbai. He was given a tour of the house and art collection, and at the end, instead of applause and admiration, Shrimad Rajchandra asked a simple question – what is all this for?[51] This inspired Tata to transfer the whole business to a charitable trust – it is now one of the world's rare multinational corporations owned entirely by a charitable trust.

HERITAGE, MEMORY AND HONOUR

History and a sense of history also help with sustainable finance leadership. Heritage suggests a tradition and an obligation to a tradition. It gives purpose and meaning to leaders and a spirit of accountability to the past, not just the present and future. It is easy to forget but for much of our human past, money played no role in society and cooperation was the norm. The absence of money and consumerism also gave people time to think and reflect even in the absence of literacy. Religion gave them a way of coping with risk and uncertainty and building communities. For ancient cultures, time is seen in a continuum, rather than a period or phase. It also makes leaders very aware of their own morbidity and the importance of leaving a legacy rather than a temporary act of profiteering and wealth creation. Material culture and progress are then seen not as a primary goal, but a partial and relative objective within the larger context of life, service, purpose and sustainability. History can be taught and learnt or studied, but also having a communal sense of history can give leaders an extra strength and spirit.

As science has become more sophisticated and knowledge more specialised, it has come to dislike the phrase 'experience' and the personal subjectivities it implies. Business education in particular, having become very commercial, has consciously and subconsciously sought to diminish this, encouraging the need to learn scientific theories as a precursor to business success. However, in all my research interviews for this book, experience was highly valued and often passed on inter-generationally, through culture and family up-bringing. The interviewees admitted that it did play a role in their achievements and success. Nitin Mehta lost both his parents at a young age but did not lose his thirst for commerce which he had inherited from growing up in Kisumu, Kenya. Even after qualifying as an accountant, he took greater interest in the commercial aspects of accounting and relatively early on, set up his own business, even though he had little capital. Chapter four in this book is devoted to tacit skills and experience as keys to finance success.

COMMUNITY AS 'VIRTUAL BANK' OF SOCIAL CAPITAL

One of the central foci of this book is community. We can theorise and analyse communities, but to experience them is something very different and unique. Communities do not neatly fit into categories, subjects or even paradigms. Yet they are rich with so many different dimensions of history, wisdom, relationships, networks and trust. To dismiss or ignore them, as finance education has done so deliberately and consistently, is like seeing a rainforest as simply a collection of mindless and dumb trees who need to be taught how to maximise happiness and wealth. In reality, a rainforest is a vast ecosystem of history, tradition, complexity, interdependence and wisdom about living in harmony with nature and creating a healthy climate and environment for one and all. Communities are the social banks from which money originally emerged and to which money must now return to be authentic and sustainable.

Approached in this way, finance education becomes creative and inclusive, not cold, logical and formulaic. Its messiness is discussed rather than suppressed. This approach is beneficial both for the lecturer and the student, encouraging dialogue and debate. In my experience, it has made them feel included, and their experiences are real and important for everyone to hear and listen to. Not all of these experiences are good ones – some may relate to debt and reckless spending, or admissions of financial illiteracy about credit cards and interest rates. Even family break-ups and divorce have come up in these discussions – it is now well documented that divorce can be a major cause of personal financial distress, so it is important not to ignore it. Sometimes students have said that they just want to get rich quick and fast, irrespective of the consequences. Such honest statements can become a basis for a classroom dialogue about the variety of objectives, and about the personal and emotional consequences of certain actions and decisions. Some students have also worked for very aggressive soul-less businesses and met some of the leaders and managers. They say to me that they do not want to become like them.

MENTORING AND TRADITION

When someone is training to be a Chartered Accountant, a senior mentor is allocated to ensure that over a three-year period, they get sufficient breadth and depth of financial experience, alongside the professional studies and examinations. This mentor is also someone to go to if one is having personal problems with colleagues, bosses or simply office politics or work pressures and stresses. The aim behind such a structure is personal and cultural – to mould the future professional and encourage their growth in self-confidence. Much depends on the personality and character of the mentor and the time and dedication they devote to the unpaid task. However, such a structure is designed to be constructive and holistic, covering any gaps in training or knowledge and supporting emotional and character development. It is not dissimilar to the clinical training given to doctors. However, the quality of the mentoring depends very much on the selflessness of the mentor and the degree of time and care they are willing to give to the young mentee. This is not in any textbook or rulebook but can make a vast difference to the future behaviour and character of the young novice. If the mentor is transactional and materialistic, they would encourage these behaviours. That could have adverse consequences. Given growing selfishness and commercialisation, the general neglect of training in all organisations and the negative attitude to young novices in places like investment banks or the global Big 4 accounting firms[52], a big opportunity to mould good character is subverted. Furthermore in terms of cultural diversity, finance leaders are extremely weak in respecting it and being sensitive to differences. This can make matters much worse.

A professional banker or adviser is likely to come across a variety of clients from different cultural backgrounds and beliefs. Being an expert does not mean that one has to understand and study all the different cultures of their clients, but simply to be sensitive to the differences, and if unsure, asking clients how certain things are done in their cultures. In this way, even the client feels listened to and engaged, rather than being sold a standard product or service which does not relate to their needs. Honesty in recommending a different provider for the service would not necessarily mean loss of the client – rather a greater trust and respect, as the professional has genuinely acted in the clients' best interests. Such advice shows a long-term patience and attitude to service, rather than a short-term greed to profit from the client. Such advice is an example of sustainable service and professionalism. In protecting a relationship, trust and respect grow, building bridges of hope and potential.

INTER-CULTURAL LITERACY AND MULTI-FAITH WISDOM

Satish Kanabar, whilst regional Director at Barclays, decided to host training seminars for his team at different local community centres, which may or may not be faith-based. This was highly innovative and pioneering for its time and courageous too. These were not commercial hotel rooms with five-star luxury or professional seating and dining services. Instead, they were local and belonged to people who valued volunteering, relationships and social capital. In this way, his team was able to see different cultures and communities from the 'inside out', rather than the 'outside in' that is the normal approach of Banking, especially as it is often steeped in power and arrogance. When cultures are so organised that they are able to build their own community centres and manage them through charity and resourcefulness, without any reliance on public funding, this shows a degree of cooperation and resilience, which is very necessary for us to build a sustainable society. Hosting training meetings inside mosques and gurudwaras (Sikh temples) would help Bankers who are non-religious to experience religion without being afraid or converted. Similarly, the community hosts would come to appreciate that here is a Bank keen to understand their culture and respect their spirit. Wider bridges of trust and relationship are cultivated through such creative acts, and a local intimacy is developed.

What these stories and examples reveal is the critical importance of good mentoring and experience to learning and personal growth. Belonging to a family and community can be a very important part of the nurturing of a social conscience and an opportunity for young people to meet potential role models and learn from their example. The fact that such stories and lived experiences are nowhere in accounting and finance textbooks is a major loss, precisely at a time when we need morality and character to be at the centre of business education. Furthermore, the strong bias against faith in the academy is based on a lot of ignorance about the diverse nature of faith and its relationship to culture, character and community. The more tradition and culture are separated from the accounting and finance theories and education, the more damage we will be doing to society. We are deliberately making it unsustainable. Academics need to be trained in the diverse nature of faith and tradition, and instead of spending all the time in their analyses and calculations, they need to visit and experience these communities without overwhelming suspicion and scepticism.

In his book 'The Third Pillar', former World Bank Chief Economist and University of Chicago Finance Professor Raghuram Rajan, laments the breakdown of community in modern society[53]. Markets and States cannot replace the importance of relationships and trust to human life, he argues. It is in communities that we develop identity, connection and co-operation, a local sense of belonging. The value of this cannot be calculated, but its importance to peace, social and economic cohesion is fundamental. It reduces the need for laws and lawyers and enhances bonds between people. Rajan argues that contemporary economics and finance have forgotten this critical ingredient, at a time when the world needs it more than ever. Similarly, world-famous economists Paul Collier and John Kay[54] in their latest book called 'Greed is Dead' devote half the book to 'communitarianism' – the importance of shared co-existence. Both of them are very clear that the science of economics is directly to blame for the breakdown of community in modernity and needs to be reversed to make community central to its future. In the next chapter, we explore community in more detail.

CULTURAL EXPERIENCE AS KNOWLEDGE

Experience is not classified into subjects or disciplines. It involves trial and error and family training, even if it is as simple as standing on the counter in the family shop when one is young. In fact, sometimes these formative experiences can be very powerful and influential in many different aspects of life and career. Experience helps people see the nature of commerce, its opportunities and challenges, its risks and benefits. It also trains young people about responsibility and even accountability. It often helps them understand the potential freedom that can come from commerce, which an expert job cannot provide. It can also give courage and self-confidence, qualities critical to success in any enterprise. Where education is scientific, risk can easily be seen as a calculation rather than an experience or judgement to be made and lived through. There is a big difference between these two aspects of risk, and the technical mindset can sometimes create an illusion of experience, or even make experts think that they do not *need* any risk experience in order to effectively manage it. Intellectually, there is a big battle between technocracy and subjective but rich cultural experience. Often, technocracy wins, but this is deeply damaging.

In the business classroom, it is very difficult to model or quantify experience. It will be different for each student and also varies depending on the country they come from or the culture and faith they belong to. In a similar way, cultures and upbringings vary – someone who is Jewish may be raised in a secular household as a non-believer, even though the behaviours and lifestyle would have many Jewish antecedents, like a natural skill for commerce and industry. There is a lot of research on the taxonomy of cultural differences and the measurement and analysis of this[55]. However, the focus of this book is on a variety of cultures and beliefs, and the different influences people experience at different stages in their lives. That is why no attempt has been made to do an exhaustive analysis of different finance cultures and traditions, which would be impossible to do. Instead, what we are trying to do is to help readers understand the nuances of culture and the implications of ignoring faith and culture in the research and teaching of finance, especially given the significant moral challenges posed by the Anthropocene.

Whatever cultures, beliefs, experiences or characters students bring with them, the biggest mistake we can make in the finance classroom is to dismiss them or avoid engagement with their identity and heritage. Sadly, this is very common in today's business education factory. This gives students the false impression that the truth in finance lies in learning the theories and formulae, without any need for culture or reflection. Narratives when discussed in the classroom help students understand the intricacies and complexities of finance. When asked to bring their own narratives to the classroom, students are found to engage much better with the subject and grow in their confidence of it[56]. It makes them have a personal and real dialogue with the subject, rather than a technical and impersonal analysis of it. In Chapter 4, we examine the role of experience and tacit skills in depth. Before that, we will explore the meaning and value of communities in finance in the next chapter. Like rainforests, communities are clusters of interdependence with priceless social, cultural and relationship capital which are keys to a sustainable finance. Why would society want to ignore them?

Notes

1 See Bakan (2020).
2 Whyte (2020) details this story in its first chapter and documents how damaging multinationals have been to the planet, being its primary polluters.
3 For a detailed analysis, see Gray et al (2010).
4 Azevedo (2019) p.68.
5 United Nations (2015).
6 Brooks (2018) is a detailed account of the highly aggressive commercial culture of these firms and their frauds and exploitation. Cooper et al (2005) examine the role of accounting academics. Shah (2022) appeals for a much more ethical and conscience driven academy.
7 ODwyer and Edgecliffe-Johnson (2021) evaluate the Big Four's opportunistic ambitions in ESG.

8 Innes (2021) explains that Britain is particularly notorious for 'state capture' – 'Under the New Public Management agenda of the last forty years, agenda-setting and policy design have increasingly been outsourced to professional consultancies, third-sector agencies, law and accountancy firms and corporate sponsored think tanks.'

9 Harari (2015), Ferguson (2012) and Finel-Honigman (2010).

10 See for example Eisenstein (2021), Akram and Rashid (2020), Bouckaert and Heuvel (2019) and Pruzan and Mikkelsen (2007).

11 Sacks (2003) Chapter 6.

12 Pruzan and Mikkelsen (2007) and Bouckaert and Heuvel (2019).

13 Friedman (2021) and Sandel (2012) expose the moral limits of markets, and the ideological roots of modern capitalism. Franklin B. (2021) Religion and the Rise of Capitalism, Vintage Books.

14 See Darcy (2010) to understand what happens when power is held without responsibility or conscience.

15 Hines (1988) shows how like money, accounting is also a social construct.

16 Sacks (1990) devotes a whole BBC Reith lecture to this experience.

17 See excellent critiques such as Chang (2011), Stiglitz (2019), Ekins et al (1992) and Daly and Cobb (1994).

18 Muradoglu and Harvey (2012).

19 See Soros (1998). He is founder of the global Institute for New Economic Thinking, INET.

20 See Thaler (2013) for a history of behavioural economics.

21 Said (1994).

22 Alpers and Goswami (2019).

23 See Poros (2011).

24 www.londonmandir.baps.org.

25 www.jaina.org ; www.jainelibrary.org.

26 Redding (1990).

27 Weintraub (2014) and Perlman (1996).

28 Sacks (2003) devotes Chapter 6 to this concept.

29 Sacks (1990) – these lectures are free and available online at https://www.bbc.co.uk/programmes/p00gq0dl.

30 www.sobellrhodes.co.uk.

31 Shah and Rankin (2017) explain the philosophy and its practical implications for an ethical finance.

32 See Dalrymple (2019) for the history and looting of the East India Company as an example of such abject expropriation and discrimination over a very old and talented merchant culture. Lewis (2020) and Annisette (2003) document racism in the accounting profession.

33 Appiah (2016) in his BBC Reith lectures exposes the deep racial prejudice in the academy well into the twentieth century, which also continues to this day.

34 See, for example, Minhat and Dzolkarnaini (2021) and Akram and Rashid (2020).

35 British Business Bank (2020).

36 Fraser (2015) provides an excellent account of this.

37 See Marett (1988) for his biography and legacy across three continents. M.P. Shah was a rare visionary and finance pioneer, whose conduct was rooted in morality and public conscience. Even with his philanthropy, he took strategic risks.

38 Augar (2019) is an excellent account of this history and transformation.

39 See Perman (2012) and Shah (2018a).

40 Ross et al (2012).

41 See Shah (2018a) Chapter 4 for a detailed account of the audit failure.

42 Tyrie et al (2013). Angelides et al (2011) came to the same conclusion in the USA.

43 Tyrie et al (2013).

44 Fraser (2015) is a bestselling account of the broken and corrupt culture at RBS Bank and the GRG debacle which destroyed viable businesses after the rescue.

45 See Fraser (2015) which exposes the sales and bullying culture very well.
46 Bukovinsky (2019) explains the history and transformation of Handelsbanken.
47 See Shah (2020).
48 Shah and Rankin (2017).
49 Gandhi (1982).
50 Desai (2000).
51 Desai (2000) p.22.
52 Sikka (2008) exposes the strong entrepreneurial culture of the Big 4 with a focus on profits and growth as opposed to ethics and public interest.
53 Rajan (2019).
54 Collier and Kay (2020).
55 Meyer (2015) is an excellent analysis of the different ways in which diverse leaders think and act.
56 Shah (2018b) gives several examples of how this was achieved in the University classroom, with transformational effects on student confidence and self-esteem.

3
COMMUNITY

Paradoxically, the etymology of the word individual comes from the Latin *individualis* – that which is NOT divisible. However, economics has made the selfish, materialist, individual the epicentre of all action and science. To economics, a community is simply a collection of individuals – a multiplier of selfishness. In its desperation to become scientific and rigorous, it forgot to enquire even about the nature and meaning of its primary agent and instead decided to misuse the word. No one can be separated from family or community – as the African phrase *ubuntu* explains, it takes a village to make a person. By ignoring or dismissing the value of community, economics has created a big rupture in our understanding, as even top economists now admit[1].

Leaders in finance and accounting carry a huge responsibility – they are handling other people's money, and therefore need to act with extra care and diligence. In my tradition, it is believed that one should look after other people's money better than one's own – their trust should be returned with the highest degree of stewardship. Professional actions need to be in the best interests of their customers and not in their own best interest. Such rules are enshrined in banking regulations all over the world. The expert knowledge and resources banks have should be applied for the benefit of their customers. However, the reality today is that most leaders act in their own best interests, and finance theory and education legitimate and encourage this. Organisations and institutions serve to multiply selfishness instead of containing it, through materialistic incentives and poor leadership, greedy practices and corrupt symbols. We desperately need communities with a different, caring and public-interest orientation. They can potentially create an ethical virtuous circle which could result in responsible and sustainable finance[2].

Moral economic practices and communities lie at the heart of Catholic Social Teaching (CST), which over 1.5 billion people in the world follow[3]. Morality

DOI: 10.4324/9781003164746-3

ought to underpin every aspect of economic activity and should not be overtaken by greed and selfishness – morality and economics are inseparable. Human dignity is central to moral life, and every human being needs to be respected and valued for their own intrinsic worth, irrespective of culture, wealth or creed. For CST, markets are not autonomous but founded on morality and fully accountable to society. There is no magical 'invisible hand' which is just and equitable. The freedom and efficiency of markets and the power of markets to automatically allocate resources to needs are rejected as a false belief in the CST. Profit-seeking is not abhorred, but the means are very important to the ends, and kindness and sustainability need to be embraced in the methods applied, and the products and services rendered. Human agency and government action matter in creating equality and justice in society, and people should understand the fundamental importance of fairness and morality in their economic behaviours. Collective members of the Catholic Church driven by such values play a very important role in building moral communities and societies. Given the global footprint of the church, and the vast diversity of followers, from nations as far apart as Philippines and Mexico, we have a significant movement to help transition the world towards a sustainable finance and economy. The pro-active leadership of Pope Francis in this arena is a significant source of global transformational leadership at a time when we need it so urgently.

By their very nature, communities are hugely diverse and cannot be easily classified or analysed[4]. It takes time to know and understand them, and their rules and methods of operation will vary even within a region, let alone a country or faith. This complexity may seem daunting to an investor or analyst, who may prefer instead to rely on legal contracts and market-based transactions. However, this may be a short-term outcome rather than a long-term solution. Given the challenges of sustainable development, we have no choice but to understand different communities and work with them rather than undermine or disrupt them. The temptation to over-ride them or exploit them in the name of growth and profit should be resisted, as the costs of doing so can be priceless. The very formation of communities takes hundreds of years and many generations, and to destroy them overnight or in the name of short-term profit maximisation is unsustainable and deeply damaging for society. The fact that contemporary finance ignores the value of communities means that the decisions and actions it promotes can easily undermine them.

FAITH AND MIGRANT DIASPORAS

All over the world, we observe communities where people feel a loyalty to one another, have a shared sense of living and mutual support and where charity and public service are celebrated and encouraged[5]. These may not have the credentials of a 'profession' or certain special talent or expertise. Often faith and belief are what binds them together. However, this is not always the case. Groups could be brought together by other motivations like charity, a good example being

Rotary International or the Scouts movement. In traditional societies, the village was often a community, a place where peace had to be maintained and respect for neighbours was critical to mutual growth and prosperity.

Children growing up in these villages often failed to see the family as a boundary, instead they experienced interdependence as a living reality, not a theory or philosophy. It is even possible that children through their innocence and creativity, encouraged communities to stick together and support one another to protect present and future generations. Socialisation and play were a core part of their childhood experiences. The friendship and camaraderie that such communities create led to a high level of trust and selflessness. They give members a sense of identity and purpose and a 'home' where they can go for guidance or advice in times of confusion, distress or even crisis. I consider myself fortunate to have been raised in this way, thousands of miles from our cultural origins in India. The resilience of faith and culture to migration, risk and change is also something not to be dismissed. Often, it is a symbol of hope in shaping a shared and dignified global society.

Given that one of the primary roles of accounting and finance professionals is to enhance trust in society, one would think community of this kind should be their core identity and support network. Once they pass the requisite entrance exams and have the necessary expertise, they ought to feel a sense of belonging and pride in their objectivity, independence and duty to protect the public and act in the best interests of their true clients. Unfortunately, in many cases, modernity has turned business professionalism into a brand for personal gain and expropriation. In the accounting profession, there is considerable authority, but little collegiality, loyalty, humility or even fear of spoiling the name of the profession – judgement has been replaced by tick-box compliance[6].

In fact, one of the big problems with all large organisations is that they can easily break the bonds of community, especially when they are driven by individualism, money and greed. If we value community, we need to be alert to these possible flaws. Both in banking and accounting, modern history is littered with examples of egregious and fraudulent behaviour, at times bringing down whole global organisations like Enron, Arthur Andersen, RBS, Lehman Brothers or HBOS. Modern accounting and finance leaders often do not belong to faiths or communities, nor do they understand the importance of public interest protection. They have come to believe private interest is all that is important and everyone should act in their own personal interest. They also perceive that everyone else is selfish and made in their own image[7]. To them, the professional license is to be used for their own self-interest – they do not feel a duty of care to uphold the reputation of the profession. We can only *speculate* as to possible reasons for this – a lack of faith; inexperience about shared coexistence when growing up; others have not done any selfless favours for them. It is also very likely that conditioning by university economics and finance teaching which ignores community and society and focuses on individual selfishness diminishes an appreciation of mutuality and collective moral efforts.

Rajan speaks of community schools as a core network of mutuality in nineteenth-century America[8]. The same applies to the UK – faith and charity schools were the most common in the Middle Ages. I went to a Jain community school in Mombasa – governed and managed by a community, but open to all students. This is a primary institution of learning and development, and in such schools, even parents have a stake in their success and longevity. They do not 'purchase' education in the same way that many wealthy parents do today when they send their children to private schools. Here there is no expectation of parent engagement or participation – their fees often focus on outcomes and results, and parents delegate education through the marketplace. Community schools are often class-neutral and shape an experience of equality and are more local and grounded. They help in weaving a community together as children often build unity among adults.

LABORATORIES OF TRUST AND RELATIONSHIP CAPITAL

Community also becomes a breeding ground for relationships, trust and social capital. In community institutions, people come to know and meet one another ostensibly without any private or personal agenda. They come to share in cultural events, festivals and celebrations, thereby coming to know one another over a period of time. In this way, trust is nurtured slowly and naturally, without any specific orchestration by a club leader or official network. Over time, interdependence becomes a lived experience, rather than a theory or dictat from politicians or business leaders. In this way, a sense of patience is cultivated and a respect for mutuality and loyalty rather than constant suspicion of the motives of 'others'. Advice is often sought from community members and given generously and selflessly, making communities a hub for shared information, risk management and knowledge. All over the world, there are hundreds of thousands of such communities, where the ideas which bind them may differ, but the experience of shared living and a peaceful neighbourhood is common. They may be small or large, local or national, faith based or secular, but they do exist and bring peace and cohesion to society.

Subhash Thakrar was born in Uganda, and coming from the Hindu Lohana community, he naturally inherited commerce and entrepreneurship skills from his upbringing. The Lohanas are a highly skilled and accomplished merchant community all over the world. When Subhash migrated to the UK, he went to Birmingham University and then qualified as a Chartered Accountant, very quickly using his technical skills to give clients outstanding service, working longer hours than the rest of his partners. He was ambitious and confident about his skills and soon developed a personal reputation.

Subhash could see in the 1980s that while Asian businesses were growing and aspirational, there was a barrier towards integration into the wider business networks and so it was difficult for them to expand their trade. Subhash suggested to the London Chamber of Commerce to set up an Asian Chamber. Through his community networks, he was able to integrate and grow this very quickly and everyone benefited from this expansion in membership and participation. Through diplomacy, tact and sheer determination, he managed to break the barriers of race and class that prevailed in London businesses at that time, an achievement which was pioneering. Subhash's early experience of community in Africa was translated into a foreign country, the United Kingdom, and he used his leadership skills to build a new 'business family' in Britain. In this way, through his character, leadership and professionalism, Subhash nurtured a whole new bridge between very different communities, providing a win–win opportunity for all the members. Catalysts like him and Satish Kanabar (also a Lohana) have played a significant role in the success of the Indian merchant diaspora in Britain, many of whom now run global businesses which are still family owned. History will record how they grew trust in society through selflessness rather than deplete it through selfishness.

MIGRATION AND MOBILE SOCIAL CAPITAL

Communities need not be fixed in time or geography. They can travel, even migrate together, as my own community has done. In this way, the priceless social and trust capital built over decades is carried with them, rather than left behind in the country of origin. They can also exist as a global diaspora, where relatives and friends live in different parts of the world, giving the community a global network of trust and relationships. Training in business and enterprise, especially in the early days when one is trying to break through barriers and is often a novice, is hard to come by. As an educator, I get very frustrated when my students cannot get summer internships even though they have significant skills and capabilities and are dying to get some experience. Such training is win–win as it gives the student a chance to explore what he or she likes or dislikes, and the employer can also test them before they recruit. Such experience can never be given in a 'classroom' and yet it is vital to their learning and development. Clinical experience is a must in medical training, but is virtually absent from business education. Young people bring a fresh energy and curiosity to a workplace and are in touch with latest developments and technologies, which businesses can benefit from. Even their questions could make employers think whether there are better ways of doing the same task. When businesses provide internships, they are also acknowledging a public duty to train future generations and give them opportunities for growth and progression.

Having 600–800 guests at an Indian wedding is very common. I attended my niece's wedding in Nairobi where we had 3000 guests. My wedding had 1000 guests. One of the first questions people ask me when I give them this news is how come I know so many people? And I respond by saying I know even more and had to cut the list several times for my own wedding. This is because in Indian culture, family and relations are given significant importance and must be invited to a wedding whether one likes them or not. In addition, belonging to a community helps expand your network of contacts and relationships significantly. The names and addresses of these relations are maintained and they also regularly invite us to their family events. We can then add other friends like those from university or work, or neighbours and soon the list adds up. For us, sharing and hospitality are central to culture, so a wide range of people are invited to the wedding. In this way, networks keep on growing, not diminishing and are also retained and nourished rather than being allowed to wither and die. Through such gatherings, whole communities get regularly nourished and reinvigorated.

Co-operative banking or Credit Unions are very common in many parts of the world, especially in developing countries, where the banks do not support small businesses who have poor track records[9]. It is financed by the community, for the community, sensitive to its needs, abilities and aspirations. Just like students without experience find it difficult to get the first job, small businesses find it very difficult to get their first loan even when there are clear growth opportunities. This becomes a vicious cycle, and society loses if it cannot facilitate growth and development. Groups of entrepreneurs club together to form a saving and lending pool and they meet every month to put money in or take money out on an auction mechanism. No laws or external regulations apply – the whole network works on trust and honour, and if one person defaults on a loan, they are never allowed to enter the club again. Over time, such networks also become mutual business support and advice hubs, and some may even start trading with one another. Co-operative banking grows trust in society rather than depleting it and is outside the control of the state or market[10]. It is community in its raw form, and mutuality is experienced and nourished at the same time. My cousin belongs to one such finance network. His actions speak much louder than words ever could. Even medium-sized businesses belong to cooperative finance networks as a way of channelling their cash flows.

In actual fact, communities redefine the breadth and depth of the meaning of the word 'capital'. In finance, it tends to be a very narrow and material phrase, and there is an assumption that financial capital can buy labour, skills and networks of experience, so its power is overwhelming. In this book, we have elaborated on the varying cultural, relationship and community dimensions of capital, which can have financial benefits, but in their origins and definition, are much more broader and deeper than financial wealth. Within communities, capital is seen as a collective asset, and its worth comes from morality, values, relationships, trust, skills and resilience. Its retention and growth come from vision and patience, an ability to live with risk and to operate in organic and home-grown methods which value wisdom and continuity, even when they are open-minded to external theories and science.

TRAINING IN THE COMMUNITY

In the presence of a community, students can get their first job or internship. A start-up business can get its first loans and lessons in growth and prudent financial management. Mentoring also becomes available as others have a stake in the success of a new or growing business. It is therefore paradoxical that in the theory and education in accounting and finance, such diversity of practices, or an appreciation of the value of community, is absent. Social capital is completely ignored. Trust is replaced by contracts and transactions and its importance is assumed away. And lawyers can be costly and greedy too, making contracts invalid or unenforceable. The role of training and mentoring in financial success is replaced by 'science' rather than human interaction, experienced guidance or mutual generosity. Most of finance is reduced to a calculation, contract or formula, giving the impression of credibility and objectivity, when the truth is often far away from it. The fact that trust and relationships are never on a balance sheet as an asset, even though they add real value to a business, often means that it is taken for granted or depleted as businesses grow and become more powerful.

A major branch of finance theory and ideology, agency theory, which was highly influential in the last four decades, focused on ways in which managers could be financially incentivised such that even when they were selfish, the outcome would benefit the shareholder owners[11]. This was a positive theory (instead of a normative theory), and assumed greed, individualism and distrust as given, focusing on material incentives to align the interests of owners and managers. Management bonuses and share options were encouraged, leading to multi-million-dollar fat cat payouts. It drew from American culture, rather than the diversity of cultures and finance practices in the world. It is no surprise that we have had several global financial crises since these theories grew in influence and reach – management remuneration has sky-rocketed, and so have frauds and bankruptcies. For the founders of Agency Theory, the very concept of community must have seemed to be impossible – they never believed such a thing could even exist.

Where entire communities have traditions and histories in business and entrepreneurship, the significant inter-generational power of these hubs of knowledge, information and networks cannot be underestimated. We have already discussed how the Jews and the Jains are good examples, but so also are many other communities all over the world – the Kikuyus in Kenya, the Sindhis originating from India, many Chinese diasporas, Yoruba and Ibo in Nigeria, early Quaker families, Wesleyan Christians, Coptic Christians, Memon Muslims, Ismailis and Mormons or Protestant communities. In these communities, there is an innate ambition and hunger to build, make and provide, and grow and nourish society. Given their socialised upbringing, young people in these communities find it easy to make friends and build trusted relationships, something which is critical to sustainable enterprises. These communities become merchant innovation hubs and universities combined into one, and through globalisation and migration, they are able to trade across the world through these trusted networks. This is further evidence why in our urgency to build a sustainable planet, the harnessing of these communities is critical, and we must begin with respecting their entrepreneurial wisdom, influence and drive.

Given that risk-taking and daring are critical to entrepreneurship, it is often believed that education and professional training are anathema to genuine entrepreneurship. In the UK, the story of young entrepreneur and university dropout Steven Bartlett has become very famous, and he now has a seat in the famous TV show the Dragons Den[12]. He credits the same series for giving him early training in commerce which he had followed from the age of twelve – from an early student, he has now become a Dragon investor and teacher (through his podcast series 'Diary of a CEO'). By definition, the business academy is institutionalised into thinking that entrepreneurs are made not born, and there are rules and techniques which need to be learnt to succeed. However, this is not always true and can be a biased viewpoint. Although Steven was self-made, such success stories are extremely rare. Communities can provide crucial early support and training for entrepreneurs which is later proven to be priceless. It is important to recognise the limitations of delegating thinking and training to institutions, who are often governed by their own norms and self-interest.[13]

BELONGING

Belonging to a community can also provide purpose and meaning, something which a market-based education is unable to give to students. As business educators, we often get complaints from employers that our students are not team players, and we ought to do more to ensure they have experience of shared working and cooperation. It is true that the examining and measurement systems reward individual performance, and therefore pose a big constraint. It is also true that businesses do not want to pay their fair taxes and continue to expect ready-made graduates whom they can rent to improve business profits. Education and training are critical to sustainable development, and teamwork needs to play a critical role in this.

Due to their social histories and festivals, communities give young people a sharing experience from an early age. They have the potential to train future leaders, often giving them very early opportunities in leadership and management (through volunteering) which they would not get in a large organisation for years. The global Scout movement is an example of a community driven by values[14], but also one which is very open and accessible and local too. It is open to all, secular and inclusive. For children, Scouting can be excellent training in the outdoors, and they are often pushed into leadership roles early on and asked to mentor other children as they grow older. Training children to experience nature can only be a bonus for sustainable development – they begin to value it from an early age and are more likely to protect it in future. In this way, people skills are built and valued, and shyness is overcome. Good peer groups are nurtured at a very important time in their lives, especially when they grow into the teenage years where they stop listening to parents. I saw how this experience had a big influence on my own son, who in his first year at university, won an award for outstanding contribution to community life at the University. Giving his service and building communities became very natural for him. The volunteer scout group seniors gave a lot of their time and patience to these young children, in a selfless way, helping to breed future leaders without the need for any external finance or market transaction. They are role models of selfless public service, whose ripples can last a long time. A lot can be learnt when no money changes hands – sadly, money often blurs and distorts trust and relationships.

Pure materialism and individualism can detach finance professionals from a wider inter-generational perspective of time and investment. Even responsible investment may seem difficult, as finance theory is 'morally neutral'. Communities on the other hand help people to feel the impact of their actions and decisions. They often provide inter-generational connections and experiences which are critical to human development and sustainability. Elders are respected for their wisdom and patience, and the breadth of their life experiences and not ignored or dismissed. Experiential capital is also not valued on a balance sheet but can be priceless both to an individual and an organisation. It is rooted in personal interactions, in failures and mishaps, in raw effort, risk encounters, resilience and perseverance. It cannot be put into an equation or formula, but in spite of this, it has value and to ignore it can be very costly and discriminating. This is true especially in finance where long-term projects require inter-generational vision, understanding and sensitivity. In a large family business, several generations are working together so there is an active sharing of experience and a living 'community' at the helm of the organisation. We now turn to examine financial institutions and professions.

ARE PROFESSIONAL FIRMS AND INSTITUTIONS SUSTAINABLE 'COMMUNITIES'?

The institutions of customer 'financial' care, like global accounting firms or financial institutions, have become profit-driven commercial businesses, and this cultural driver conflicts deeply with the duty to act in the best interests of the customer. Paradoxically, in the case of corporate clients, the 'actual' owner may be very remote and invisible – so often proxies (like management) are assumed to 'act' as customers. To protect our natural environment, social ecology is critical – communities need to be understood, respected and protected. Due to their commanding roles and influence, experts ought to be particularly virtuous and reflective in protecting society from falsehood and fraud. They need to be driven by a moral conscience and a deep desire to do good and take responsibility for people and planet.

Communities represent a key link for the efficient functioning of states and markets – Rajan (2019) has called them the 'third pillar'. Communities are places where people connect with one another and develop a sense of mutuality and respect. It is in community that trust and confidence in money and finance are nurtured and nourished. Also shame and dishonour are self-regulating mechanisms within communities – members want to build and uphold a reputation of trust and honesty so as to continue their sense of belonging and camaraderie. When communities are ignored, this core fabric of lived interdependence can be eroded, with significantly adverse long-term consequences.

Professionals belong to expertly trained and certified 'communities' which were created to put specialist knowledge and public interest at the heart of their professionalism – profit and fees were incidental, rather than the primary motive[15]. In the UK, we have the origins of global bodies like the Institute of Bankers or the Institute of Chartered Accountants in England & Wales to uphold independence and integrity and the Certified Financial Analyst (CFA) is a fast-growing new profession emanating from North America. In world history, the UK is one of the major hubs of the creation of finance professions in accounting and banking. Ethics and public interest were at the heart of this early history – in the City of London where they are headquartered, there once were 104 churches in the square mile, showing that faith had a major influence on the concept of professional service. Today, to say that these bodies are failing in their duties would be an understatement. Lord Sikka claims that they do not even deserve to be called professional bodies, but in reality, have become trade associations, helping to maximise the incomes and trades of their members to serve their own interests[16]. Quality knowledge and expertise, with a strong moral conscience, have become removed from the practice and regulation. Profit-making has largely become institutionalised and normalised as a professional right, and 'public' interest has disappeared. These organisations have also forgotten what professional duty actually means and instead enhanced a culture of private interest and commerce, seeing nothing wrong with the contradictions this raises.

The Big 4 global accountancy firms (KPMG, EY, PWC, Deloitte) are a classic example of this corruption and institutional failure, and their huge power and influence on global political economy make this subversion hugely concerning and problematic[17]. Brooks (2018) details examples of global scandals and profound conflicts of interest which have become embedded in their organisational structures and DNA. One of their core businesses is audit, something which is licensed and required by governments, through laws about the independent verification of reported financial statements. As a result of this, not only do these firms get a guaranteed annual revenue stream, they also get access to the corporate Boardroom, where there is a significant concentration of power and resources. In theory, the audit is performed not for the managers of the business, but for the benefit of the shareholders and other stakeholders who are remote from the business. Instead, the Big 4 routinely develop a relationship with the management 'clients' and consistently fails to challenge them on aggressive or inaccurate reporting. In fact, evidence shows that they enable management to influence financial reporting and support them in tax and regulatory arbitrage – they have been dubbed the 'Pin-Stripe Mafia'[18]. Business crises and scandals continue to grow, with fraud even escaping undetected, so compromised the Big 4 have become with their commercial priorities and profit-making[19].

In her study of leadership in these global professional law and accounting firms, Empson (2017) discovers a competitive internal politics, with partners vying for influence, and 'insecure achievers', who perform to please. The fact that they are corporate and profit-oriented is a given, and notions of public interest and professional ethics get subsumed in these large organisations. Her comprehensive interviews reveal the significant power politics in these influential firms which are internalised and normalised. In this sense, partners do not behave as members of communities of public interest and protection, but more as private competitive agents, vying for status and position and often insecure within themselves. From an ethical finance perspective, such decadent leadership cultures, combined with the significant regulatory and consulting powers of these firms, expose the deeper crises of the finance professions and their commercialisation. When communities have little moral reflexivity, and at the same time have significant power and influence, they can become harmful to society and nature.

LEGAL FAILURE

Lord Andrew Phillips trained as a solicitor gained invaluable experience in business law. What he saw happening gradually and then like a flood was more and more laws and regulations, without any thought of their policing or enforcement. Every year, twenty thousand new pages of laws are issued in Britain. Lawyers became busier and richer, but their skills became narrower, specialist and pricier. From this experience, he concluded that the legal system has become unsustainable and equally unenforceable. Instead of encouraging conscience, trust and good character, the legal system became a force for destroying both character and community. He experienced this and wrote and spoke about it with passion on platforms like the BBC, where he was a legal eagle.

As a member of the UK House of Lords, Lord Phillips actively campaigned to change this state of affairs which often made government seem paralysed and inefficient. The costs of litigation have become very high, and governments are not able to curb excessive tax avoidance, pollution or corporate damage to society. In fact they have become captured by corporations and their lobbyists. Access to the law is unequal and only those with lots of money can try to get fair retribution in a business dispute. This often means that smaller businesses struggle to get justice against giant firms when they are suppliers. As a contrasting communitarian example, he explained that there were three law courts in his home town of Sudbury in Suffolk and now there are none. Local courts helped administer local justice and helped the community stay grounded and involved in the administration of fairness and equality. Instead, justice has now become remote, making it more and more difficult for the local community to engage with rules and regulations.

Rules and laws also need community to help them become respected and enforced. They cannot easily operate in abstraction from community. Social customs, relationships and norms can mean that disputes are resolved amicably before they reach the courts, at low cost and leading to better social welfare.

Arbitration and dialogue become much easier in resolving such disputes where there are communities of trust and honour. A community is the space where an individual connects with markets and the state. Good communities are price-less in finance – they are able to channel investment to worthy projects and ensure that judgement and trust are not compromised in the process[20]. Through networks and relationships, community fund-raising becomes easier, and infor-mation and skills are shared, increasing the likelihood of success of a project or investment. The educational, health and religious needs of a community create a focus for action, bringing people together where the collective benefits are directly experienced. Communities also create opportunities for leadership, pur-pose and meaningful enterprise.

HEALTH AND WELL-BEING OF FINANCE LEADERS

As a rule, health and well-being are never discussed in a finance or accounting classroom. They are simply assumed, or when we dig deeper, money is seen as a proxy for health, well-being and happiness. It can 'buy' good health if needed. If finance is to be sustainable, health and well-being of individuals, finance leaders, families and communities are critical – they cannot be compromised for the sake of profit or wealth maximisation, nor can they be selectively available just for the elites or the rich. We have examples from the past where employers used to provide housing and healthcare to their staff, acknowledging that their performance is not disconnected from their healthcare and accommodation. In this way, employers actively built and nurtured communities of their employ-ees, making them feel they belonged to a larger family, and their work was guaranteed for life provided they were loyal. This is an example of sustainable finance in action. There were costs of making such provisions for the employers, but these were seen as duties rather than costs, and employees were not simply human resources, but people who built and grew the business – direct stake-holders in its success.

Potter was a senior Vice President in Communications at a major American health insurance company (Potter 2010). He found deceit and lies were normalised, and finance and profit motives overwhelmed any sense of care or well-being for Americans – the driving force was financialisation, profits and share price growth, at any cost, including honesty and genuine insurance. He personally wrote the press releases when profit announcements were made, and saw how much spin was applied, and the constant pressure to report ever higher profits. It is well known that the private market for healthcare in America has been a public failure, and it is over-costly and inefficient, with no access for the poor and the marginalised. This is a raw and living example of extreme finance, without any sense of concern for the well-being of society – enterprises whose sole purpose is to exploit and extract. Over the years, health insurance companies have grown bigger and bigger and more and more powerful, leaving ordinary people very insecure and vulnerable. The market has encouraged monopolies instead of competition.

However, when organisations start to see their workers as family, rather than separate individual units, whose skills are purchased for performance, a very different finance and management culture is inculcated. Sadly, these kinds of employers have virtually disappeared from society today, and the stock markets would punish companies who were socially oriented, as that would mean less returns for the shareholders. The long-term culture of a corporation is simply not valued, nor is it on the balance sheet in the reporting of financial performance. As to workers being seen as communities, that phrase has disappeared from the textbook. To the contrary, there are examples where workers are so exploited that they are forced to break up the communities that they belong to, having to travel far to find a job and then feeling totally isolated from their families and homes[21]. This is the increasing feature of large-scale manufacturing businesses, where even pay and conditions of workers are such as to undermine their health and well-being. This is not in any way sustainable.

SUPERMARKETS

In his book 'Tesco-poly'[22], Andrew Simms elaborates how giant chain stores destroy local communities, first by removing local small businesses like grocery stores and then by employing anonymous workers who have no time to take any interest in their customers – just cashiers whose productivity is measured by how quickly they process customers. Chatting and engagement are timewasters and prohibited. 'Whereas locally rooted businesses irrigate wealth around a community, remotely owned chain stores can suck money out like giant cash vacuum cleaners' (p. 146). He gives the example of Josephine who owned a small grocery store in his local area and explains how she took a personal interest in every customer, exchanged local information and even took pains to enquire about their health if they had not come to the store recently. Such businesses nourished communities rather than expropriate them. Josephine is unlikely ever to have become very rich, but it seems her priorities were different – she actively cultivated social and relationship capital.

After successfully building large supermarkets all over the country, Tesco decided to go into the small local grocery store business, by opening smaller convenience stores all over the country. If they wanted to, they could have done this using a co-operative or franchise model, to ensure that local wealth and connectivity remained within a neighbourhood. Instead of opening their own new branches, Tesco could have worked in partnership with existing local businesses, by giving them franchises and thereby, some local ownership and responsibility. However, they chose not to do that, so even smaller family-owned local stores were hoovered up. These new Tesco stores are open long hours, taking away the one competitive edge which smaller local businesses had. Staff are on shift patterns, so there is little recognition between customers and personnel, nor is there any feeling of loyalty or trust. When calculations in accounting and finance do not factor local relationships, trust and responsibility, they end up helping businesses destroy such communities. Today in the UK, small local grocery stores struggle to barely survive and constantly go out of business, destroying any sense of community.

COMMUNITY CAPITAL

The destruction of community capital is never measured on a profit and loss account or balance sheet, but it is real and irreplaceable. In Britain of the 1960s, 1970s and 1980s, immigrant Asians came to own and manage what were then known as *Corner Shops*[23] all over Britain, and the personal service they provided is still missed by many. As an example, if customers asked for something and they did not have it, they got it for them the next day or guided them as to where they could get it. They brought their culture of community to their enterprise, by *nurturing* a community of customers whom they cared about, knowing many of them by first name. Even the newspapers and cigarettes customers preferred were ready as soon as they walked through the entrance – such was the memory of the owners. The supermarket chains today have removed the Asian community from this business, and the remaining shops run by immigrants are all struggling just to survive.

Global hubs of finance like London, New York or Hong Kong are located in mega-cities. In the case of London, we have a political and financial centre located within one geographical boundary. In fact, the 'City of London' which is the square mile where financial institutions are headquartered is regarded as the largest concentration of financial and political influence anywhere in the world[24]. Even today, the Queen needs permission from the Lord Mayor of the City of London before she can enter it. It has its own laws and taxes and has a very powerful influence in parliament – its own City Minister. Such a significant concentration of capital and decision-making creates a very deep fracture for sustainability – it is simply incapable of understanding the local and community influence of its allocations. The City of London is very distant and removed from both the shareholders and the businesses where its markets exert influence. Whereas once it had one hundred four churches in its midst, today it has nearly seventeen hundred pubs and wine bars to nourish the finance leaders with regular alcohol throughout the day. There is no more visible evidence of culture change than this.

Within this same geography, we have the EMEA (Europe, Middle-East and Africa) headquarters of the giant global accounting firms – PWC, Deloitte, KPMG and EY. Therefore, both finance and its 'independent' accountability are located within one geographical jurisdiction, breeding significant revolving doors and conflicts of interest. When the science and teaching of accounting and finance completely ignore these geographical factors[25], it is making a statement that they are irrelevant to actual practice and decision-making. In fact, they are highly relevant, because within these cities, we have 'communities' of experts and professionals who can and do collude to undermine responsibility and accountability[26]. Networks of evil in finance and accounting can be deeply damaging for planetary sustainability. London is home to hundreds of elite private members clubs. In the UK, KPMG built a private members club in the heart of Mayfair for its executive and elite networking[27].

GEOGRAPHY

In theorising and teaching finance, geography is important. Cities can breed huge concentrations of power and conflicts of interest at the expense of remote investors, pensioners, savers or communities and societies[28]. Here in London, we have a community of pilferers rather than a community of responsible citizens. Nicholas Shaxson calls this a 'Finance Curse'[29] – large concentrations of finance bring curse and devastation to societies, rather than nourishment and growth. A Spiders Web of offshore secrecy jurisdictions is run from London with disastrous tax evasion and avoidance, leaving an unsustainable tax burden on ordinary hard-working citizens. Large floods of money going through very narrow funnels can and do bring pain and misery. We need to build dams and filters if we wish to create a sustainable planet. Despite the regulation of banking and accounting, what we have at present is failing in a number of serious ways.

Just as trust can be grown and enriched by communities, it can easily be depleted and destroyed by the *wrong* types of communities and networks. In London, faithless and drug-fuelled concentrations of power have become deeply damaging[30]. The Big 4 global accounting firms do not just provide audit services – they also provide tax advice and an A-Z of consulting services to large multinational corporations which also change and evolve depending on the latest fashions or buzzwords. One of their main sources of revenue is change in laws and regulations – this means that they can help their clients adopt to the new rules[31]. Volatility is good for professional business, especially if you are large, branded and global. Even if the Big 4 brand suffers damage due to audit failures or corporate frauds, their oligopolistic power and political influence mean that no one goes to jail. They keep their resilience, threatening to governments that if one of them were to be closed down, there would only be Big 3 which would mean even less choice![32] Too big to fail has become a safety net for both banks and accounting firms. Is this really sustainable?

Even inside a bank, there is often no community – but instead competition and back-stabbing prevail, and there is a culture of bullying and exploitation which can be very cold and ruthless[33]. Given that Banks are guardians of 'other people's money', such a culture would seem antithetical to good banking, but has grown and prevailed in large international banks for decades, especially in their high-risk areas like the trading floor or investment banking[34]. Within the geographical boundary of one institution, there can be tension between individualism and cooperation. Rewards and incentives can act to undermine community. There is evidence that in the trading floors, top dealers have their own executive powers and often command their own salaries and bonuses – yes they are more powerful than their bosses![35]. Banks have to compete to 'keep' their top risk takers[36]. Here again, sustainability can be easily compromised, and there have been cases like Barings in the past, where aggressive traders have brought down whole institutions or created billions in losses for them.

CHARACTER AND INTEGRITY

The ethics and integrity of members of a community matter significantly to the success and longevity of the group. There should be feelings of trust and empathy and a conscience which warns against wrongdoing and unfairness, especially when one is in a position of power and influence[37]. Honour and reputation need to matter and help in regulating behaviour and elites should be prohibited from hiding behind institutional brands so that they can be personally named, punished and shamed. The impersonal corporation today has become a protective shell for unethical expropriation. The weak and illiterate ought to be protected and not exploited. Measures of performance and valuation need to incorporate such ethical ideals, not exclude or ignore them.

When HBOS Bank was expanding very quickly out of proportion to its capacity and risk management, its Head of Regulatory Risk, Paul Moore felt very uncomfortable. Instead of buckling down and keeping mum, he decided to speak up and challenge the leadership[38]. Most people in a similar position would not do this even when they know wrong is happening in front of their very eyes – they are afraid to lose their job and reputation as the risk of speaking truth to power is very high. Paul was a Catholic by faith and belonged to a community of faith, with a strong sense of social and moral conscience. He decided not to think about himself, but instead the customers and employees who worked hard and stood to lose by the high risk-taking. Unfortunately, he lost his job and was never again gainfully employed by the sector. However, when HBOS eventually collapsed a few years later, the Parliamentary investigation regarded him as a key witness and someone whom both the Board and regulators ignored, to the peril of the customers and investors. In the end, fifty-two billion pounds of losses were accumulated and the Bank had to be bailed out[39]. This proves that leadership, faith and conscience can have a big influence on culture and resilience.

People who belong to communities, bring culture and wisdom to an organisation and even conscience and character. At present, due to cultural ignorance and impersonal science, finance organisations do not appreciate or value these qualities at all, and as we saw in the above case, suppress or even dismiss people of conscience. We need to find a way of changing this huge loss arising from ignorance and bias if we are to improve the leadership and character of financial institutions. This book is a step in this direction by encouraging better education and research. It is very clear to me that such training cannot be limited to the classroom – it can be delivered on the field by taking leaders on culture tours and cultural experiences, where they are able to see and experience a community on its own terms[40]. One of the biggest fortunes we have is that all these finance megacities, whether it is London, New York, Hong Kong or even Frankfurt, have very diverse communities living in their geographies. These can be places where such visits can be coordinated and facilitated, so that the context does not feel remote and distant, but local and real. However, one tour would not be enough, but is a start.

SPIRITUAL COMMUNITIES UNDERSTAND THE LIMITS OF MATERIALISM

Global multinational corporations also increasingly remove themselves from communities, as there is a growing distance between the boardroom where decisions are made and the local companies and subsidiaries in different parts of the world where the impact of these decisions is felt[41]. Information and reports cannot easily replace the local voice and experience, but they can give the impression that such impact is being monitored and measured. Proxies are used to measure social and community impact through strategies for CSR – corporate social responsibility. In this way, a 'fictional' feeling of social responsibility is created, which can be far from the truth and therefore mis-direct the strategic decisions that are taken.

David Korten[42] was a development economist and consultant who travelled all over Asia to advise governments and corporations on development. He started with strong American ideals of progress and civilisation which he wanted to take to Asia to help transform it. Initially, he set out to impose solutions on the people, top down, as part of the strings attached to development funding. His education had convinced him that the American model of development was very advanced and superior. However, on his journey, he discovered that local communities in Asia were far more civilised than professionals gave them credit, and they often knew the solutions to their own problems without the need for foreign 'experts'. What they lacked were resources to fund their solutions and political and corporate support to back them. *Experts and distant finance or corporate interests became a big part of the problem, rather than a sustainable part of the solution.* As early as the 1990s, Korten warned society against the growth of giant corporations, predicting that their size and influence would undermine growth rather than enable it. His predictions have all come true – corporations do rule the world today, for their own commercial and financial interests.

One key ingredient he found missing from his own training in economics was the vital importance of *spiritual development* to growth and sustenance. In Asia, he found communities had a lot of spiritual resources and resilience – they had an innate sense of trust and connectivity which was absent from the West. They also had a sense of history and identity. They were proud in spite of their material poverty. Not only can spirituality bind communities, but it can also give them an added sense of purpose and resilience which could help them transcend their problems and challenges and build new futures which are both local and sustainable. Enterprise is often sparked by this deeper sense of purpose, which gives birth to courageous leadership. Korten also observed that spiritual strength also gave them inter-generational respect and fairness, making communities sensitised to the impact of their actions on people and nature. It also gives people humility and a profound respect for the environment, something which is not easy to teach through textbooks or laws. As an example, I come from a farming background, and during times of harvest, the first actions by my grandfather were to share the fruits and vegetables with the local community for free, acknowledging the role of land, water and sunshine in growing the vegetables. The profits and produce did not just 'belong' to the farmer – they were for everyone.

GOVERNANCE AND REGULATORY CAPTURE

Members of a corporate boardroom make up a community, with significant leadership qualities, powers and responsibilities. Non-executive directors are meant to *challenge and critique* corporate actions where they are damaging to stakeholders and society – they have a duty to police corporate action and prevent hubris and arrogance. Cultural and experiential diversity in the Boardroom is critical to this challenge.[43] Independent directors are supposed to monitor corporate social responsibility and not encourage greed and expropriation. After the collapse of HBOS Bank[44], which was Britain's fifth-largest retail and commercial bank, forensic parliamentary investigation and questioning revealed that none of the Board members had *any* banking experience whatsoever. The Chairman even explained that as a matter of rule, the Non-Executive Directors did not criticise the Bank on its business strategy as they did not wish to interfere with it! Neither did the auditors KPMG warn society of the enormous risks being built up in the systemically significant financial institution. During its short seven-year life, the Bank flooded the market with cheap loans, helping shape a huge housing bubble which burst in 2008. Not only did this significant pillar of finance collapse, it acted irresponsibly during its short life, and its leaders failed to challenge the high-risk high-growth strategy in a timely manner. They *facilitated* corporate hubris and failure.

When a finance community is motivated by the desire to grab 'other people's money', a very different culture and mindset develops, which still involves people and relationships. However, the motives of these are to exploit and expropriate as the owners of the wealth are distant and divided, e.g. groups of pensioners or investors (indirect shareholders) spread out in various parts of the world[45]. Sadly, evidence shows that a lot of modern finance is driven by such a community, even while the textbooks are totally silent about the existence of it. In fact, this 'social silence' among experts legitimates this expropriation. Collusion among bankers, lawyers and accountants is critical to the growth and expansion of such communities, and the ability to escape any justice whatsoever. The sums involved are often very much large, which mean that the losses for society are unsustainable. In the case of large financial institutions, the ramifications are system-wide and therefore affect the whole economy as we experienced in the

2008 crash[46]. However, in practice, it is very difficult to directly identify this collusion, or break such networks, because they operate in the shadows and are usually driven by experts who know very well the gaps in the legal and account-ing rules. Often these networks also use their power and influence to lobby and capture regulatory processes, making it impossible for society to govern or police them effectively[47]. Whereas many of the communities identified in this book are identifiable, these 'hidden' communities can be much more dangerous due to their opacity and skill in staying above the justice system. Instead of regulating corporate abuse, networks of bankers, lawyers and accountants become enablers of exploitation.

Also such selfish communities have very little sense of history, conscience or responsibility and yet have significant latent power and influence. In this sense, they can be more dangerous and harmful during their temporary existence. Their subtlety and invisibility mean that they are unidentifiable, opaque and impenetrable by outsiders who wish to unlock the real nature of the networks and relationships. Those allowed to enter may be forced to behave in sinister ways and even policed for any misbehaviours outside formal legal systems or transparent methods of justice. They may not have definite physical meeting spaces like churches or temples. Private selfish networks do not wish to be sus-tainable in the social or environmental sense – only to themselves. They could also be communities of self-harm which could and often do bring wider social inequality and discontent through unequal and hubristic power and influence.

IMPACT MEASUREMENT

There are practical ways in which Boards, especially non-executives, can monitor corporate impact on communities. They could go into the field and talk directly to different stakeholders, like customers and small business suppliers, about their experiences of dealing with the organisation. How are they treated? What hap-pens when things go wrong? Are the products and services provided ethical and respectful of local communities? Instead of simply sitting in the Boardroom and looking at reports, they must go into the field on a random basis, unannounced, to really engage, listen and thereby discern what is really going on. Board papers can easily be filtered by the executive, such that non-executives only see what the executives want them to see. Primary evidence can be very powerful in helping leaders understand the degree to which products and services are really sustain-able. Non-executives could also appoint their own investigators and researchers to discover these facts on their behalf. This would compose an independent audit of management decisions and strategies.

For corporations to understand, respect and protect communities, they also need to behave like one and set an example to others. This is especially true in banking and financial institutions where they are at the apex of managing other people's money. Employees need to be trained in terms of morality and character, and team building and collaboration should be encouraged. Social activities for employees can act as bonding exercises, and charitable projects for the benefit of local groups could help the firm engage with the wider community. It may even be that some of the groups supported are those that employees are already volunteering for and passionate about. This would bring added appreciation of the employer and its respect for the staff. Communities need to be nourished by education, participation and social impact. Large employers could do all these things and thereby experience the value of team and engagement capital.

For corporations listed on stock markets, with access to very large financial resources, and operations all over the world, the power and influence are often even greater than those of Prime Ministers or Presidents, and the Board members are not elected democratically. This makes the psychology of this power, and the methods leaders use to apply it responsibly and sustainably, very critical. The fact that they do not 'own' the finance that they are allocating is very important to understand and requires significant humility and accountability. These skills and traits cannot easily be 'taught' in a business school or even necessarily in the world of business. Often, they are nurtured in the families and communities from where leaders come and their personal values and integrity and how these are upheld even in challenging times. Leaders need to come from 'grounded' experiences, not just clever-clever techniques and formulae learnt from scientific experts. When they are interviewed for board positions, these questions become critical to their appointment to such senior positions of influence. Their raw experiences and track records of using power responsibly become very critical in deciding on their leadership capacities and resulting impact on business sustainability.

NATURE AS COMMUNITY

In the last four decades, evidence of a growing *disruption* of community within stock market quoted companies has been growing. Corporate raids, mergers and takeovers, new aggressive financial vehicles like junk bonds, private equity and hedge funds have resulted in significant restructurings, even bankruptcies and consolidations[48]. More and more effort has been devoted to the pay and bonuses of senior executives, and the financial nature of their incentives, at the expense of social responsibilities, with employees increasingly seen as workhorses to serve the interests of management. Even the appreciation of the key stakeholders of any business, the workers, has been declining and their loyalty is undervalued – trade unions have been broken and undermined. As a result, corporate locations and geographies keep changing through these financial manoeuvres. For workers, the inability to live stable lives disrupts their own family life making communal and collective experiences more and more difficult. This leads to unstable societies and growing anonymity and alienation. Instead of encouraging stability and sustainability, corporate financialisation has had the opposite effect – a constant state of restlessness. The insecurities of the leaders have been passed onto the workers, spreading the cancer of individualism and selfishness. Far from being an example to the world, these corporate leaders have had the opposite effect. Given that global business and financial flows are directed from these boardrooms, such disruption has also been globalised.

The current global leader of the Catholic Church, Pope Francis, has provided strong leadership in the urgency to save our ecosystem. He has issued a special 'Encyclical Letter', *Laudato Si*, on 'Care For Our Common Home'[49]. In it, he explains (p.11): 'If we approach nature and the environment without openness to awe and wonder, if we no longer speak the language of fraternity and beauty in our relationship with the world, our attitude will be that of masters, consumers, ruthless exploiters unable to set limits on their immediate needs.' For the Pope, nature is an extension of family and community. It is us and our very own home which we must look after with the utmost love and care – violence to nature is violence to ourselves. He explains the centrality of spiritual wisdom and community to our appreciation of the environment – mere calculation and analysis, with laws and regulations, will not bring about sustainable change. There is a whole chapter in the *Laudato Si* devoted to 'Integral Ecology' (Chapter 4). Here he introduces concepts such as cultural ecology, the principle of the common good and justice between the generations. Pope Francis also attacks technocracy and anthropocentrism, explaining that we need to fundamentally change our knowledge systems and dominion of nature to one of caretaker and community-builder.

HISTORY AND HERITAGE

Building and nurturing communities take hundreds of years, even thousands for some. Like Rain Forests, once they are destroyed, they cannot be resurrected, because each community is an ecosystem and a place where there is history, memory, trust, loyalty, character, self-regulation, adaptability and resilience. Just as replanting trees does not bring back a Rain Forest ecosystem, once destroyed, communities are impossible to resurrect. That is why it is so important that modern finance science and education engage with the understanding and value of communities and ensure that in its equations and techniques, these macrocosms of social and ethical capital are valued and not destroyed by ignorance, prejudice or simply an inability to understand their timeless wisdoms and qualities. Communities are 'whole' organisms, holistic in their approach to life, not specialised or boxed into technocratic expertise and knowledge which is removed from its wider social and environmental implications. Networks of trust and loyalty take many lifetimes to build and grow. They are not dependent simply on material interests or welfare – they go far beyond, maintaining mental, physical and emotional health of whole populations. Instead of money, they put well-being at the heart of their priorities, and collectivism stumps individualism inside these groupings.

When the science and practice of finance directly or inadvertently diminish or damage communities, the loss to society is significant and often cannot even be priced. Just as society is now realising the devastating implications of environmental destruction, economics and finance ought to start measuring and acknowledging the harm their science has caused to cultures and communities all over the world. Just as environment has been treated as an externality, so has community, as a result of which economics has damaged both society and nature at the same time. The cure to this malaise is not to patch the science but to re-examine its fundamental assumptions, prejudices and outright fictions and false narratives or fundamentalisms. If the very content of our disciplines of accounting and finance is prejudicial to the importance of communities, then this damages society irreparably. I have seen from my decades of teaching experience in the West that academics rarely ask students about their cultures or community experiences even in the field of business. What is known and present in the classroom is not even acknowledged, let alone celebrated and allowed to nourish business and finance knowledge.

SOCIAL SILENCE

There is a profound intellectual disrespect of communities which creates a barrier to their sustenance. By the denial of their very existence, through abstract and impersonal finance and economic theories, there is a subtle but harmful attack on communities and their traditions of trust, wisdom and interdependence. The religion of secularism has also enhanced the illiteracy and ignorance of what really happens within faith communities, and how business and finance operate. Not only is this veil harmful in terms of our understanding of truth and sustainable human society, it also attacks these communities directly by the conscious promotion of materialism and individualism. Trust takes decades and generations to build and nurture and to destroy it means that it cannot be resurrected easily, precisely at a time when we need it the most. To pursue the millennium development goals, we have no choice but to acknowledge and work with existing communities, however diverse their beliefs and traditions. This means a non-standard and inclusive finance, rather than a hierarchical top-down mechanistic and materialistic science, devoid of human and social relations.

I know this is a big ask and will take time to shape and mould. However, we must recognise how short a time it has taken to deplete nature and indigenous cultures which were thousands of years old, living in peace and harmony with animals and the environment. The structures, framing and ideology of the multinational corporation, combined with the fiction of free and competitive markets, are deeply damaging. None of this blood is on the hands of the powerful elites, but it should be, if only to remind them that the status quo is no longer sustainable and respect for culture is not just a nice to have. Science should take moral and ethical responsibility for its claims and valuations and not wash its hands from the moral consequences of its actions. Respect for traditional communities should be core to the science and cultures should also be allowed to be wiser than our present knowledge and practices in finance. Whilst we are struggling to 'find' sustainable finance, we are ignoring the vast bank of sustainable knowledge that lies within these communities which is hiding in plain sight. We must rise to the challenge of understanding traditional wisdom within their own contexts and not rushing to judge or diminish them.

What this chapter, and the practical cultural leadership and community examples demonstrate, is that there is a very important dimension of knowledge, beyond the rational or the cognitive, that is missed by modern social science – the dimension of living spirituality, cultural diversity and human collective experience. This is not hard technocratic knowledge, but soft nuanced wisdom which has moral responsibility and accountability often at its core. We cannot make finance sustainable without re-examining our anthropomorphic science and education systems and reforming them fundamentally. Even the university campus can be nurtured as a community of aspiration towards a sustainable and inclusive society, which does not deny faith or spirituality but includes a diversity of world-views, cultures and beliefs. Here students should get an experience of interdependence and feel that all together is better and more fun than all alone. Academic prejudices about belief and spirituality need to be addressed rather than suppressed or ignored. In the next chapter, we focus in detail on tacit knowledge – skills obtained through upbringing, culture, tradition and community living. Even though they are not in textbooks or classrooms, they are very helpful in accounting and finance leadership.

Notes

1 Rajan (2019) and Collier and Kay (2020).
2 Kinley (2018), a Human Rights lawyer, makes a strong case for finance to change direction and protect human rights through its institutions and practices, instead of destroying them. He calls finance a 'Necessary Evil', the title of his book.
3 See Mea and Sims (2019) and Katona (2020). There are many Papal edicts on the Catholic Social Teaching, and we have also discussed the Laudato Si earlier.
4 Sacks (1990) – in particular his lecture, 'A Community of Communities'; Sacks (2003).
5 The BBC Reith Lectures by Jonathan Sacks (1990) are outstanding in their illumination of the morality, versatility and resilience of faith communities.
6 West (2003); Sikka and Wilmott (1995); Shah (2018b).
7 See Luyendijk (2015) for an analysis of Banking culture and hyper-individualism and back-stabbing.
8 Rajan (2019).
9 Ekins et al (1992).
10 Prieg and Greenham (2012).
11 Shaxson (2018) and Erturk et al (2007).
12 www.stevenbartlett.com.
13 Parker (2018a) exposes this failure well.
14 Rosenthal (1986) calls it a 'character factory' which shapes civic virtues and citizenship at a tender malleable age. In a similar way, communities can also be dubbed character factories, with all their virtues and imperfections. They are agents of socialization and morality.
15 Abbott (1988); West (2003) Chapter 2.
16 Sikka et al (2018).

17 Sikka (2008) and Mitchell and Sikka (2011).
18 Shah (1996a) and Shah (2015a,b).
19 Brooks (2018); Mitchell and Sikka (2011) call them the 'Pin-Stripe Mafia'.
20 Rajan (2019).
21 Hertz (2001), Bakan (2004), Korten (1995) and Hutton (2010).
22 Simms (2007).
23 See Sharma (2019) for a first person account of one such shop and its history, and how the family learnt entrepreneurial and social skills whilst growing up above the shop.
24 Kynaston (2011) *City of London – The History*, Chatto & Windus, UK.
25 See Sassen (2001, 2012) for the political and economic geography of cities.
26 Shaxson (2012) and Palan et al (2010) report on the worlds off-shore secrecy havens run from London. Bullough (2018) reports on the frauds arising from the City.
27 See Brooks (2018) Prologue.
28 See Folkman et al (2007), Augar (2005) and Hall (2009) for the influential networks and their power in global banking.
29 Shaxson (2018).
30 Shah (2014).
31 Shah (2015b) explains their role in 'systemic regulatory arbitrage' and Shah (1996a) analyses the 'Creative Compliance' phenomenon.
32 Brooks (2018) examines this power in depth.
33 Luyendijk (2015) compiles a number of true stories of the *real* culture in the square mile.
34 Tett (2010) details how such networks centred around New York and London served to enable the 2008 global financial crash – they were obsessed by private returns and pushing risk to society without blinking an eye. Cohan (2011) describes the networks shaped by Goldman Sachs, which became the world's premiere investment bank. Vampire Squid is how Taibbi (2009, 2014) describes the firm.
35 Augar (2005).
36 Strange (1986) foresaw this 'Casino Capitalism' as highly speculative and dangerous for the global economy.
37 Polman and Winston (2021) explain how companies can give more than they take.
38 Moore (2015) is a detailed account of his personal ordeal and whistle-blowing experience.
39 Shah (2018a) details the networks which mis-managed the bank and got away without any punishment, including the auditors. Tyrie et al (2013a) is a forensic parliamentary investigation of the debacle.
40 Shah (2007) explains how the richness of diversity can be understood and celebrated.
41 Hertz (2001), Simms (2007), Bakan (2004), Rajan (2019) and Collier and Kay (2020).
42 Korten (1995) is a very pioneering and prescient analysis of the dangers of multinational corporations and their profound unsustainability.
43 See Shah (2012) for explanations and examples on how this can be achieved in practice.
44 PRA (2015a,b,c); Tyrie et al (2013a).
45 Kay (2015) and Collier and Kay (2020).
46 Shah (1996b, 1996b, 1997a).
47 Shah (1996a, 1997b).
48 Hertz (2001), Tett (2010), Gray (1998) and Froud et al (2006).
49 Pope Francis (2015).

4

EXPERIENCE

Picture the scene. Mumbai in 2021. Twenty-three members of a global business family live together and eat together every day. Present are the founding brothers, their wives and siblings, all of whom share their work life and their home. Offices are not very far away. Meals are taken together on a regular basis – alongside banter, deals may be discussed, challenges may be shared and the upcoming generation, while playing begin to hear the business language. And this language is repeated every day, reinforcing the subconscious development. Is this a Board meeting? Is it a Business School, where entrepreneurial training and incubation are provided? Or is it simply any other household – except that several families are living together? This is the true story of Waaree Group[1], one of India's largest global solar energy businesses, led by CEO Mr Hitesh Doshi. Is it a surprise that the business is growing rapidly today? When I set up a meeting for them with a top energy group in the UK, they ensured that at the meeting, one of their youngest sons, Ankit Doshi, was also present so that he could be trained in international business. One thing is for sure – this family would not need any lessons in unity, mentoring or teamwork – they practise it every day.

Finance decision-making and execution are ultimately done by human beings, not machines. How these humans think, operate, trust, manage risk and decide is therefore critical to a deeper understanding of the discipline. In this chapter, we look at the tacit skills that are critical to success, from communication and socialisation, to role models and mentoring, character, honour and relationship skills. How is trust built and defended, at times even at a loss? What happens when leaders place a high value on reputation and family name? What role does family business play in the character, vision, judgement and training of young novices? Communities play an important role in the training and development of business acumen, often very informally. Migration involves risk but

DOI: 10.4324/9781003164746-4

also opportunity and is cushioned when trust capital becomes accessible – mutual hard work and sharing provide a springboard for entrepreneurial success.

In previous chapters, we looked at tradition and community. Tradition comes from hundreds or even thousands of years of history. It represents knowledge percolated and sieved by experience. Community and festivals bring alive traditions and give new generations a direct sense of experience of that heritage, memory, art and the spirit of sharing and caring. When children and young people are raised in this combined milieu, they are given a unique trajectory into the world of business and finance which is too often ignored, undervalued or simply dismissed as backward and regressive. This chapter will show what is lost when this is done, and what can instead be harnessed if this upbringing is recognised and discussed. The significant importance of volunteering experiences for finance professionals in an era of financialisation can never be underemphasised.

HOLISTIC COMMUNICATION

Formal methods of communication like emails and meetings have their disadvantages. They are never whole – the mind, body and spirit of the person are not visible – only a partial aspect is displayed. In contrast in a relaxed setting like the dining room, there is deeper communication and engagement, where both problems and opportunities are shared in a natural intimate way. There is no question of hiding risks or information – the family home encourages trust and mutuality, reinforcing it every day. Problems and losses are shared, not denied or hidden. Conflicts are not suppressed but instead addressed through communication. In this way, business gets done, and the variety of stakeholders in an enterprise, be it customers, suppliers, future generations or wider society, and community are understood and the long-term approach is beyond question. Future owners are real, not imaginary, and inside the family home. Inter-generational equity does not need to be put in the risk calculations – it is central to investment decision-making.

Amish Tripathi is the Minister of Culture at the Indian High Commission in London. A banker by profession with an MBA from the Indian Institute of Management, he is a rare finance expert who has become one of India's most famous best-selling writers of ancient epic narratives like the Ramayana and Mahabharata in contemporary language (5.5 million books sold)[2]. Whilst recognising that his own finance education was very technical and neo-liberal, he says that in truth India is moved by a 'Dharmic Capitalism' rooted in faith, tradition and cultural and community relationships which have travelled through generations. He agreed that the curriculum needs to embrace narrative and culture as it is through culture and relationships that finance often operates in India and not cold transactions and autonomous contracts.

Amish Tripathi spoke of various communities among Hindus, like the Sindhis, the Marvadis, Gujaratis, the Chettiyars and the Punjabis with skilled business acumen and thrift in their DNA. He also recalled the vast amount of charity done by business leaders, often anonymously in India, to help run schools, colleges and community institutions, including temples. This gave flow to their wealth and reduced accumulation and greed and enabled the leaders to experience the smiles on the faces of the beneficiaries. Regular contact of business leaders with monks and nuns gave them a sense of humility and simplicity which kept them grounded and rooted. Family business flourishes because family is such a profound institution of India, and its tentacles extend to hundreds of relatives for each person, which tradition bound together, in pain or gain. This gave people resilience and mutuality in times of hardship.

When several generations work together in a business, a fact which is unusual in society today, there is a natural sharing of wisdom and experience. There may also be an active questioning of assumptions and traditions by younger generations. Power and authority are not always taken for granted, and young people may ask fundamental questions which would otherwise have been normalised as habits for many years. As in all organisations, there will be hierarchy and politics, but leaders of a family business can help set a tone of openness and critical discussion. This dialogue may be challenging, but where it happens on a regular basis, it has the potential to carry the force of memory, experience and tradition giving a deeper resilience and sustainability to the enterprise.

New products and investment strategies can be soundly debated in this way prior to launch and execution, helping to manage risk. In a family business, this inter-generational dialogue would happen in a respectful and trusted manner, and there could be active listening from all sides. This can give a sense of robustness and longevity to the business. It also reminds the founders that they need to pro-actively think about business transition, rather than leave it to others to sort out when they die. Personal and regular oral communication is key to sustainability of leadership. Based in Nairobi, Kenya, top management consultant Deepak Shah often found that when family businesses break down, a lot of the problems stem from poor communication and established hierarchy. Openness and engagement are keys to growth and progression, his experience has shown.

THE SILK ROAD

Business schools and professions are fairly recent innovations in human history. Prior to that time, business was conducted, trade was done across countries and commerce led to economic growth and expansion in many parts of the world. India was one of the largest trading economies in the world, before the British occupation and looting.[3] A lot of international trade was done peacefully, where each side of the deal wanted the other to win too and come back for more. In fact, we forget that for a long time in history, trade was an active form of peace-making between cultures, communities and nations. The 'Silk Road'[4] through Asia and linking Europe was an excellent example of this. It was much more than a transport route – it became a flow of ideas, goods, a place where the great religions of the world were born and disseminated. Furthermore, traders of that time were often contented, faithful and grateful, not greedy, materialistic and selfish. They often used trade as a means of learning about other people and cultures and their beliefs too. It was as much adventure as a source of economic well-being. In finance, the phrase adventure is never used today – instead it has been replaced by 'venture' capital, which is often tax avoiding and focused on fast-paced wealth creation, spreading greed more widely in society. The history of the Silk Road has a lot to teach modern finance students about inter-cultural sustainability.

There were no borders of the mind, body and spirit in those times. Trade enabled people to communicate across barriers of language and belief – a skill we seem to have lost today, in spite of global travel and cosmopolitan cities. In the rush towards secularism, modernity and technology, we have sacrificed the patience and value of relationships which is critical to sustainable trade. Ancient peoples understood this and valued it. Trade has prevented wars in the past, and this value is never discussed in finance. The Silk Road became a tributary for wisdom, the knowledge which is beyond the physical or material world and transcends the limits of a selfish materialistic existence. Its real capital lay in the treasury of human curiosity, aspiration and community.

In 1688, a Dutch East India company Director observed this about the skill and thrift of Indian merchants[5]:

> The merchants … are exceptionally quick and experienced. When they are still very young and in the laps of their parents and hardly able to walk, they already begin to be trained as merchants. They are made to pretend to engage in trade while playing, first buying *cauris (sea-shells)*, followed by silver and gold. In this training as moneychangers, they acquire the capability of engaging in large-scale trade. They are always sober, modest, thrifty, and cunning in identifying the source of their profit, which they are always at pain to maximize. They have an exceptional capacity of discovering the humour of those who are in a position to help or hurt them. They flatter those they know they need to be in the good books of. In case of loss, they console themselves easily and can hide their sorrow wonderfully … In general, they are a people with whom one can get along well so long as one is on one's guard.

The above quote explains the cultural nature of business acumen and skill, which we dismiss to our peril. Much can be learnt from observing this firsthand. I take students on field trips to see small-scale enterprise in action – not large corporations, whose behaviours are often remotely controlled. Instead, I take them to market traders or small businesses, where the whole can be seen and experienced visually through observation, oral enquiry and communication. I find that they learn a lot from such micro-experiences, then when they are in the small branch of a giant, soulless corporation, although I take them there also to experience the contrast. When students learnt of the scale and pain of debt problems faced by ordinary people at the UK Citizens Advice Bureau, they instinctively rushed to volunteer and support them.

TACIT KNOWLEDGE – VALUING 'KNOW-HOW'

Tacit knowledge has multiple meanings – it comes from experience, is often immeasurable and intangible and it is about know-how not know-why[6]. It also comes from social and relational customs, awareness and sensitivities. It cannot be codified, nor can it be easily aggregated or generalised. By its very nature, a university or professional accounting or finance classroom struggles to give tacit knowledge. In business education, it is a component of the subject of knowledge management. It is about feeling and wisdom, rather than calculation and technique. In trade, it is as much about relational knowledge as about specific skills relating to the product or service. In accounting and finance, there is no mention of tacit knowledge – the silence implying that scholars do not value its existence or importance at all. How wrong they are you will discover as you read this chapter. It shows that the ignorance of this skill is one of the core reasons for the massive problems we experience today in accounting and finance practice. The professions have become overly technocratic and insensitive to systemic risks, social and environmental impacts, and institutional badges and zero personal punishment have served to perpetuate financial fraud and expropriation.

The current fad of trade through technology and contracts is a major barrier to relationship building. Information was needed about what goods were in demand and where and how to sell them. Finance was needed to facilitate transactions and invest in production, storage and transportation. Skills were needed for land ownership, management, trade negotiations, accounting and financial management. Risk was experienced rather than delegated to the compliance department or the insurance company. Losses meant penury for the business family, and trade had to be conducted prudently and in a measured way. The responsibility of ownership created discipline and a culture of measured risk-taking.

Another major problem with contemporary business and professional training is increasing commercialisation, specialisation and separation from industry knowledge, context and a professional ethos[7]. Even when experts in certain subjects are needed, they need to be able to communicate with others and have a broader understanding of commerce and investment methods. This communication needs cultural appreciation and sensitivity. Investment appraisal and discounted cash flow may be fine in the classroom, but on the field, there are a host of other factors which need to be considered in business decision-making. Payback is a simple and age-old method of decision-making which is still in use today and requires little formal finance teaching. How well a manager knows a particular industry and its production process is critical to making a sound judgement for investment purposes. However, this intimate knowledge is not needed in the finance calculations, nor can it easily be priced or valued. Even where there is an intention to provide this training, the classroom is limited in its capacity to educate and enable deeper awareness and understanding.

CULTIVATING GOOD HABITS – VALUING TACIT SKILLS IN FINANCE

The concept of tacit skills is never even discussed in accounting or finance – it is assumed that these subjects can only be taught by experts. As we have already seen, trust is central to finance, and it's not a skill that can be imparted in a business textbook or classroom. Good understanding of risk and return is crucial to investment appraisal, and while there are some elements of this which are technical, there are also other elements which are intangible and depend on intimate understanding of the industry. Good relationships can enhance trust and also help manage risk. Networks are key to raising capital – whether it is equity, debt or other types of capital like the ability to recruit skilled and reliable project managers. An ability to value assets and spot under-valued assets help with success in finance. The resilience to hold on to risky assets in tough times helps can yield larger rewards in good times – here again trusted banking networks can extend lending and working capital in tough times, to avoid a liquidity crunch. Knowledge of budgeting and accounting is critical to good financial control and is as much a commercial skill as it is a technical one. An ability to check greed and be able to 'digest' financial success and not get too obsessed by money is a very important financial skill for long-term sustainability. The character and personality of finance leaders ought to be in the curriculum.

In an increasingly globalised world, migration can give tacit skills such as risk-taking, inter-cultural knowledge and sensitivity, multiple languages and international networks, which can be priceless to a global firm or enterprise[8]. Research shows that immigrants boost economic performance of their host countries, instead of impoverishing them[9]. They play a significant role in start-ups of small businesses and innovation, as with zero assets and huge determination, they have little to lose from risk-taking and everything to gain from hard work and sacrifice. Immigrants also provide a loyal and disciplined workforce, with a hunger and determination to succeed. Unfortunately, what we often find in the West is discrimination, illiteracy and an active and subtle suppression and devaluation of migrant skills[10]. This in turn has a huge economic cost to leaders and managers who hire external consultants to guide them on international trade instead of talking to their own staff for suggestions and networks which they may already have. Diversity at best is seen as something to be tolerated, rather than to be harnessed or valued, least of all a source of critical advice and innovation. This is why large global organisations fail.

There is some recent emerging evidence of employers demanding 'soft leadership skills' of communication, self-awareness, motivation, empathy and social skills[11]. Some business schools are changing their curricula to accommodate this training, with resulting success, although in terms of time and effort, such

training is costly to deliver as it is by nature personal. It also needs to be culture sensitive, recognising the cultural nuances of the student and their customs
and beliefs. Soft skills cannot easily be taught with a factory mindset and
require a personal and subjective approach, which is antithetical to conventional
business education.

The stories and examples in this chapter will demonstrate how communities are often excellent (and often informal) training and mentoring grounds
for soft skills, but are hitherto ignored in the literature. The time span for community training is long and can begin from childhood, giving young people a
wide breadth and depth of social and cultural experience. The informal nature
of such training has advantages and disadvantages too, but it does give young
people valuable 'experience' of volunteering, relationship building, social and
inter-personal skills, team building and management. I am a personal beneficiary
of this training, and it gave me a rare perspective on life purpose and the centrality of morality in public life. These traits then became instinctive and helped
shape my teaching approach and research priorities.

FAMILY AND COMMUNITY AS TRAINING AND MENTORING HUB

If one is raised within a family business, or has prior experience working for it,
there is much more potential for understanding the wider nuances and context
of production and its relationships to fields like finance and marketing. Specific
industry and trade knowledge is cultivated in the family from a young age – and
leaders do not wait for university 'professional' coaching. It is often very difficult
to provide such diverse skills and knowledge in the business classroom, even if
one intends to do so. A family business becomes a laboratory where information
and knowledge are collated and skills are tried and tested in the field of practice[12].
Elders and founders become repositories of this wisdom and may devote a lot
of time and effort in training and mentoring younger siblings. I have heard of
stories where even risks are permitted, and failure is seen as an opportunity for
young people to learn of their limitations and hubris. In contrast, if the first business experience or training is obtained in a large firm or corporation, it is specialised to begin with and can mislead the student into thinking that business is all
about knowledge, technique and outcomes. The Big 4 global accounting firms
train large swathes of talented graduates all over the world, but rarely do they
help them in understanding the nature of the client businesses they are auditing.
This was a regular complaint I heard from clients when I was a trainee – the
auditors simply do not understand our business. As West (2003) shows, auditing
has become a tick-box exercise rather than an exercise of discerning and author-
itative professional judgement. How can audit ever be effective without basic
commercial and industry acumen?

Within a family business, learning happens in many different ways – through
listening, observing, coaching, critique and questioning. Even overhearing

conversations can be a form of learning, conscious or otherwise. Work experience is easy to obtain in the holidays – in fact, the family is likely to encourage such interaction. The family business school is open 24/7 and education is personal rather than distant or technology based. Most importantly, culture and values are modelled and learnt best in an environment where one is raised and trusted. Relationships between buyers and suppliers are also an important form of tacit knowledge acquisition, new product innovation and skill development[13]. If the leaders want to, they can translate the learning in an intimate bespoke way, relevant to the character of each member of staff in the family. This training can be holistic and personal, rather than distant and impersonal. While one person may be skilled in selling, another may be very good in building long-term relationships or developing new products and services. Through regular contact, intimate awareness of skills and talents helps business founders direct junior people towards growth and expansion of the business. Furthermore, if elders do not behave the way they want their children to, they will fail in maintaining the core business ethics that they espouse to customers and suppliers. In this way, ethics are taught through lived example rather than books or case studies. The history and heritage of trust within family networks also become a significant commercial advantage in terms of recruitment, training and trading. It's an intimate, secret route to financial resilience and sustained growth.

Dr Jasvant Modi is a physician based in California. When he opened his first medical practice, he was not a business expert, but through asking questions, he learnt about costs and revenues and how these were recorded. He began to understand how medical insurance worked and alongside good patient care, he saw opportunities for business – today he owns several hospitals and is a generous philanthropist. From his Jain tradition, basic skills of commerce were in Dr Modi's DNA, and through patience and diligence, he learnt the rest. He saw medicine as more than a profession – an opportunity to give good service, health and well-being to patients. From the beginning, he saw his employees as a critical part of his business, and even when they struggled to get work permits or migrant visas, he was happy to sponsor them without exploiting them, remembering that he too was a migrant once.

Dr Modi's father was a schoolteacher, and they were brought up in relative poverty in India, but he did not feel much suffering and regards his childhood as a blissful time. There was culture and community all around, and this gave him considerable joy and helped his early socialisation. When in the 1970s he needed funding to travel to America for medical training, relatives scraped their resources and supported him. The day Dr Modi received his first pay cheque in America, he went to the local bank and took out a loan to repay everyone, with interest. He was brought up to honour his debts and to work hard to earn his living. Instead of seeing leverage as an opportunity to maximise profit, he saw it as an obligation for which one was duty-bound to repay. Prudence was a core part of his mindset and habits. Similarly, when Dr Modi saw patients dying, without any plan for their wealth, he saw the limits of a material life and decided to make philanthropy a core part of his personal life in retirement. He has donated millions of dollars to universities. Dr Modi did not allow his wealth and fortune to distance him from truth and equality. One of his favourite mottos is 'when we walk together, we can move mountains'. There is no fun in walking or accumulating alone.

RELATIONSHIP SKILLS

Social and relationship skills are critical to success in any business – how else would one find the customers or suppliers willing to sell their raw materials? Management and teamwork require an understanding of human psychology and an experience of working in groups and appreciating the strength of partnerships, creditworthiness and collectives[14]. The faith centre, temple or the mosque becomes a meeting place where information is exchanged, relationships are cultivated, recruitment is done and skills in trading and negotiation are nurtured. If one walks the streets of Mumbai, we can see this physical history – the temple was often very close to the shops and offices – there was no separation between faith, community and enterprise. Growing up in Mombasa, I too saw this regular meeting of business and community, with 'Jain Street', a major trading hub, an extension of the Jain temple (thousands of miles away from the origins in India). Tacit skills do not recognise international boundaries, especially when they are rooted in diaspora communities. Some of these modest appearing wholesale trading businesses in time became very significant in their turnover and size, but still maintained their simple offices, where anyone could walk in without appointment. All the directors would be sat at desks and directly visible to the visiting customer – such was the ease of access even in wholesale business. When they could not supply you with your order, they often knew someone who could and would be kind enough to point you to them.

Habits and values inculcated at home were imported in the minds and hearts of the new merchants – and executed in foreign lands, without enslaving the local peoples or bullying them into subservience. On the contrary, the native Africans in Kenya were given goods and services at a fair price, jobs and training and an economic boost which would help the whole society, not just the business class. Even when the power of business was understood and experienced, it was used responsibly rather than overwhelmed by greed. An upbringing where interdependence is a daily lived reality helps nurture a sense of shared existence and humility. No separate rules and regulations are needed – harmony is learnt and practised at the grassroots.

Eynour Boutia, an Ismaili banker[15] with experience of international securities trading and structured finance at an international bank, confided in me that while the technical knowledge of models and pricing are important, relationships are even more critical in deal-making. Through relationships and conversations, one builds a sophisticated understanding of the market and customers, and the risks and opportunities. Social and networking skills can be very helpful in knowing where to focus, whom to ask and what are the limits of reliance on models and calculations. We know how valuable relationships are to international corporate finance and investment banking – they are also important on the competitive trading floor. The social silence of the importance of this in corporate finance theory and education is significantly problematic.

HEROES AND ROLE MODELS IN THE FAMILY

Business training can also be provided informally in the community hall, during public lectures, gatherings or festivals. Furthermore, the management and governance of community institutions, like schools, hospitals and temples or mosques, also require skill and dedication. These can be important grounds for learning and networking, where skills are shared and experience is nurtured. Huge amounts of volunteering time and talent are required for efficient management and transformation. Volunteering also has the profound ability to help business leaders understand the complex challenges of society and keep their work grounded as opposed to remote and distant. It helps them value society as a stakeholder, not just a CSR tick box.

Growing up as a child, I remember a musician from India, Shantilal Shah, singing a song about charity and profit whose verses were simple, yet the meaning was profound. He explained that if we wish to earn *karmic* merit in life, then charity has to be a natural dimension of profit and wealth creation. If this same message was given in the form of a lecture to business leaders, it would not have the same impact. However through art and music, the message comes across more subtly and deeply. A community gathering is much more intimate and trusted than an anonymous lecture hall. There is a deeper connection between the speaker and the audience, one which also carries with it the batons of history and memory.

It is small wonder that in Mombasa, business leaders vied to serve the community, seeing it as an honour rather than an obligation. Public values and responsible leadership cannot be taught in a formulaic way, although they are extremely important. Today we have all heard about the importance of role models and mentoring, but what happens when your teacher is also a close family member? Then the training is personal, intimate and possibly more patient, memorable and lasting. Furthermore, the respect for the teacher is also deepened, and trust makes the mentoring very effective. While books and courses on leadership may help with some tips and strategies, nothing can replace the role modelling of leadership and the intimate coaching that is nurtured in the home and community. It is evidence of sustainability in practice, an inter-generational transfer of social capital, knowledge and skills critical to economic progress.

TRUST AND HONOUR

Given that trust and honour are at the heart of sustainable finance, how can they be taught as 'technical' skills and behaviours? The finance textbooks I have seen are all silent on this – pretending as if trust and honour are irrelevant and can easily be replaced by efficient contracts[16]. This is a big challenge, especially in a world dominated by market transactions, where all too often there is no personal meeting between customer and supplier. Proxies like customer ratings and Trustpilot are used to help us monitor behaviour through technology. However, for small start-up businesses, needing significant finance, technology is not enough. There is little track record to fall back upon to give investors a sense of trustworthiness. It would be an asset to show that the founders come from these rich ethical customs and traditions, where honour is given very high importance and value, and other people's money is not seen as a resource to exploit and expropriate. The ignorance or dismissal of faith-based knowledge in the business curriculum is damaging and regressive, given its rich history of influence in business training.

In the profession of accounting, I have observed how rare trust-worthy accountants are, and also how often good accountants are rewarded with more and more work and less and less questioning of their bills, once clients develop a degree of trust. Those I know who are trust-worthy tend to come from old cultures and traditions and have a conscience which prevents them from expropriating their clients and directs them instead towards guiding and supporting them in their growth. I have heard many stories where the reputation of the accountant develops organically and there is no need to search, market or advertise for new business. Furthermore, clients would involve them more in their commercial decision-making once good trust and reliability are established – so the depth of work from the same client often increases when honest professional advice is rendered. Even when clients want to minimise tax and their accountants say that this would be illegal, the clients respect them and do not walk away. If clients were to walk away from truthful accountants, the reputation of the accounting firm would still be solidified and in the long term, more business would come their way.

Law and governance mechanisms have taken the place of trust, but these are also not fool-proof as plenty of finance experience shows. Something very important is lost when we replace the importance of trust and honour in society, with legal rules and instruments. The self-regulation of conduct and behaviour diminishes, at the very time when we have an urgent need for responsible leadership. Similarly, the kinds of leadership which emanate from people who are not concerned about trust and honour are very different from the leadership where these values are guarded tightly. For rooted leaders, responsibility and integrity are the outcomes, and these values silently ripple out to the employees through observed actions, rather than speeches or dictats from the top.

BUSINESS IN THE DNA – THE 'BAZAAR' ECONOMY

In the seventeenth and eighteenth centuries, one-third of the world's trade passed through India. There was a 'Bazaar' Economy 'staffed by Bhagdadi Jews, Gujarati Hindus and Muslims, Armenians, Greeks, Iranians, Chinese and Portuguese'[17]. In such an economy, language and inter-cultural skills became central to business success. The ability to understand different cultures and methods of business trade are critical to growth and expansion, risk-evaluation and the building of relationships. Cultural nuances are difficult to teach in a classroom, but if one is trained to observe different behaviours, or speak different languages, it is possible to break down the barriers.

Migration often automatically gives people inter-cultural skills. If in addition, one comes from a cultural community where the importance of nuances and character is understood, it helps to discern these dimensions in others. References for trust and reliability become very critical to success in the *Bazaar Economy*. These can only be obtained from people whom you trust, deepening the importance of lasting relationships and honour. Given these operational challenges, it is no surprise that certain business families and communities thrived in these times, because they were able to cultivate the tacit skills of trade in these arenas[18]. These skills would not have been available in the marketplace of jobs or schools.

My home state of Gujarat in India was blessed by numerous safe harbours and accessible ports, and a rich 'cultural and entrepreneurial' hinterland, which traded with Africa, Europe, China and Asia from as far back as two millennia[19]. Such trade relations became a huge tributary of knowledge, products and services, helping connect different cultures, customs and belief systems in a peaceful manner. Today the Gujaratis are known as some of the world's best entrepreneurs and traders, but there is a long history, and this history and heritage was an important training ground for the tacit skills that are now so instinctive among Gujaratis all over the world. Even Mumbai, India's world-famous business hub, has a very significant Gujarati merchant population which is central to its economic growth and development in the last two hundred years. Gujaratis also occupy top positions in banking and finance in India – Enam Securities is only one such example.

In her study of global Gujarati migration, Poros (2011) finds that there are strong network influences on commercial and professional success. Ties included family and relations, neighbours and friends, faith and belief, and historical occupations and new employers in host cities. Trust that was cultivated in Gujarat was exported to London and New York, and the geographical clusters in these mega cities helped the community to rebuild in the new host city very quickly, and flourish too. An Uncle once told me that when he arrived in the early 1970s, the Shahs had an excellent reputation in John Lewis Oxford Circus, a retail megastore which was growing and needed reliable and hard-working staff. The moment you arrived and applied for a job, they accepted you because of the 'brand' the community had developed. This was a unique example of positive discrimination which is a very rare experience for migrant minorities in Britain.

In an increasingly transactional world, the importance of relationships gets diminished, but at what cost to society? Through relationships, an understanding of interdependence is cultivated which is deeper than any technology or transaction. Somehow, we need to rekindle that understanding and respect for relationships in the business of finance. To do so, we can observe trading and faith communities, and their business practices, in products and services where technology has not yet taken over. We can research and write business case studies of such practices and present them to students in the business classroom – even better, we can help them to visit some of these businesses and learn at first hand from the leaders.

INTER-CULTURAL INTELLIGENCE

To engage students in seeing that good relationships are important, we can ask them to share their own experiences of business transactions as customers or employees. An open dialogue could help raise issues about culture and training, both when they succeeded and when they became problematic. What was the role of relationships in those deals? What about personal relationships – be it with friends, family or partners? What is the role of trust and honour in these relationships? What would happen if we were to make them material and transactional? What would the consequences be for the student and their life and well-being? Such reflection in the classroom could help nurture an understanding of the importance of tacit skills, and the need to invest in them and respect them if one is to succeed in business.

The importance of history and case studies of family businesses is critical to explaining the nature and dimensions of trust in society. Such stories could showcase both the successes and failures, exposing the risks of trust, but also the possibilities and opportunities. Links between risk and trust could be discussed and elaborated, explaining that the evaluation of risk as more than a mathematical calculation – it depends on personal relationships, history and experience, skills which are tacit. Inter-generational wisdom and experience can help both reduce risk and also sustain and enhance relationships if practised in the right way. Dimensions of trust can also be discussed – how do businesses decide upon levels of creditworthiness and who can be trusted for what amount and over what time? Here again, there may not be a magic formula, but the skills nurtured over time and within families can be evaluated. More research needs to be done to discern how small businesses evaluate and manage risk and develop methods of trust monitoring.

Case studies of businesses from a variety of faiths and cultures, and in different parts of the world, could help illustrate the different nuances of culture, and the variety of contexts in which such organisations operate[20]. Guided field trips to Chinatown or Little Italy or African markets would give students a direct experience of cultural varieties and enterprise – they could ask questions to market traders about their immigration stories. I often feel that even though culture and politics are important to understand when students enter a workplace, they are ill-equipped to analyse it before accepting a job, or even after they start a new employment. Toolkits on evaluating culture from an employee perspective could be developed, although these would vary both within and across countries.

Whilst it is impossible to teach about all cultures in a classroom, to educate students about cultural sensitivity is critical in a globalised world. Ignoring it signals that culture is unimportant – mere knowledge and technique are sufficient. Cultural training helps them to see the world from other people's perspectives – fulfilling Steven Covey's famous motto – 'seek first to understand, then to be understood'[21]. The West has a history of imposing its culture and systems on the rest of the world and talk down to them, because of ignorance and arrogance. The results of genuine cultural dialogue can be very surprising as I discovered in my classroom experiments. Dialogues can be done through role play – as often the class is multi-cultural, but as culture rarely gets discussed in finance, the discussion is superficial at best and seen as irrelevant. Genuine deeper conversations can be enabled, and one may not be surprised to find many similarities or connections between students that they did not know existed. Similarly, time given to helping people understand one another's cultural approaches to finance can also open a deeper conversation about meaning and purpose in business enterprise. Cultural sensitivity requires patience and listening – we have two ears and one mouth because we are meant to listen twice as much as we speak.

Similarly, the two eyes can be used to observe how people respond to suggestions – deals always have a human element, and it is helpful to meet face to face. The lived experiences of students from different parts of the world can help immensely in developing cultural sensitivity, something which cannot be easily transplanted to someone from one country. Nowadays there is a growing appreciation of cultural diversity, especially by international business and financial institutions, as they realise that this is a skill which cannot be replicated but can be harnessed by a diverse workforce. There is also a greater degree of value attached to this skill than before, although the lack of cultural knowledge in finance courses may make some believe that none of this is necessary in deal-making.

RISK AS 'TACIT' EDUCATOR – TRIAL AND ERROR

My friend Mr Sobhag Zaverchand Shah has lived and conducted business in three continents – Tanzania, India and UK. These are three very different contexts, and in all countries, he has suffered misfortune and success. Whenever I meet him, these stories come to life, and they are so vivid in his memory even at the ripe old age of eighty. Above all, he is most proud of the friendships and relationships he has built over the years with the various people he met through his business. For Sobhag, which literally means luck, business was a journey not a destination, and good honest service much more important than short-term profit. Along the way, he has trusted people, and at times paid for his innocence, but still he has no regrets.

Sobhag says it is better to trust and lose than to live a life where we distrust everyone, all the time. I cannot help feeling the joy of enterprise after listening to him – and joy has the power to radiate to others, and to give purpose and meaning, tacit skills which are priceless yet cannot be taught in the classroom. On reflection, the stories and experiences have become a deep a part of his narrative of life, and its purpose and meaning, which he has discovered through enterprise. The stories also remind me of the oral tradition, in times when literacy and the absence of printing made access to knowledge difficult – it was stories which communicated wisdom and provided training. They also carried an intimacy which is lost when technology or media become the conveyor belts of narrative.

There is a big push towards purposeful business in today's era – our final chapter is devoted to this. At the same time, science is showing that meaning is more important to people than happiness[22]. Happiness can often be fleeting but meaning can give a clear motivation to us. However, individuals must discover their own sense of purpose and what it is that provides them meaning in life. The process can be one of trial and error, and good coaching and mentoring can help. In these respects, belonging to a close-knit family can be a huge bonus, as it provides the comfort and stability for people to discover their own identity. The business can provide those trial-and-error experiences which help people decide what they are good at, and what they enjoy doing. Business networks and relationships could become an additional resource for guidance and even work experience. If in addition the family is part of a faith community, then participating in community gatherings can also give people the social interactions and wisdom needed in discovering self-purpose and meaning.

The skill of judging others and knowing whom to trust and whom one cannot trust is also very critical in finance and business. This skill cannot be put into a formula – this is why in fact both accounting and finance textbooks have nothing to say about trust. Often people learn about trust from direct experiences, and these betrayals can be very costly in real life. Even the branded and technocratic mechanisms of 'regulated trust' often fail with huge losses for savers and investors. Family businesses in practice cultivate a good degree of experience in trust and relationships, and this can be a teacher and guide to novices entering the business world. The social capital that has hitherto been built can help the new generation expand and grow the business as critical relationships have already been established. In contrast, building relationships from scratch is very challenging, and takes considerable effort and patience. When family businesses directly carry the risk of failure, they have no choice but to develop a sharp skill in deciding whom they can trust, especially with money, finance and any lending, even if it is short-term. Such experiences, sometimes nurtured over decades, concentrate the skill of discernment and retain this very important tacit knowledge within the family.

ACCOUNTING FOR TRUST

Good financial record-keeping and monitoring are critical to business success. This is especially true when a business grows and expands, and operates from many different locations, far from where the immediate family resides.

Accounting, budgeting and financial control are very important technical skills, but they are not separate from understandings of culture and relationships. It is often very difficult to conduct and monitor business from a distance, and even where there is technology to track stock movements and orders, trust is still critical in ensuring good service and financial control. The teaching of accounting focuses on calculation and measurement, but its real value is in its interpretation and analysis, its ability to warn about impending risks and to control and monitor financial flows. The classroom is limited in its ability to give such skills – narratives can give students an appreciation of how accounting can help business analysis in different industries and countries. An Indonesian study found that accounting soft skills and language training were significantly missing and needed for effective trade in Asia[23].

In growing and expanding family businesses, trusted members of the owner's family cannot be everywhere – delegation is inevitable. Similarly, the handling of cash, and banking and credit-checking also needs to be delegated, and this involves risk, trust and opportunities. Good culture and values set by the family can help attract similar-minded employees who stay loyal to the business and do not feel they are being exploited but instead respected and paid fairly for their dedication and reliability. The cultivation and retention of a good culture within a business organisation is itself a tacit skill, and ways in which employees are treated will circulate throughout the enterprise, as workers do talk to each other. Where there is a high standard of integrity set by the leaders, this can percolate and lead to long-term loyalty from staff and managers. Failure to have a good culture would lead to high employee turnover and significant loss in terms of the costs of training and monitoring.

In practice, it is difficult to teach 'good' culture to business students. No simple formula would reveal itself, but the richness and complexity of culture could empower students to explore its variety rather than to ignore or misunderstand it. Also dialogues about culture would help them recognise their own good habits and customs and empower them, growing the learner's self-confidence. Stories are good ways of communicating culture, and these can be shared and discussed in the classroom to enable students to come up with their own interpretations.

FOLLOWERSHIP + TRUST + MENTORING BRINGS 'TACIT' SKILL REWARDS

Organisational culture requires not just good leadership, but also good *followership*. Employees need to value the importance of good character and conduct and the need to be patient and work with honesty and integrity. Modelling the behaviours and habits of good finance leaders can be priceless. This would help them to not only keep their job, but also to be promoted and recognised for their efforts. It is possible that when employees join family businesses managed with a sound culture, they can be more motivated to work hard and stay rather than to be lazy and keep hopping from one company to another. After graduation, most business students look for a job as a step on their career ladder, and if they are armed with cultural skills and good moral character, alongside technical knowledge, they are more likely to succeed and progress. If they come from faith backgrounds and families where their character is moulded by trust and integrity, these dimensions can give them an extra strength and resilience in the workplace, even when these factors are not monitored or measured.

Not everyone is a good teacher or communicator. However, these skills are essential if there is inter-generational transfer of knowledge and experience. In a family setting, there is likely to be genuine interest in the growth and development of younger members, and trust, care and compassion in their personal development. This is something which big organisations may lack, especially if managers are transactional and selfish. This can be a drawback for family businesses or a strength depending on how these skills are nurtured and harnessed. Family businesses also involve politics, like any organisation or enterprise. And how these political tensions are resolved and alleviated depends on culture, leadership and peaceful means of resolution. It is therefore possible that when students from family businesses come to learn about professional methods of business and management, they learn new skills which they can take back to the family business by exposing themselves to different tools and methods. However, these teachings would be much more effective if students are allowed to share some of their personal business experiences and cultural wisdoms in the classroom. In this way, everyone gets to understand the stories and nuances of a variety of business customs and practices.

Students need to understand that just as important as it is for people to be able to rely upon and trust others, it is similarly critical for them to behave in a trustworthy way to build personal reputation and sustain their jobs and careers. There are two sides to the trust coin. To be trusted, one may need to be fair and transparent in transactions, and even when opportunities for private gain or profit arise, one would need to avoid them and instead give them to the employer. Depending on the context and situation, this honesty could give them significant long-term rewards. It would also help them to have a clear conscience and protect their character and integrity, rather than give in to short-term gains and temptations.

Knowledge management is a big field in business education – usually applicable to large anonymous corporations where people come and go and mergers and acquisitions lead to an absence of memory and skill banks. Formal systems are then needed to 'capture' and 'retain' knowledge. A family business often develops its own methods of knowledge storage, transmission and retrieval, which can prove invaluable to sustaining an inter-generational business and retaining wealth and success. Training and mentoring are a key part of this, but so are dinner table conversations and family gatherings and festivals. These methods may not be formalised or stored on computer drives, but that does not mean they do not exist. In fact, through real-life stories and examples, they have a longer term capacity for survival and retention than data which is impersonal and unfamiliar. Trust and loyalty also help in knowledge retention and retrieval.

RELAXED 'TRUSTED' NETWORKING – FESTIVALS AND LARGE WEDDINGS

Within business and faith communities, there is a regular reminder of values like discipline, duty, sincerity and co-operation or mutuality. When these subjects are taught in the classroom, they could be learnt and quickly forgotten. However when this 'ethical nourishment' is experienced in a community setting, on a regular basis, whether it is done consciously or sub-consciously, it helps to encourage and sustain ethical behaviours. Such experiences bring conscience to the fore and remind people of the limitations of materialism and possessiveness. They also teach humility as often in prayer meetings everyone is an equal – no VIPs are given front stage. This humility can be a very important check on hubris and greed.

Festivals, marriages and public events provide significant opportunity for business leaders to congregate and exchange ideas in a relaxed and trusted setting. These are often very large gatherings, so there are a huge variety of people who come together – business managers, professionals, artists, teachers. When in 1963, the Mombasa Jain temple was first opened, a whole procession went through the town, so everyone became aware of this new cultural space which was open to all. The same story was repeated in London in 1995 when the BAPS Swaminarayan Hindu Mandir was first opened. Pride and joy in the culture and community were celebrated and reinforced.

There is a variety of skills and experience at such venues and communal gatherings – they are warehouses of shared wisdom. Even religious lectures often carry business and trading examples, such is the deep relationship between business and faith in many cultures and diaspora communities. This really does give people a direct 'experience' of the varied skills and dimensions which comprise an aspirational community. Advice about what to ask, whom to ask, what is happening in the marketplace and how to deal with challenges in finance and investment can be obtained here for free, without a need for a formal appointment. Top business leaders are easily approachable at these venues – such intimate and trusted access would not be easily available elsewhere. Through such experiences, skills and expertise are grown and reinforced, rather than decaying once people have left school or university.

Jaggadu Shah was an eminent Indian Jain merchant based in Gujarat in thirteenth-century India[24]. He controlled the shipping trade and traded in spices, textiles and other precious commodities and his ships sailed to Africa and Persia and Middle East. These were high-risk journeys, and not all ships came back. Once he himself nearly died. He is celebrated today not only for his wealth, but also for his generosity. When a famine was predicted, he stored vast quantities of grain, not for the sake of profit, but for free distribution. When the famine struck many Kings depended on his generosity to protect their people – he never saw his society as a source for profit extraction. In fact, he understood that without his people, he had no customers or suppliers – there was a long-term understanding of interdependence. It is important to understand and value this wider social and public conscience.

Today, Jaggadu Shah's stories are being staged in plays to remind the community of this legacy of leadership and wisdom which has brought us where we are today. Such myths and fables play a very important lesson in creatively conveying business leadership skills to new generations and reminding them of the risks and opportunities that wealth brings. One of his trading partners was the refugee Ismaili community who had fled from Persia. To help them, he financed the first-ever Ismaili Mosque in India. This also shows a significant degree of cultural empathy and open-mindedness, in spite of the differences in beliefs. It is also another example of the interdependence of trade.

At community gatherings, not only does networking happen naturally, but a generous approach to training and sharing emerges, without any need for external facilitation. Interdependence and not independence are taken as a given, so there is no need for a quid pro quo. Often people who trade with one another meet in these settings, reinforcing their partnerships. Business owners often invite customers and clients to family weddings – implying they see them as stakeholders and an 'extended' family. I have been to these lavish weddings, and business partners feel obligated to attend and show their presence as it would be embarrassing otherwise. At a nephew's wedding in Mumbai in a five-star hotel, I met a Swiss supplier who had flown especially. When I asked why he made all that effort to come, he said that this is one of his first customers of a new product who was never sceptical and made a deal without any suspicion, even though they had never met before. How can he forget such a supportive customer? It seems that one transaction established a life-long relationship.

Whilst these discussions may not be certified or formalised in the form of exams and qualifications, their potential to transfer market information or convey and reinforce ethical norms should not be under-estimated in any way. Instead of competition, cooperation often results. Instead of distrust, trust is reinforced and rejuvenated. These regular meetings make it very important that people who live in the town preserve their honour and not bring themselves in disrepute. The Gujarati word for this is 'abru' – name and reputation are priceless and irreplaceable. Bad names and reputations travel fast through whispers at such gatherings. There is no easy way for deceit to hide in such communities, and this method of self-regulation is so much more effective than external laws and rules.

CO-OPERATIVE FINANCE

We saw earlier how in many parts of the world access to commercial finance from Banks is very limited, so people are forced to use alternative sources of finance to fund their growth and expansion. For very small one-person businesses, where the amounts of money needed are tiny, no Bank would be interested. Co-operative methods of lending and borrowing emerge in these settings and not only do they provide precious funds, there are also meetings where information, products and strategies could be exchanged, as there is a growing degree of trust. Alongside the provision of micro-finance, financial training is also given, which could be priceless as it is not accessible in remote areas or for very poor or illiterate communities. For business growth and expansion, this combination of funds with training can be priceless.

Prior to attending a single course in finance, I was raised and brought up in a very active social and communal environment, where there were many aspects of life conducted without any need for money. Take food for example, something which is a very basic human need. I remember regularly going to the temple or community centre for meals shared with the community – either by invitation, such as a wedding or during festivals and spiritual events. Without any money, I experienced a lot of sharing, caring and joy – and this is true in so many cultural traditions. Often, I volunteered – as this seemed very natural and fulfilling – there was no cost-benefit analysis done prior to the act of volunteering. The Sikhs believe that serving food to any visitor is the highest religion. And they too are a very successful global business diaspora today. The Chief Executive of Mastercard for many years was a Sikh – Ajay Banga. He explains that 'Listening is the first step to true knowledge, and a good leader knows that knowledge is invaluable'[25]. Active listening helps build relationships and trust and shows that different perspectives are valued rather than suppressed or ignored. The experience of sharing has been etched deep into my psyche – so much so that it has led me to a teaching career, where one is focused on sharing knowledge, rather than possessing and profiting from it.

When I meet accountants in our community who have their own practices serving family businesses, they often say that they have become business mentors and 'finance directors' of businesses who could not afford to hire their own full-time director. The fact that money is so deeply interwoven with personal lives also means that some of these accountants become de facto personal advisors for big client family decisions. The bond of trust is built in such a way that there is a partnership which is not codified, but vital to the growth and sustainability of the business. Given that the accountant serves a wide variety of clients, they become a repository of contacts and information about what is happening in various industries, and what problems and dangers to look out for, and the opportunities that clients may want to benefit from. Relationships and trust are at the heart of this tacit learning.

Andrew Pike of Handelsbanken, with three decades of banking and commercial lending experience, shared with me and my students a lending secret. When Andrew meets a market and sales-driven entrepreneur, he wants to closely examine the financial systems and controls and ascertain whether the finance director has the power to 'rein him in' when necessary. His experience has taught him that charismatic and ebullient salesmen can also be high-risk takers and start believing in their hubris – so there needs to be balance in the business. This statement relies on the traditional form of relationship lending which has been drying up and replaced by cold transactional financial calculation and technical analysis. However, it says a lot about the importance of personal experience and knowledge when it comes to loan evaluations – the hubris of the CEO may not be captured at all in the technical analysis as it cannot be measured.

ORGANIC FINANCE – GROWTH WITHIN NATURAL LIMITS

When businesses are challenged to get external finance, they have no choice but to grow finance organically. Also external finance may be costly, even if it were available. Prudence may dictate wariness in getting into debt, even where there is tax relief for interest. Despite running a very large manufacturing business, Dr Firodia explained that their family are 'net lenders' to Banks – that means they are cash positive. Modern finance theory and science encourage leverage as a way to maximise growth and profit opportunities. What these theories do not consider is the burden that leverage can bring during downturns, and the longer-term costs of losing a family's reputation or credit worthiness, which may be very important to them. Also often these businesses do not wish to grow simply for growth's sake – they can be quite content. Organic growth is that which is within manageable limits.

Culture or scarcity means that businesses have to conserve their cash and capital for future investment or growth needs. Whilst this practice may sound tough or limiting, it also creates an important discipline of capital maintenance and liquidity control which is critical to the sustainability of any business. Systems of budgeting and accounting need to be working and operational all the time, with someone monitoring the performance and cash flow reports and acting quickly to fix any problems. External finance, even when it is obtainable, can suffer from a potential for recklessness. This possibility of waste is limited in the case of organic finance – as there is little room for failure. Once again, such control practices create a self-discipline in financial management which can easily be absent from large, quoted businesses or transactional corporations, where the employees do not have their own skin in the game. We saw earlier how Francine McKenna described this as a 'waterfall problem' – when problems strike, corporate managers pretend that no one is to blame as no one was monitoring the big picture or responsible for acting on it.

When we have a combination of culture, family ownership, patience and community rootedness, business finance and growth have a very different meaning and motivation. This does not mean ambition is denied or disabled, but it is exercised within scale and scope and with careful planning. When leaders are themselves vegetarians, they are likely to only pursue non-violent products and services, ensuring harmony with the environment and animals. There is no need to please anonymous and often speculative stock market investors. Also the lack of desire to make a quick buck from cheap finance, and a responsible attitude to borrowing, shifts management culture and philosophy. The calculations are tempered by prudence and a sense of awareness about the possibilities and limitations of expansion which are difficult to describe, but very real.

KNOWLEDGE NOURISHMENT AND RENEWAL

Business leader and pioneer Subhash Thakrar regularly reads the 'Bhagvad Gita' for personal inspiration towards life purpose, management and leadership. So did Mahatma Gandhi, who quotes widely from it in his autobiography. From the Gita, Subhash has learnt that action is more important than outcomes – instead of pursuing goals and targets, put the best of your efforts, and the results will come automatically. When he first discovered this, he found it very difficult and challenging as a concept – as he had been trained to pursue measurable goals and targets. However, once he understood the sustainable wisdom philosophy of the Gita, he changed his leadership and management style completely and feels much more at ease as a result. And the results have not been diminished either. In fact, this philosophy could itself be classified as an 'organic' approach to finance – give the best of your actions and character, and the products and services will grow naturally. Similarly, the example such leadership sets for employees is such that they too feel motivated to be the best of themselves, without being punished for failing to achieve specific goals or targets.

Scriptures and verses have stood the test of time and were often conceived in times which were much less materialistic than the world is today. Reading and reflecting upon their content can be a continued source of inspiration and wisdom which can be very nourishing and enriching for leaders. My friend and highly successful social entrepreneur in Kenya, Mr Chuni Shah sets aside some time every day for reading and reflection – he says he cannot sleep without it. He is particularly fond of poetry and philosophy. This is in spite of him running several national and international business and community projects and juggling them during crises like the pandemic. While business immerses him in the material world, he also likes to keep a distance from it through his reading and reflection – Chuni understands the limitations of worldly existence and does not live in denial of death to suit his material ambitions. In fact, his life is so simple that there is little ostentatiousness and he constantly gives anonymously to the poor and the weak.

Contemporary books and courses on leadership and management often have embedded cultural assumptions which may not suit diverse audiences. The idea that good principles of leadership and management are universal and 'culturally neutral' can lead to a denial of personal context, beliefs and values. Often secularism is another deep-seated assumption. The training can subconsciously diminish the importance of these private cultural beliefs and emotions, which are often very valuable to the practitioners and their identity and reflexivity. In particular, assumptions of growth, expansion and material prosperity are so deeply embedded in these courses that they are rarely questioned. Even enrolling in these courses is often very costly, so it is assumed that the tutors will be giving 'value for money'! However, modern global crises require leadership which is much more humble and reflexive, and leaders need to understand their own limitations and social and environmental responsibilities.

UNDERSTANDING THE NATURE AND LIMITS OF MONEY

Mastery in finance requires a sophisticated understanding of the nature and limits of money. This understanding is not just intellectual, but spiritual and cultural too. This may seem paradoxical – that to make money last and sustain itself, one needs to not see it simply as external and given, but central to unlocking the secrets and growth of any enterprise. In a similar way, when one has earned and made money, if one sees it as personal possession, the sustainability of that wealth is going to be questionable. Somehow, the skill of making and 'digesting' money is crucial to avoiding loss and indigestion. However, this skill cannot be given like a formula in a business class. There is a strong intangible and tacit aspect to it which requires regular reflection and renewal. We have seen in human history how entrepreneurs who misunderstand this often experience severe ups and downs, sometimes losing everything they have made. Unfortunately, as contemporary finance education has impersonalised and depersonalised finance, this understanding and reflexivity is missing, making it very difficult for business and finance leaders trained in this way to sustain their wealth.

There is some fascinating academic work on this theme, which is outside the discipline of finance. German philosopher George Simmel wrote extensively about this in the nineteenth century and latterly, sociologist Nigel Dodd has conducted a multi-disciplinary contemporary analysis of the nature of money which shows that it is much more a process than a measure and a social, cultural and political construct[26]. We have also earlier spoken about the pioneering work of anthropologist David Graeber[27] and Coggan (2012) exposes the deeper history and politics of paper money. Dodd explores the many layers of meaning ascribed to money and its impact on trust, relationships, social and community life. He explores the deeper context of money which is ignored by technocratic economists, who *want it to be* an objective and independent measure of activity, production and profit. Such thinking and analysis ought to be part of economics or finance 101. It would also help the subject to be less reductive and more interactive.

'Experiencing' death by attending funerals or memorial services is also a way of reminding ourselves of the temporality of human existence. Here again, if one listens to the prayers and services, shares in the pain of the family who have lost a loved one, the limits of wealth begin to soak in. At the very least, we begin to understand and accept for ourselves that we are not going to be able to take our money with us to the next life. When one attends funerals regularly, which is a duty and not a choice in my community (when we have such large extended families and relatives and friends whom we have known for many years), then this understanding gets etched more and more deeply. Social and cultural experiences help one to avoid distancing oneself from seeing the long-term perishability of material wealth and possessions.

Another key aspect of the nature of money is that it is a flow of resources and power, not just a stock. Hence there are dangers when one sees it as an item of ownership rather than a means to an end. One simple way of learning and reminding oneself of this nature is through philanthropy and charitable giving, provided it is selfless. With success in business, giving some money away on a regular basis helps leaders and managers to detach themselves from money rather than becoming cold and calculating all the time. It frees the businessman from the clutches of money and possibly even helps them enjoy the way in which it nourishes needy people or organisations. More than corporate social responsibility, such actions help financiers experience the need to avoid too much indulgence and arrogance that may result from wealth creation. I know many businessmen or women who also get directly involved in charitable activities, either by becoming trustees or by actively volunteering at festive or community events. This could be something as simple as organising car parking for visitors, or serving food, or even cleaning up after the party, doing some of the dirtiest work with all humility and sacrifice.

Eynour Boutia was born in Mauritius, educated in Paris and now lives and works in London and Paris. By tradition, he is Ismaili, a global business diaspora, renowned for its diplomatic and inter-cultural skills. The Ismailis are also hugely successful in business and finance. He speaks four languages and says that trading and deal-making were a basic part of growing up. Eynour's father had to go into business at the age of twelve to shelter and protect the family at a particularly difficult time when they had lost everything virtually overnight. Risk has been a part of the family history, and out of that a culture of prudence has grown. For his new boutique banking enterprise, he says relationships are everything. Eynour is fluent in French and finds it easier to think and speak in French. When I spoke to him, I could see how diplomatic he was, almost by instinct. He knew about my culture and history. This helped establish a good rapport. In fact, it turned out that both our vernaculars are similar even though our faiths are very different – Gujarati. We would not have discovered this if it was a transactional or impatient conversation where there was a rush to cut a deal. However once discovered, it helped open the door to a deeper relationship. Common languages are also important bridges between faiths, which people can easily forget, but are so critical to building sustainable relationships.

This chapter has taken us deep into the world of tacit skills and experience, something which modern professional training subconsciously denies and implies its worthlessness. The stories and examples show how powerful and influential such know-how can be and is often equal to or more important than professional scientific training. It is hoped that readers will come to see the value of their own cultural experiences and to look for this in potential employees or colleagues. Encouraging people to share their cultural experiences can open new ways of seeing and relating to one another and to customers and suppliers. Denial of the value of tacit skills, and their suppression in the organisation, can lead to potentially large speculative risks and reckless losses. Different cultures will have different strengths, attributes and weaknesses too. Inter-cultural awareness helps to understand these and then we can use education and science to enhance skills and training. In the next chapter, we examine purposeful leadership in finance. Sadly, this is a very ignored but important topic – the contemporary science denies its importance – projects with positive net present values should be accepted, irrespective of purpose! The Anthropocene makes good business leadership and purpose central to corporate sustainable strategy. Once again you will see from the stories and examples that many purposeful practices are often hiding in plain sight. Clarity of purpose checks greed and selfishness and instead can lead to better equality and inclusion for all living beings.

Notes

1 Mr Hitesh Doshi is founder and CEO – www.waaree.com.
2 Amish Tripathi's books and writings can be found at www.authoramish.com.
3 Tharoor (2016) provides exceptional evidence of the vast ocean of cultural and trade skills that India had in its history prior to its looting and expropriation.
4 Frankopan (2017) details the relationships and trust that was nurtured on this historic trade route, which was also a tributary for culture and wisdom.
5 Prakash (2004).
6 Oğuz and Elif Şengün (2011) is a good research summary of the different dimensions of tacit knowledge. In finance research, there is negligible literature on tacit knowledge – it is subconsciously deemed irrelevant and unscientific.
7 Pfeffer and Fong (2004) see the American business school template and its global export damaging as it is profit-oriented rather than a training ground for ethical professionals.
8 Baláž et al (2019) study Slovak migrants and their experiences and entrepreneurial skills, explaining new skills acquired through migration.
9 See Legrain (2007) for a forensic analysis of the wide range of economic talents and benefits immigrants bring.
10 See Kandola (2018). Winder (2004) is an excellent account of the highly mixed and mongrel nation that is Britain today – for thousands of years, immigrants came to its shores to start a new life. Every Briton is an immigrant of some kind or another, something which most have forgotten today.
11 Marques (2013) is a case study of the effectiveness of such training in a Californian University.
12 Ugoani (2014) is an empirical study of Nigerian Igbo traders, which finds that tacit skills to give them a significant commercial advantage. Among the Igbo, academic business knowledge is seen as a disadvantage, and there is 3–5 years of apprentice training required with successful entrepreneurs before one gains respect or trust.
13 Sikombe and Phiri (2019) is an extensive literature review of tacit knowledge gained in this way.
14 Goyal and Heine (2021) study the Indian footwear industry based in Agra and explain the tacit knowledge relating to credit-worthiness which is critical to sustainability among small shoe-makers.
15 Followers of the Aga Khan, a Shia Muslim sect which has a very successful global business diaspora.

16 See Hillier et al (2016), Deegan and Ward (2013), or Lakshmi (2018), which review undergraduate finance teaching.
17 Timberg (2014), p. 19.
18 Poros (2011) is an excellent account of Gujarati migrants to New York and London and their business prowess and diaspora networks.
19 Alpers and Goswami (2019) is an excellent analysis of this rich history and business heritage.
20 Meyer (2015) is an excellent collection of examples and case studies of inter-cultural nuances.
21 Covey (1989) is excellent on leadership with values, and he was a Mormon by upbringing.
22 World famous psychologist Petersen (1999) shows the science of myth-making and meaning that is derived from faith traditions – it is not just mumbo-jumbo, but practical and relevant to personal psychology, mental health and motivation. In finance, myths and stories carry purpose and meaning which help make leaders and professionals resilient and contented.
23 See Adhariani (2020).
24 Patel (2021) explains the unique merchant ethics in Gujarat in those times.
25 See Banga (2017).
26 See Simmel (1978) and Dodd (2014).
27 See Graeber (2014).

5

PURPOSE

The focus of this book has been on interviewing finance leaders from diverse cultures and countries, to understand what it is that drives them and connect their answers to what we know about finance science and education. One of the most critical and influential persons in any business organisations is its founders and/or leaders. They are able to command resources and set the cultural tone at the top, the example that others can follow. Furthermore, in an era of financialisation, the roles and importance of finance in any organisation have grown significantly. It is therefore critical to understand how responsibly this power is exercised and to what end. The true stories shown in this book demonstrate how many leaders are motivated by a clear sense of mission and public interest, without necessarily boasting about morality. It is through their decisions and lived examples that they convey a culture of care and long-termism. In this final chapter, we focus on purpose, the motivation that drives finance leaders and how this can be directed towards social and environmental sustainability.

There are thousands of books and articles on business leadership. And most of them are either secular and normative, trying to give readers a formula or method for success, or a personal story of a 'successful' leader[1]. They seek a universal platonic 'science' of leadership and avoid discussing the problematic politics and power that derives from leadership – it's assumed to be a good thing to aspire towards[2]. As a result, leadership training often fails in achieving its objectives. There is little debate about the definition of business 'success' – which is primarily secular, materialistic and wealth oriented. In his famously critical book 'Leadership BS', the renowned Stanford leadership scholar, Jeffrey Pfeffer explains that most leaders see employees as a burden and a cost, and in this sense, are highly financialised in their management ideology[3]. In practice, finance floods and overwhelms purpose, even when the theories and literature are in denial. It is therefore critical that we reform its leadership and

DOI: 10.4324/9781003164746-5

practice to build a sustainable and inclusive world. And purpose lies at the heart of this.

Leadership researchers Collinson and Tourish (2015) draw from their own teaching and research experiences to recommend a different, more nuanced and reflexive approach to leadership training, which engages with its complexity and power politics. The examples in this book reveal the cultural diversity of the world and the different beliefs and contexts in which businesses operate. The superiority of 'whiteness', patriarchy and its leadership science, is often subconsciously woven into the business textbooks, with very little exposition of the cultural assumptions and biases underlying the analysis. There is also a lot of emphasis on large corporate business leadership, rather than the small, local or even sustainable business for the family and community. Such businesses may (although not always) be low on power and material wealth, but very high on wisdom and purpose, as we have seen from the examples in this book. They may also contribute much more to a positive social ecology, by providing locally needed goods and services at a fair price.

The environment can only be understood at an aesthetic, spiritual level. The writer and Nobel laureate Vaclav Havel[4] calls this 'transcendance' which he explains as:

> ...the need to be in harmony with even what we ourselves are not, with what we do not understand, with what seems distant from us in time and space ...

Transcendance enables us to keep learning, to allow nature to speak its own truths in a way we can understand and to stay in awe of the miracle that is life. It does not stop at leadership, or success, but instead focuses on evolution and personal growth, both in wisdom and in humility. It puts materialism in its place and enables leaders to experience the joy of giving and sharing, which is very much larger than the practice of accumulation and rising insecurity.

For this chapter, I understand purpose to mean motive, and in particular, the motivation of the business leader. In contemporary accounting and finance, it is assumed that the leader wants to maximise wealth and profits, and hence there is no need for any 'subjective' theory of leadership or purpose. The challenge today is that to reform society and nature, we cannot avoid making the task of business leadership personal and humane, compassionate and caring, and above all, one which leaves a long-term legacy and a light footprint on the planet. This would require a substantial change in the very nature of finance theory and education. This chapter demonstrates that through a deeper, holistic understanding of the nature of finance, we can transform leadership behaviour and make it in their interest to do good by being good. Sustainable finance leadership ought to be to promote kindness and generosity, and inter-generational equity, with a minimum harm to living beings and the environment. For purposeful leadership in finance education, our science also needs to be purposeful – knowledge should inform practice, as this book has shown.

'IDEOLOGICAL FINANCE' – FALSE AND RECKLESS INDIVIDUALIST NARRATIVES

The Anthropocene is evidence of a corporatised human attack on nature. Methods of accounting and finance have fuelled the forest fires. Slavery was a human attack on other humans. Empire was the human-led robbery of the wealth of whole nations and their peoples. The feudal society was an attack on peasants by the aristocracy. The culture of exploitation and expropriation has been deeply woven into human history especially through European colonisation of the world. Looking at the rich and diverse cultural influences on finance presented in this book, one cannot help but conclude that acultural economic ideology was just an extension of empire. It was an intellectual and moral conspiracy to help subjugate the rest of the world into economic subservience[5]. In the name of science, cultures and societies were forced to become selfish, corrupt, fraudulent and individualist[6]. Multinational corporations and globalisation were used as vehicles to build new colonial empires in the name of free markets and neo-liberal capitalism. Cultural diversity was ignored precisely because it had the power to challenge this orthodoxy and is still being ignored today in the drive towards standardisation and financialisation. All the equality rubbish being spouted by multinationals is a mere smokescreen – what they really want is conformity and people who are easily dispensable and replaceable.

Whyte and Wiegratz (2016) argue that neo-liberalism is pernicious in shaping a 'moral economy of fraud'. It promotes a particular model of economic growth which concentrates corporate power, reduces worker rights and wages, idolises 'free' markets, encourages tax avoidance and minimisation and the privatisation of public services[7]. It is an alliance between the state and elite capital interests to undermine democracy and increase inequality, where there is no such thing as community or society, merely individuals with 'private' beliefs and cultures. Given this ideology, morality is made subservient to materialism and therefore becomes subverted to an atomistic culture of greed and selfishness. The 2008 global financial crash is an extreme example of the fraud embedded within neo-liberalism, and hardly any bankers went to jail. States bailed out the corrupt banking system at a significant and continuing cost to humanity.

In short, the political climate undermines conscience, community, social capital and belief of the type I have taken pains to emphasise in this book. It also encourages the kinds of technocratic corporate finance that are being taught in business schools all over the world today. In such circumstances, white-collar crime and fraud become 'normalised' according to Whyte and Wiegratz. To reform finance, we also need to deal with these systemic threats. When the University of Chicago Finance Professor Rajan (2019) pleaded for a third pillar in society in addition to states and markets, the pillar of community, he did not critique utilitarian neo-liberalism. It is a miracle that the stories in this book show a very different and positive culture, but this may not be sustainable under the sweep of monocultural neo-liberalism and its pernicious inequities.

Economics starts from a foundation of scarcity, when in reality there is abundance in nature. This makes it very puzzling why modern accounting and finance science and education do not directly address these expropriative behaviours and vices. Evidence shows that the modern business school, and its very construction and pedagogy, are racist.[8] No surprise then that the plurality of faith and cultural diversity has little place in education and training in accounting and finance, in spite of the huge diversity of the student population. Dar et al (2020) explain that 'white supremacy' should not be forgotten, and the diverse stories and experiences of the marginalised need much wider engagement and dissemination. This ought to be the purpose of the business teacher.

The implication is that business science is trying to cover up the reality by spinning narratives of corporate social responsibility, rationality and fairness, objectivity even, whilst expropriation and financialisation remain the actual practice. It appears as if there is a conspiracy by the experts to avoid direct engagement with the motives and excesses of the Masters of Finance. If leadership in accounting and finance is genuinely debated and taught, it would bring the whole house of finance down – exposing its deeper and malicious motives, politics and expropriation. That may be the real reason why the subject is so under-researched, despite its significant importance. The narrative of a rational and scientific corporate finance, or techniques of asset pricing or risk management help protect the expert species and knowledge systems. The result is social and economic inequality and outright fraud by financial institutions and markets, without any personal criminal culpability and punishment of finance leaders[9]. Their power is such that they constantly remain above the law, especially in the western world.

In his reflective address, the President of the highly influential and conservative American Finance Association, University of Chicago Professor Luigi Zingales[10] provides stark evidence of the nature and extent of financial scandals over recent decades and the cost to society. He laments that there are serious flaws in finance theory and science which have contributed to this scenario, and even amoral teaching is no longer sustainable. Academics can no longer say that they do not need to take a moral position, he argues. Sadly, the analysis does not examine the deep cultural malaise that is institutionalised, nor the structural and political problems of financial markets and incentives, although these problems are admitted. In truth, the academy has become very distant and removed from nature and society for far too long and has built up a big power base through its technocratic jargon.

Fortunately, there is an even deeper identity crisis in leadership teaching in the field of management too, with scholars arguing that it has done little to advance knowledge or improve humanity[11]. It perpetuates the power of the 'white-male' leader and assumes that leadership is a type of formula which can be learnt, rather than a culture which needs to be shaped or can be inherited. Followership is also often seen uncritically. The discipline is marginal, self-referential, too obsessed by theory and often research is poorly conducted, in spite of the hundreds of international journals in the field. It has little or no impact on management practice and is often completely disengaged from it. Management scientists have created their own inner world of what counts as good science, and in the process created a deep identity crisis for the scholars, who feel they have to write to appease journal editors, rather than what truly motivates them. They too have lost a sense of purpose, belonging and meaning and are currently providing very poor academic and educational leadership to business students. Critical leadership education offers an alternative way of addressing these challenges, which is more nuanced and reflexive, rather than formulaic and ignorant of the power dynamics and politics of leadership.

Over the last four hundred years, since the time of Spinoza, there has been a direct attack on purpose and meaning by Science and Modernity[12]. Even the idea of a deeper moral and spiritual purpose, beyond the present rational and material world, had been challenged by philosopher Friedrich Nietzsche's attack on religion – what he called the death of God. Instead, science has tried to discover universal logic about cause and effect and leave moral judgement to the individual self. The role of religious cultures and collective communities of morality and conscience in providing purpose and meaning has been seen as regressive and irrational. Therefore, it should be no surprise that contemporary finance has not even sought a sense of purpose and meaning. In this sense, what this book has done is to unravel centuries of ignorance and falsehood about faith and morality, and this is never easy to achieve. When traditions fundamentally based on morality build a finance practice to serve the community, we have a very different outcome. It is not rooted in the rebellion of the renaissance, but in the truth-seeking of wise faith pioneers.

CULTURAL IDOLS: AYN RAND, OBJECTIVISM AND THE SELFISH INDIVIDUALIST IMPERATIVE

The cold calculating, rationalistic and utilitarian logic of contemporary economics require an accompanying cultural narrative – a story which justifies it, even celebrates it. A 'silent' story which endorses the scientific assumptions and removes them from critique and helps sustain a bankrupt ideology. The foremost and most influential writer of these stories is Ayn Rand[13]. Born and raised in a wealthy Jewish family in Russia, and an American migrant, she became totally convinced of the failure of collectivism and through her novels, especially 'Atlas Shrugged' (published in 1957), she celebrated the beauty of individualism and selfishness for productive enterprise and economic growth[14]. She founded the school of 'objectivism', and her narrative appealed to a post-war capitalist America going through mechanisation and industrialisation. Her writing is very elegant and forceful, converting readers to her beliefs in a very persuasive way and convincing them that there is nothing wrong with selfishness. Business and finance leaders could keep their wealth without any fear or conscience – it is right for them to do so as they are contributing to wider economic success. Religion and faith had no place in her utopia, even though her narrative itself was ideological and 'religious'. They were seen as backward and regressive. No society can survive without public government, laws and health and safety. People like the Chairman of the Federal Reserve, Alan Greenspan, and the University of Chicago Nobel Economics laureate Professor Milton Friedman were significantly influenced by her writing. Such scientific ideologues became strongly anti-regulation, with Friedman even arguing that business has no social responsibility. Even today, there is an active attempt to promote Rand's materialist 'objectivism' in universities all across the US through the well-endowed BB&T Banking Corporation[15].

The stories and examples in this book have described leaders who never believed this and instead, found joy in sharing and giving, helping others to start their own businesses, or providing jobs and security, or affordable public transport. The environmental crisis and the sustainability imperative are now forcing us to think and act differently. Even then, there are deep ideological and political forces in denial of climate change and promoting materialism and selfishness. For transformation to happen, we cannot do it simply by changing the equations of finance. We must deal with the narratives and beliefs which celebrate materialism, greed and selfishness and expose their fundamental flaws. It is such narratives which have led to the Anthropocene – the one species which has caused irreversible havoc on the planet has become super-selfish and powerful, when there are plenty of cultures which have behaved in a completely opposite win-win manner. When we look at the economic principles of different cultures, like Islamic Finance or Jain Ethical Finance, the beliefs are expressed openly and up front so that there is no deceit and morality is central and all-important. Ayn Rand's influence on economic theory, institutions and practice is hidden and therefore deceitful. Hers is a narrative which sustains inequality and a cold, unemotional mindset. It is no surprise that we are in such a global mess with high finance and its towering ideologues of expropriation. Can we say that there is a consistency between the fiction of money and the corporation and the unsustainable fiction of free markets ideology? The evidence and analysis presented in this book suggest so and require us to tackle the very roots and politics of finance thinking and belief, before we can reform it.

A DISTINCTLY AMERICAN HUBRIS, GOES VIRAL WITH GLOBAL INFLUENCE

Finel-Honigman (2010) has analysed two hundred years of American financial history, and it is littered with fraud, deceit and hubris. One would think most countries would be deeply ashamed and there would be huge public uproar to transform this deep-rooted culture. However, her research finds that the fiction of a dreamy, capitalist, free-market utopia for hard-working entrepreneurs still prevails, and neither the politicians nor markets or institutions are capable of controlling it. She demonstrates a systemic and more specifically, American, root in the academic and intellectual narratives of the possibilities and opportunities of finance. She writes (p.215):

> American capitalism and the culture of profit and money is so unique because it is fundamentally devoid of moral content, it is self-perpetuating, deemed essential rather than existential in the collective psyche ...

From this viewpoint, precisely the separation of moral and ethical content is what gives American capitalism its magnetism, hubris and dynamism. At the same time, its practice alienates its leaders from a personal sense of identity, belonging and mortality. This is when the institutions they run become positively harmful and unsustainable. The challenge facing this book, given the huge economic and intellectual power of America, is demonstrated to be deeply moral and cultural. This immorality cannot be changed overnight by better science, as it has a deep-rooted behavioural and political barrier at its core.

As this book has demonstrated, pluralism and diversity can help shift the thinking and maybe even some of the theories and science of finance. However, the American juggernaut of influence means that transforming the paradigm, which is so urgently needed, is quite far from reach. Not only is it deeply hard-wired in the textbooks and curricula, but also in the markets and institutions that America have been exporting to the world. The political, intellectual, cultural, economic and spiritual resistance to the Anthropocene should not be under-estimated. As we know, even Climate Change Denial has pride of place in America, with huge amounts of funding and economic power[16]. Dogma and false belief are often more comfortable than truth or social justice. For finance professors, it gives them permanent tenured jobs and high salaries, topped up by consulting with big corporations – money drives their ambition. It is not in their interest to upset the apple cart.

MULTINATIONAL CORPORATE PURPOSE – A FAILING AGENDA

The subject of corporate purpose and leadership has attracted significant research and analysis from the world-renown 'British Academy' and led by Oxford Professor Colin Mayer. The research results were published in 2021[17] and it was based on four years of work on the behaviour of large multinational corporations with the help of hundreds of business leaders, policymakers, academics and practitioners. Forty researchers and two hundred academics were involved in the project and twenty-nine roundtables were held. When we read the findings of this research, it is difficult to hide the scale of management, governance, accountability and regulatory challenges facing the modern corporation. Without spelling it outright, the report admits that the modern corporation has run amok especially in terms of purposeful business practices, policies and investment. It is selfish, difficult to control and regulate, greedy and materialistic and abuses its position of power by growing monopolies and avoiding genuine accountability. The corporation actively tries to reduce competition, to capture regulation and lobby politicians and influence elections, not to mention the minimisation of tax liabilities. Paradoxically, despite leadership beliefs and values being central to purpose, the report avoids discussing this at any length, nor does it deal with cultural diversity. It has a deep platonic, universalist paradigm, in spite of the abject failure of this approach. Instead of embracing the reality of subjective leadership, it forces objectification and standardisation of corporate purpose.

The British Academy report makes a spate of recommendations about fundamental reforms to laws, accountability, business character and conduct, if corporations are to be sustainable. These require new globally agreed legal rules, new regulatory powers, direct policing of corporate leaders and directors to make them personally responsible for corporate abuses and greater investor engagement with corporations about their sustainable purpose. There is a strong self-regulatory bias in the recommendations, implying an allegiance to corporate power, rather than any rigorous challenge – a model similar to stakeholder capitalism which has become a constantly failing rhetoric. Most of the aspirations will not be achieved, because the political capture and regulatory arbitrage by these corporate behemoths are a systemic problem lacking any global governance mechanism. Large fund managers and proxy investors like Blackrock and State Street have also become far too powerful instead of being independent and challenging to corporations. The report's social silence over the political hubris of these giants is most disappointing, and it makes no reference to faith or belief in guiding leaders towards sustainable moral purpose. This shows the continuing deep intellectual prejudice against faith communities and their beliefs.

The report demonstrates how captured even experts and academics have become by the giant corporate behemoth and its global power. At least they are blinded by their platonic world-view and avoidance of transcendence, faith and spirituality as solutions for the climate crisis. The British Academy is giving an independent and scientific endorsement to what will result largely in business as usual, with regulation of the powerful, by the powerful. The report reads like another technocratic solution to a problem created by a morally bankrupt technocracy. Purpose becomes a fig leaf in this chimera. It has no soul, nor is there any serious curb to the growth and materialistic ambitions of these businesses. The words 'conscience', 'tradition' and 'community' or 'tacit skills' are missing from the analysis. So is monopoly politics and power, which is often the real driver of multinational purpose. Somehow, they bear no relationship to corporate purpose. The report does not address the fundamental 'demoralisation of discourse' that has been at the core of our purposeless businesses and society today. Paradoxically, the extensive British Academy research fails to recognise that for purposeful corporations, we cannot escape talking about normative ethics and mission, and the platonic approach to an objective business science abjectly fails when we engage with sustainable purpose. For me, this report is evidence of the fundamental problems of finance education.

VIOLENT FINANCE

Most readers would have rarely seen these two phrases connected together – finance and violence. Sadly, the reality has been otherwise – finance has been violent towards nature and society. Business behaviour, especially of large corporations, has been a major part of the problem of modernity's attack on nature and society. The British Academy report suggests a whole range of regulatory and structural reforms to rein in this behaviour towards more long-term, meaningful and sustainable practices. The research admits that private interest alone is insufficient to direct sustainable finance and investment – there needs to be a wider partnership with public and social organisations and projects. It avoids the question of personal leadership, preferring instead to focus on a set of principles and practices which would lead to purposeful organisations. In this sense, the report is deeply secular and avoids engaging with the conscience and collective responsibility that is demanded of leaders today. A similar problem is found in the widely celebrated corporate finance book by Alex Edmans – 'Grow the Pie'[18]. The role of leadership, culture, and conscience is submerged in favour of larger questions of the principles of purposeful profit-seeking. Technocratic principles are preferred as compared to subjective personal beliefs and preferences. The obsessive pursuit of objectivity in finance eats personality for lunch. The failure of technocracy is resolved by more technocracy and 'better' governance!

As this book has shown, this problem cannot be generalised or avoided, and the subjectivity of leadership behaviour and culture needs to be understood and acknowledged in the teaching of corporate finance. Purpose, spirit, upbringing, culture and community cannot be separated from business analysis, especially when we are seeking meaning and social & environmental responsibility. Principles and objective science cannot replace personal conduct and character moulded by history, belief and culture. Meaning is a belief, not a formula. In this sense, it clashes with platonic and rational science. When sustainability demands purposeful leadership, we are opening up a scientific chasm – universal beliefs cannot accommodate subjective purpose. Where this accommodation is done as a patch, we should be very wary of the applicability of the results. They are not embedded in the very soul of the science of finance, but accommodated due to the climate crisis.

United Nations Human Rights legislation and global policies have been designed to ensure that states and corporations do not exploit human beings and instead take a direct interest in their health, well-being, social and economic development[19]. Finance plays a hugely influential role in this, although one would not see it if one were to read a finance textbook. Finance helps create or destroy jobs, is needed to improve public health and can be directed to avoid inequality and pollution – such that human lives become meaningful and sustainable. Unfortunately, many finance teachers would laugh if we asked them to connect finance and human rights – they simply would not see the connection, or call it an oxymoron. The record has been very troubling – finance has taken an active part in corruption, fraud and inequality, damaging human rights and well-being in the process. At a very simple level, it does not believe in paying taxes, even when they are core to public safety and well-being and creating a rule-based legal justice system to protect private property and assets. The connection between finance and human rights needs to be reinstated urgently to ensure finance leaders act with responsibility and protect human rights rather than destroying them. At the very least, finance leaders need to fully acknowledge their 'responsibility' (and not choice) in protecting human rights. This also means that at an educational and intellectual level, much more work needs to be done to integrate finance with human values and societal well-being. We need to find innovative ways of putting purpose, rights and well-being into the valuation and capital budgeting equations.

DELIBERATE IMPERSONALITY

Like the British Academy report, accounting and finance science have deliberately tried to be impersonal and therefore platonic – believing that there is a universal natural science, beyond culture, belief, tradition or community. The track record of this science has been abysmal in terms of frauds, failures and corruption even among its most elite institutions both in banking and in accounting. At the same time, the political nature of finance has been deliberately avoided in the pursuit of this objectivity, leading to widespread fiction and devastation of economies and societies. The analysis and evidence in this book not only expose the flaws of these theories and pedagogies, but also show that another richer and more sustainable world has long been hiding in plain sight because of such intellectual prejudice. This world is rich in belief, social and community capital, respect for equality and nature and inclusive and cooperative, rather than competitive and expropriative. It is hoped that this book encourages researchers from these cultures and communities to articulate their own wisdom and their relevance for building a sustainable future. These chapters merely scratch the surface of this vast ocean, opening a lens into what is possible and articulating a language for wider intellectual and pedagogical enrichment. In particular, it exposes the deep ignorance of the renaissance, which tarred all faiths with the same brush, and led to the demoralisation of discourse[20]. Instead, there is a vast diversity of faiths and beliefs in the world, and in terms of sustainable finance leadership, these traditions play a vital role in helping take society out of its abyss – there is dignity in difference[21].

Due to the various scandals and frauds, elite institutions in both accounting and finance have begun a new rhetoric on good culture and how it is central to their businesses[22]. However, the ideological conundrum, that sustainable culture has no place in the technocratic science, is completely ignored. As a result, the assumption is that somehow pragmatic rules and processes will bring about a sustainable culture change, without addressing the fundamentals. This book and the stories and examples in it have shown that this contradiction lies at the heart of our broken financial system. The science has encouraged materialism and individualism, and an ideological market triumphalism which is unsustainable and a direct reason for the Anthropocene. Unless there is a transformation in theory, institutions and pedagogy, we are not going to change the world. Whilst we do not deny the importance of rules, laws and regulations, the book shows that personality, character and culture matter too and need to be understood and harnessed for social and environmental transformation.

The interviews have also revealed the significant role of spirituality, faith and conscience in regulating leadership actions and character. Good moral leadership matters, and good leadership can and does make a difference, even in accounting and finance. Faiths are diverse and have different ways of seeing truth and reality. They also belong to large living communities, spread out all over the world, people who have a sense of moral purpose and a desire to care for others, including plants and animals. There is an inter-twining of faith and culture, which is often misunderstood by a secular and technocratic academy. The boundary between faith and culture is never sharp, and sometimes, even people who claim to be secular may behave with a strong moral conscience, because of their history and upbringing. Faith also helps leaders manage risk and develop lasting and meaningful relationships, with patience and perseverance. Faith educates leaders about the limits of money and tempers greed and selfishness often much better than any rule book or moral code. In fact, in the deep denial and dismissal of faith, modern accounting and finance have themselves often become fundamentalist and dogmatic in the reliance on technical codes and calculations.

In this book, we explored what good finance leadership looks like when people are influenced by a deeper sense of mission and purpose, drawing either from their faith and belief or from their upbringing, socialisation, character and public spirit. They have taken finance personally. We found that there is no magic formula for ethical finance – and often a lot of pain and perseverance. Membership and belonging to a living community, with historical roots and memory, helps them build the stamina to progress and grow. For such leaders, interdependence is a living reality not a dashboard or governance target. The relationships they have nurtured help them to learn and attract finance even in challenging times. They can cope with the risks and rewards and stay resilient in the face of crises. The results show that when leaders have a deeper sense of meaning and public purpose, they are more likely to succeed and help others succeed and grow at the same time. Instead of being selfish, they are instinctively selfless and generous. They do not need to be told or governed to act in protecting wider stakeholders, including employees and the state. For such leaders, social responsibility is simply the right way to operate, not a legal code or governance dictat.

THIN AND THICK MORALITY

Lord Jonathan Sacks compared universal human rights and ethical philosophy with faiths and beliefs which many people have[23]. The scientific approach to ethical education tends to be abstract and philosophical and therefore generic and impersonal. He calls this a 'thin' morality. This is the morality that dominates contemporary Western secular approaches to ethical finance[24]. The extant research tries to apply philosophical ideas and concepts and connects them to practice. When such an approach is merged with a technical craft of accounting or finance practice, it has the tendency to become superficial and transactional, rather than meaningful and purposeful at a deeper personal and professional level[25].

In contrast, for people who belong to faiths and communities, they have a living experience of morality which gives them meaning, purpose and context for their lives. This is labelled a 'thick' morality, which is rooted in personal beliefs, convictions, experiences and conscience. Lord Sacks warned about not confusing and mixing the two and argued that a 'thick' morality is one we should all be aspiring for, such that we can have a life of meaning and purpose. He accepted that a thick morality is necessarily subjective, but it is deeper and richer. At the very least, teachers of 'thin' morality should try to engage students in deeper contextual conversations about their own beliefs and experiences. Research in business education has also revealed that when students are asked to personally reflect on their values, they come up with better and more engaged moral analysis than if they were only given philosophical tools[26]. Morality is not simply about an outer philosophical dialogue, but about a deeper inner dialogue and reflection, which may be uncomfortable, but should not be avoided.

As we have seen, given the technocratic domination of accounting and finance, the 'professional' approach to ethics is secular and philosophical and impersonal. It is about following codes, rules and regulations and NOT about personal values, beliefs, experiences and culture. The Institute of Chartered Accountants in England & Wales has a code of ethics which is long on words and short on meaning or truth – its most common requirement is that 'accountants should not do anything to bring the profession into disrepute', without specifying what this means[27]. This would be a 'thin' morality, which attracts a tick-box transactional approach. Paradoxically, several Big 4 global accounting firms (KPMG in US and PWC in Canada) have recently been caught with systemic and systematic ethics infringements by cheating on their exams, with partners aiding and abetting the process[28]. This is direct evidence of how the leaders perceive ethics – as an exam to be passed, rather than a culture to be practised and lived by. This is the biggest problem with secular, philosophical approaches to ethics, which continue to this day. Morality is very thin and often overwhelmed by greed and short-termism, and therefore, unsustainable. Purpose then becomes selfish and materialistic and supported ostensibly by a code of ethics.

For a purposeful finance, we need much deeper and wider engagement with 'thick' morality. We can do so by accepting the richness of diversity and valuing dialogue and engagement between different leaders about what empowers them about accounting and finance and how they derive moral meaning and purpose from it. When such dialogues and case studies are researched and taught, it is likely that ethics will no longer be seen simply seen as an exam to be passed and then forgotten, but something that helps clarify the richness of being a professional and the joy of protecting public interest. When true stories and examples are combined with personal lived experiences and beliefs of students, there is a potential to transform finance leadership towards sustainable goals. Professional bodies can play a pro-active role in hosting such deeper dialogues and facilitating leaders to support one another in this moral journey. In large organisations, the challenges of speaking truth to power are formidable, but with a support mechanism, this can be done in a timely fashion to avoid fraud and catastrophe. If on the other hand, we stick merely to the thin morality because of its 'scientific' and 'objective' credentials, we are likely to lose much of the personal passion and commitment that is needed to bring change in society. This will end up with continuing scandals, where no one is responsible and fines simply become a cost of doing business.

WE ALSO NEED TO TALK ABOUT DEATH, AND NOT AVOID IT

Sadly, death is never discussed in accounting and finance – it happens to other people! However, when it comes to purpose and meaning, death and its finality can really help bring a focus to what life is about and the role of money and possessions, given that we will be unable to take them away with us. Culturally, in the West, this may be seen as a 'morbid' subject, or a sensitive and emotional topic, but in other cultures, this may not be a difficult topic at all and students may even welcome its discussion. The denial of death can lead to purposeless accumulation and unjustified greed, removing any emotional care or concern about the methods used to make profits or wealth. Death can give a focus and clarity to purpose and leadership that very little else can. Even asking managers and professionals to write their own eulogy can be a very effective way of facilitating a deeper discovery of purpose and meaning. On the funeral pyre, it is the people who have shared and given in life who are remembered the most, not the ones who have taken and kept wealth all to themselves. Death can be a great leveller of people and a unique teacher of purpose, like no other. The examples in the book have shown how attending funerals and memorial services is normal in so many communities and even children and young people come to pay their respects to relatives. This gives them an 'experience' of death, helping them to talk about it openly.

This book has shown that it is our silences and false beliefs about nature which have played a big part in the Anthropocene. Our education and training have made us 'unreflexive' and conditioned us to thinking that this is normal and acceptable. Fictitious theories have been replicated as science all over the world, without any respect for local cultures or beliefs. Empires of the mind have come to rule the textbooks of silent destruction, in the name of economic growth and progress. This is unsustainable, and a dialogue on death can also open the possibility of inter-generational equity as a critical concern among finance leaders. Death dialogues have a capacity to personalise life and finance too.

If we avoid this dialogue, inter-generational equity will simply remain as a theoretical concept which is given lip service if at all. Legacies are shaped by what leaders leave behind for future generations and not the inequality and expropriation they created whilst being alive. Religious leaders are revered for the wisdom and stories they have left behind hundreds of years after their death. These parables are often timeless and place such a low emphasis on material prosperity and a high emphasis on giving and sharing. Purpose and meaning for leaders can only come when we make their work feel personal and give them the role models and concepts to help them experience the joy of taking finance personally. So much damage has been done by making the corporation impersonal and ignoring the nature and limits of money that this trajectory must be reversed if we wish leaders to act sustainably.

SOCIAL, MORAL AND POLITICAL SILENCES BETRAY PURPOSE

This book has exposed the social, spiritual and intellectual silence on purposeful finance leadership and shown what is suffered and lost when we ignore leaders' power and influence in directing financial markets and institutions. Its intellectual roots and corruption need much wider exposure, and the technocratic foundations of contemporary finance which serve to disguise the moral algorithms ought to be discussed and shared in the classroom. The significant power of finance leaders, and their influence on jobs, pensions, savings, equality, race, class, animals and nature, is never discussed in the finance classroom. This needs to be transformed – the lines of connection between finance practice and wider social and environmental impacts need to be discussed pro-actively, both those that are good and those that are deceitful or harmful. The disconnection is actively shaping lying, cheating and expropriation on a global scale. Such dialogues could be the beginnings of deeper debates on the fundamental purpose, impact and meaning of finance.

The Anthropocene provides us with a good framework to tackle the intellectual deceit and expropriation that has brought humanity to such a profound existential crisis. In the business school, leadership is taught as a separate subject and rarely connected directly with accounting or finance. In the professional examinations, there is no separate module on leadership or public interest. What this reveals is that there is possibly a deeper battle in the curricula between a technocratic finance and a personal subjective leadership approach. Alternatively, expert finance technocrats cannot even conceive of linking the two themes together, as they simply do not have the tools to do so and think in silos. However, the towers of financial institutions are evidence of their dominance over the economy, and the leaders of these towers, exercise even more combined power.

Modern accounting and finance have become overly specialised and technocratic. This has led to a burial of basic moral concerns like purpose, meaning, contentment, social and environmental obligations, trust and sustainable relationships. The equations hide more than they solve. In the Laudato Si, the Pope argues that technocracy has disabled us from moral challenge and critique and increased its power on humanity and nature, instead of being a servant to society. Technology has given us the false belief that experts will be able to control nature and resolve the afflictions of society. The recent pandemic has shown how little even the best experts can do to predict or control disease and infection.

Risk and uncertainty are a core part of everyday life and culture, but technocratic societies try to deny them. Risk calculation and measurements give us the false belief that it is being controlled and managed[29]. In the process, experts and institutions have increased their power and influence on society and reduced their humility, fallibility and accountability. This book has shown what happens when leaders and communities act with trust and conscience and prevent technology from ruling their beliefs and occupations. Given our significant social and environmental challenge, we have no choice but to challenge and transform accounting and finance towards sustainability and purpose, helping them make culture and morality central to their logics. Both theory and the curriculum can and must change in fundamental ways. There is no alternative.

Given the degree to which finance concentrates power, the need for responsible and purposeful leadership is heightened at the very time when the scientific wisdom is neglecting it and denying its significance. How is it possible that top brands like Goldman Sachs or Lehman Brothers, or elite financial markets like London and New York, manage to disguise and cover up fraud for so long at such huge costs to society? What is it about powerful institutions like HSBC or JP Morgan or even the Big 4 Global Accounting oligopoly that help them cover up the past and spin a professional image which is to be trusted? Students should be encouraged to ask these questions and dig deep about the histories of the branded institutions they aspire to work for. Politics and finance need to be broken up from their divorce and exposed for the deep layers of fraud and corruption that lie hidden behind the glamorous towers and high bonuses. Communities broken and exploited by finance need to be connected to these institutions to expose the extent of their reach and disruption of our moral fabric.

Conscience, honour and humility are critical to purposeful finance and key character qualities needed from moral leaders. Through the reporting of trusted conversations, rather than standard wholesale anonymous research interviews, the book has shown that the depth and quality of evidence uncovered can be deeper and more helpful to conceptual development. Intellectual purpose has been a key driver for me in writing this book – how can a scholar and teacher help transform society such that leaders take responsibility and provide the role models and language, to articulate an ethical approach to finance? The stories and examples in this book should help inspire diverse thinkers and writers from all over the world to dig deep into their cultures, histories and leadership practices and share these stories with the wider world in their classrooms, courses, articles and books. It is very much hoped that not only will this book educate, but it will also provide a framework for cultural and moral articulation and help create new modules in student curricula. In the process, the links between finance and ethics will become more embedded and students will have the ability to actively participate in the learning process, as opposed to blind absorbers of a technocratic, faithless and immoral paradigm. Students can bring their own stories and experiences into the classroom and be set projects and research tasks to document good leadership case studies and share them with everyone. The style of writing that has been used is to empower such thinking and research and to inspire a new generation of leaders to dig deep into their own cultural heritage and memories.

THE RISE OF FIN-TECH

Over the last two decades, the growing mantra in finance is Fin-Tech[30]. On-line banking, digital currency, mobile payments have all come into society like a hurricane and made lives easier and faster, especially in terms of financial transactions, borrowing and saving. The average person in the West now carries very little physical cash, and the mobile phone is increasingly becoming a payment and money transfer system. At the same time, the 'impersonality' of finance has grown, and out of nowhere, fintech firms have launched with multi-billion-dollar valuations. Stock markets have enabled the cashing in of intellectual capital and the concentration of technological power at an unprecedented rate. At the same time, tech fraud has grown exponentially, often stealing the hard-earned savings of many people, with ever-cleverer schemes and shams.

Technology and human culture have a conflicted relationship. On the one hand, it makes social life easier, but on the other hand, reliance on it reduces human and social contact and dependency, giving the impression that it is unnecessary for survival and transcendence. It can easily eat culture for lunch, just as neo-liberalism has done. That becomes a huge problem for sustainable finance. Technology reduces the need for trust at the very same time that we need to enhance it in society. The Anthropocene demands a cultural shift from selfishness and individualism to compassion and community. Social media tools like Facebook can help create community but here again, technology interfaces are not the same as personal ones.

To have a sense of purpose and retain it, we must learn to adapt to technologies, but at the same time keep them in their place. Fintech should serve human society and not become a master which is out of human control. This requires a pro-active vetting and regulation of financial technologies, for which society is at present ill-equipped as the hurricane of tech company valuations overwhelm the neo-liberal economic sphere with big dollar signs and hidden social repercussions. The Pope's warnings on technocracy are very apposite here.

FINANCE INTELLECTUALS 'OUGHT TO BE' DRIVEN BY MORAL PURPOSE

Professor Lord Prem Sikka has for his lifetime been a Professor of accounting and finance and has published hundreds of articles, academic and professional, about the social and political nature of accounting, embracing the need to speak truth to power in both the profession and the wider economy. He has received multiple awards for this critical scientific research and is the founder of the Association of Accountancy and Business Affairs (AABA) which he runs to this day. At the same time, he has been actively speaking to the media and appearing on radio programmes and TV documentaries as an expert. As already explained, he has suffered abuse and criticism for his public statements and positions, but he has stood resolute throughout. Throughout his career, he had actively engaged with politicians and parliament, especially ex-academic Austin Mitchell MP, again trying to question government actions which were against the poor and marginalised and suggesting different alternative policies which were more equal and fairer. Lord Sikka has demonstrated through research that accounting practices and the behaviour of large professional firms 'actively perpetuate' inequality – the assumptions woven into the calculations are cultural, political and divisive[31]. He has long campaigned against the Big 4 accounting multinationals and ensured tax avoidance was shown up for what it truly is – undermining the tax base, whilst using all the protection and services provided by the State. Recently, he was appointed by the Labour Party to the House of Lords, where he is now actively commenting on new laws and regulations to ensure fairness and equality. To find his hundreds of articles and writings, simply google his name and you will see the range and breadth of his work.

By its very nature, the function of the intellectual is powerful – how they choose to exercise this power depends very much on the personal values and politics. Edward Said (1993) conducted a unique 'BBC Reith Lecture Series' about 'Representations of the Intellectuals'. Over five lectures, he reflected deeply on the role, function and purpose of the intellectual, drawing examples from history and research over several centuries of the power, policy influence and status of intellectuals. He found that moral purpose needs to be central and speaking truth to power the norm of a true public intellectual NOT the exception. He also noted how 'black intellectuals' were not even recognised until after the 1960s – for a long time, blacks were not even thought to be capable of intellectual thought and only European Males occupied that space. He also explored the professional rewards and privileges that intellectuals achieved if they toed the establishment line, something which is highly lucrative in the field of finance.

In the UK, finance academics are the only academics in the entire university system that have negotiated their own separate pay scales, just like dealers in the trading floor have done with financial institutions. For Said, such conduct immediately reeks of materialism, a lack of objectivity, and intellectual capture rather than an openness to speaking truth to power. This is so true in Finance in North America and Europe where the research is very narrow and parochial, and hardly critical of power of any kind[32] – in fact, it denies the existence of power altogether, through its obsession with competitive markets. It has also narrowed critique of the finance curriculum[33] and wider dissemination of any critical theories and perspectives on finance, ensuring a particular ideology and market triumphalism dominate everything.

IS BUSINESS AND FINANCE EDUCATION PURPOSEFUL AND SUSTAINABLE?

For Said, the primary moral motives intellectuals ought to embrace are those of freedom, liberty and justice, with a quest for objectivity and an alliance with the poor and the marginalised. This is similar to the motives applied in the writing of this book – the work had no research funding. Said also explored faith and exposed how misunderstood and misrepresented it has become in the secular academy. Whilst the secular intellectual ought not to promote a particular 'higher' truth or faith, this does not preclude them from understanding the nature of faith and its cultural influences. Financial Literacy, one of the biggest problems of modernity, where the poor and weak are exploited routinely by financial institutions and corporations, has attracted virtually zero research and public interest from finance experts, exposing whose side they really are on.

Said spoke about the need for intellectuals to take risk and not become too comfortable with the badges of applause and rewards which come from their status and position. By risk, he meant writing in non-standard media like newspapers or giving speeches in public forums rather than just speaking to and writing for experts. He counselled against 'inside-ease' the technical language that experts use to speak to one another, often helping them hide from the public gaze or cheat about the real motives of their research and theories. Risk means not hiding behind jargon and listening to people's experiences, fears, concerns and sufferings, not cushioning oneself from them. Race continues to be a major issue – it is a fact even today that black intellectuals in accounting and finance have little power and influence, and there are very few who make it to full Professor. This discrimination can also be a catalyst for a purposeful intellectual 'fight' which allies with others who are equally marginalised, be they women, disabled or other minorities.

Politically, finance academics by the nature of their discipline are conservative and right wing. This goes against Said's view of the public intellectual who must ally with the under-represented and the marginal, for there will always be thousands willing to cosy up to power and the establishment. Given our pressing challenges of sustainability, social justice and equality, this political alliance is also deeply problematic. Fortunately, there are critical journals and writers who are willing to challenge mainstream views, like research centres at the University of Manchester, Sheffield and Dundee in the UK, and journals like

'Critical Perspectives on Accounting', 'Accounting, Auditing and Accountability Journal' and 'Accounting Forum'.

Not surprisingly, there are virtually NO quality critical academic journals dedicated to finance, so captured is the discipline by the technocrats and market triumphalist ideology. It is so important that critique comes from within not without – that way the discipline can reform and adapt. This means that even when academics do wish to write critically, the intellectual outlets simply do not exist. The Journal of Business Ethics, which is often cited in this book, is beginning to draw a number of critical finance papers, as it is internationally rated. However, the mainstream continues to operate in its own cave. Elite finance institutions like Harvard Business School or the London School of Economics produce hardly any critical thought which publicly challenges the issues raised in this book. This means that their experts are unwilling to speak truth directly to power or ally with the poor and marginalised who are regularly exploited by multinational corporations.

Most of the 'critical' research in accounting and finance originates from Britain, Australia and Canada, and not the main engine of intellectual output, the United States. The quality of this research and analysis is very high and pioneering in shifting the understanding of these important disciplines. However, the research so far has not led to a transformation of the education and training curriculum both for university students and for professional bodies. The separation between research and education and the differential incentives given to research output versus teaching are also a part of the problem. Furthermore, producing high-quality research is very demanding and can mean that academics are pressured to keep talking to one another rather than take risk and engage with wider media and public policy.

In terms of education and pedagogy, the situation is even bleaker. Elite research institutions, which have become the main production and recruitment base for intellectuals, are generally least interested in teaching. Most of their 'experts' do hardly any teaching, so not only do they not engage with public policy, but they also rarely take an interest in the future generation of business leaders and their moral, social and political upbringing. As we saw earlier, even accounting and finance have become separated as disciplines, so specialised and technocratic have the fields become. This means that intellectual leaders in this field have to reflect deeply about purpose, beyond being mere functionaries who write clever, clever papers in top journals to pursue promotion and higher salary bonuses. The journey to the top often involves appeasement to the received theories and methods, but even after tenure, intellectuals are unable to unshackle this cage and take risks with their writing and scholarship. Future generations, many of whom will directly suffer from the evils of inequality, racism and climate change, will be left to find their own pathways to social, ethical and political transcendence.

As discussed earlier, there is also a wider institutional malaise about the nature and purpose of the business school. Even in the intellectual engine that is North America, business schools have lost a professional mission of building a better human life on this planet and instead drifted into a technocratic and commercial mindset[34]. This has impacted the quality and ethics of their research output and public impact. Universities all over the world have become habituated to treating these institutions as cash cows, often using part-time faculty to provide teaching so that there is little engagement with research and critical thinking[35]. Many private enterprises have entered business education, with little interest in or funding for research and focusing instead on profiteering, with very high staff-student ratios. Such a corporatised education model directly subverts purpose and sustainability of the kind discussed in this book.

The examples, narratives and cases in this book give plenty of food for thought for intellectuals willing to embrace purpose and move away from anthropocentric theories and pedagogies. They show how the leadership they provide can be both purposeful and reflexive, and morality can be connected to what they study and how they choose to present and teach it. For a new generation of scholars and intellectuals, they open a whole new pathway of embracing their passion for social justice and inter-generational equity and sustainability. This is urgently needed today as business consultants are already actively claiming expert space in terms of advising organisations to transition to a green economy – for a fat fee of course. A recent ray of hope has come from the world-leading American Association of Colleges and Schools of Business, which is a certification body for elite business schools. In their revised 2021 definition of diversity[36], they state:

> AACSB defines diversity as culturally embedded identities rooted in *historical and cultural traditions*, legislative and regulatory concepts, ethnicity, gender, sexual orientation, socioeconomic conditions, *religious practices*, age, ability, and individual and *shared experiences*. When these differences are both recognized and respected through the delivery of high-quality business education, diversity becomes a powerful catalyst for unleashing the potential of an organization and individuals.

The keywords of interest for this book are historical and cultural traditions, religious practices, and shared experiences. We will wait and see how long it takes for these concepts to lead to a reformed finance curriculum, especially in the elite business schools all over the world, which are in the AACSB network.

COUNTER-NARRATIVES – PURPOSE ELEVATES LEADERSHIP

The narrative of an objective, scientific finance which is free from moral and cultural 'subjectivity' and is liberal and liberating, has been busted by the evidence of financial hubris and corruption. However, it continues, as we saw in the recent example of the Edmans book, which is re-arranging deck chairs on the titanic when it asks finance leaders to 'Grow the Pie'[37]. The separation of the person from the leadership action lies at the heart of this systemic problem in finance – when things go wrong, others, such as regulators, government or processes and systems are to blame. Rarely is there any personal punishment for financial failure, which helps in increasing the impersonality of the decision-making.

Instead, what is needed are counter-narratives of a plural and diverse finance, one which is rooted in moral responsibility and has no ambitions to grow in greed and power, but instead to rise in public service, economic empower- ment, and humility. Leaders who use their financial resources to help others do exist, and their narratives need wider exposure and dialogue. As Chapter 4 has demonstrated, the wholesale denial of 'experience' as a source of wisdom and knowledge in finance is flawed and unsustainable. We need to tackle this at its very root, as it leads to much alienation of students and their personal intuitions and values. By making finance personal and relatable in the classroom, students can understand at a formative age how meaning and purpose can motivate and inspire their professional careers.

From the stories and interviews, what we saw was that when leaders had a sense of meaning and purpose, their qualities and achievements were elevated to new heights of trust, confidence and shared success. In many cases, they drew their meaning from their faith and upbringing and the examples and role models they had seen in their families and communities. Money and profits were impor- tant to them, but never overwhelming. They rarely took the cold, calculating character of finance and instead used finance as a means to a larger goal – be it providing a public transport vehicle which is affordable (Firodia – tuk-tuk), loans which would help advance small immigrant community businesses (Meghraj and Barclays) or education and campaigning to reduce tax avoidance and protect public interest (Tax Justice Network).

Throughout, we saw a level of meaning and intimacy with the enterprise such that the leaders engaged with their inner conscience and acted in line with its wisdom. There was reflexivity and even meditation was seen as a 'competi- tive advantage in finance' (Bhansali – Enam Securities). Owner-managed family businesses can have a unique quality and character, and sustainability is often in-grained and hard-wired into the very nature, leadership and management of the enterprise. Future generations to take over the business are not distant but intimately engaged in its performance and direction, and elders see their role as passing the baton rather than milking their customers of suppliers. Finance is forced to serve the business, not the other way round. It is also kept in its place when leaders have a sense of purpose – to serve rather than to dominate society.

Belonging to living communities helped leaders to develop a direct experi- ence of public duty and social capital and reputation and honour mattered deeply to them. Their childhood memories of growing up in these communities were vivid and rich and gave them a direct experience of interdependence – similar to my own memories from Mombasa. When interdependence is experienced, its expression does not require a new rule book or law or code of governance. Lord Phillips spoke about his pride of growing up in Sudbury, Suffolk, where local reputation and networks had significant value. They also helped keep him grounded, such that he was able to provide national leadership and elevate himself in a naturally confident way, without becoming arrogant.

Serving communities as volunteers became a normal part of the lived experiences, helping the interviewees stay in direct contact with all kinds of people from all walks of life. Lord Phillips has founded a number of very important national charities. In many cultures, it is considered the highest honour to serve, even higher than being a CEO of a business enterprise. Such acts also taught the leaders humility and checked their hubris and ego, qualities critical to responsible finance leadership. When purpose and meaning are regulated or codified, they lose their power to move and inspire leaders. Purpose should come from within, not without. In the process, the task of leadership is elevated to new heights of equality, social and environmental responsibility, which a technocracy cannot attain.

BELIEF, CARE AND COMPASSION

Another way in which finance leaders can stay grounded is by joining a caring and responsible community which actively measures and monitors the business impact on human rights all over the world where they operate. Adhering to the spirit of regulations and laws, not just their form is also critical. Trade unions could be encouraged to ensure a sharing of power and accountability, instead of businesses repeating the mantra of stakeholder capitalism without allowing stakeholders like workers to influence actual practices. Even when labour may be cheaper in developing countries, it is the responsibility of finance to ensure fair wages and working conditions are provided, and even health care and housing if this is needed. The profit targets and margins on such manufacturing can be reduced to facilitate fairness to all employees, not just those living in the headquarter nations of multinational corporations.

The founder and CEO of Khosla Ventures, a top Silicon Valley venture capital firm and renown entrepreneur explained that most CEOs of Fortune 100 companies whom he has met personally have NO belief system[38]. They simply do not have their own internal compass and yet are in positions of significant power and authority. For Khosla, this is a major problem in society, as leaders need to have their own vision and sense of right and wrong. Purposeful leaders should not rely on others, be it advisers, analysts or journalists to decide which strategy to adopt or what decision to take. Leadership behaviour needs to be consistent to be effective.

For Khosla, purpose and belief are at the heart of sustainable leadership – there is no other alternative. While advising students at Stanford Graduate Business School, he repeatedly emphasised how important it was that they nurtured their own values and priorities and not rely on others to direct their life or work. Each person needs to develop their own moral compass and sense of right and wrong, truth and falsehood and a conviction to make a difference in life. He encouraged a deeper reflexivity than facts, figures and theories which are normally served in the business school in a universalist way. Khosla was very critical of working for large blue-chip professional employers to build a career and add lines to the CV. For him, risk was to be experienced personally and directly, not delegated to others, or calculated on a spreadsheet. Khosla abhorred the 'false comforts' which employers can provide – they do not lead to sustainable leadership in his opinion. Instead, they can easily lead to politics, compromise and prejudice. For Khosla, purposeful leadership is both personal and behavioural, where leaders are seen to walk their talk.

In describing his finance and investment philosophy, he was extremely critical of most venture capitalists – for Khosla, very few of them know how to run a business, and yet in their power to advise others, they help in destroying businesses rather than building them. This is a devastating critique of a whole industry of finance which is often seen in the literature as very entrepreneurial and visionary. In fact, it is perceived as the engine room of innovation and progress. There is so much waste in finance, yet we rarely talk about waste in this way – how capital is misdirected and wasted in the hundreds of millions and no one gets blamed in the process. Whilst many people in the world are dying to get small amounts of seed capital for their family's education and welfare, and we have evidence of the success of micro-finance initiatives in many parts of the world, the developed countries waste billions through venture capital and other fictitious investment projects. Khosla's finance philosophy is very simple – he never performed projected return calculations, but instead looked at the product and the people and invested, fully prepared to fail and write off the investment. He did a lot of homework early on, and then let the investment multiply through the hard work and dedication of the founders who had plenty of self-belief. If he failed, he did not blame others.

EXPERIENCE AS ASSET

From the above, we can see that Khosla values experience over education or training. Throughout this book, we have shared a variety of stories of leadership experiences in business. It is evident that finance education is responsible for professionalising the discipline and removing it from experience – technical calculation and training are seen to be enough for producing finance professionals and leaders. The wholeness that comes from *both* learning and experience is not valued in the theories and models. If we see the theories and scientific claims as a direct attack on subjective experience, emotions, and feelings, then it is no surprise that they are not valued in finance. However, in this devaluation, we have a latent and profound flaw in the science at a time when we urgently need institutions and leaders who care for both society and our ecosystem.

Khosla's sustained success is an anomaly for finance theory, whose science is rational, methodical, calculative and measured, with a strong emphasis on return and wealth maximisation. Khosla's comments actually describe precisely the flaws of impersonal anonymity in finance – whilst beliefs and purpose are highly personal characteristics, even when they may not be easy to measure and evaluate, they are critical to sustained success. The secrets to sustainability lie precisely in the questions contemporary finance has so far refused to address. The active denial of inter-disciplinary knowledge in the investment decision is also deeply problematic. The discipline seeks to direct people in a fictitious knowledge boundary which is damaging precisely because it is unreal.

Purpose and reflexivity in leadership *have to* be twin partners. This means that the leader should not just reflect on the performance of the larger organisation, but at the same time on themselves and the personal meaning and purpose that is achieved through the leadership of the corporation. The ethical values of the leaders need to be aligned with the values of the organisation and their stated goals and aspirations – leaders need to be seen to be walking their talk. The best way to achieve this level of integrity is not to distance the business from the self, but to connect both and to engage in a deeper exploration of the self and its sustainable motives and aspirations. The power and responsibility that leadership commands require the melting of any boundaries between the self and the corporation.

Contemporary western society finds reflexivity very difficult – people are simply not used to closing their eyes and facing their inner selves and spirit. This becomes even more problematic when such people occupy positions of power and influence. As the evidence of the past shows, many finance leaders accept greed and selfishness as a norm, and wealth as the ultimate road to security, happiness and well-being. When leading organisations, they make the workplaces technocratic, transactional and instrumental, subconsciously forcing their employees to be equally unreflexive about their life goals. This culture is unsustainable. Our debate on purpose must go to the very heart of finance wisdom and the purpose of finance, irrespective of the institutions which leaders take charge of. It needs to place character, trust, relationships, non-materialism, non-possessiveness, community and integrity at the core of finance. In this sense, we redefine purpose as starting with the very goals and motives of finance and the nature and limits of money. Conscience needs to be faced and nurtured.

SPIRITUAL MOTIVATION CAN NOURISH FINANCE

A common theme arising among the interviewees of this book whether they are Hindu, Christian, Jewish, Muslim or Jain is the importance of spirituality. Spirituality need not mean belonging to an organised religion or a specific church or institution – in fact none of the leaders I interviewed defined it in this way. Instead, it was more about a belief in a larger sense of duty and purpose beyond materialist goals and possessions. They valued relationships and placed a strong value on trust. Their stories illustrate how their faith and belief inspired them towards purpose and resilience in challenging times and a conscience to do good by being good. They all understood and acknowledged human mortality and were not in denial of death. In short, none of them were obsessed by finance and its power – on the contrary, it often inspired humility among them. Prior to the writing of this book, the Jain founders of Enam Securities had made a hundred-million-dollar donation to set up Flame University and kept it anonymous. It was only revealed when Oxford University decided to do a case study on them for their impact finance series.

The global founder of the Wesleyan Church, John Wesley, was a philosopher, preacher and social entrepreneur who started many businesses and helped create jobs and organisations to help the poor, including a small business loan scheme[39]. For him, belief and practice through helping the upliftment of society were entwined, and he drew energy from this sense of purpose and servant leadership. In history, there are many examples of faith-inspired servant leaders who used finance for a deeply moral purpose and help create jobs and boost the economy. For leaders driven by spiritual motives, the impact of their actions on society is often given priority and the sharing of wealth and success is normalised. In fact, one of Wesley's weaknesses was that he did not save and was always low on cash. Workers and producers are respected and not exploited, and they in turn feel motivated to go the extra mile and provide quality goods and services.

While spirituality cannot be put into an equation or a scientific formula, its connection to purpose cannot be denied[40]. In fact, we can argue the opposite, that purpose without spirituality in finance leadership often leads to emptiness and unsustainability. A formulaic or rule-based approach to purpose and the separation of ownership and management among financial institutions has often meant what is the least leaders can get away with it, rather than a pro-active approach to good culture and fair treatment of all stakeholders. The mainstream literature avoids this completely and denies the existence of spirit and its role in influencing financial conduct and leadership character.

When it comes to protecting our natural environment, which has been destroyed and exploited by finance for decades, we have a particular quandary. Finance may not admit it, but it fundamentally lacks the language and spirit to cope with nature. Recent work on the climate crisis shows that there is very little research in the finance discipline on this theme, despite its urgency[41]. The researchers found that the editorial boards of top finance journals were primarily North American, and there has long been a bias against 'policy-oriented' topics and towards an insular theorisation. They called Finance a 'House with No Windows' – self-referential and inward-looking. Its very foundation has been built on seeing nature as a resource and as 'other' rather than a core part of human survival and existence. Poets and writers of nature constantly evoke its deep intelligence and wisdom, and its ability to teach and inspire human society about truth, justice and beauty. Nature has a transcendent quality which evokes respect and tolerance, even awe for its vastness and innate interdependence. Its true understanding evokes a spiritual response, however one defines it. To reduce our responsibility to a variable in an equation is to expose our ignorance and arrogance towards nature. If finance were to understand the essence of nature, it would affect the entire ontology and belief system foundational to the discipline.

For sustainable leadership, this is a challenge the experts should not shirk but address head on. Our common future depends on it.

COMMUNITY AS 'BANK' OF LEADERSHIP CAPITAL

Finance policies and decisions affect a range of people – they could be employees, customers or suppliers or pensioners and other stakeholders. Leaders need to understand and accept the limitations of technical decision-making – through risk calculation, they can pretend to address uncertainty and at the same time completely miss it as it is outside their understanding and control. Lack of information may lead to procrastination, which can also be damaging. What is very important is that finance leaders do not distance themselves from society where real lives are lived and actions performed, which are often dependent on an ethical and moral finance. Not only should such impacts be measured, they need to be felt and experienced by leaders through direct personal engagement. The present internet world often removes leaders from direct experience of the impact of their decisions on other stakeholders, and this is a tragedy. The proxying of people with data and impact measurements can and often does blind-side leaders.

Through the focus on communities as hubs of social, relationship and trust capital, we have learnt that everyone can be helped by a sense of purpose and belonging, not just leaders. Communities play a critical role in helping people develop a larger sense of responsibility and accountability. At the same time, the alienation from any sense of belonging can have exactly the opposite effect. It can lead to leaders who do not care about their impact on others. Closeness and intimacy are critical to helping young people have role models to aspire to and neighbours and friends whom they can connect with and trust. Ideally, for communities to work, they need to be local and personal, not just virtual and distant. Each person would need a sense of rootedness and connection to feel a sense of belonging. Faith can be an important provider of this but is not the only resource for community. Large organisations may struggle to build and retain this sense of intimacy and loyalty even though they could benefit significantly from it. There are significant 'diseconomies' of scale when it comes to culture and values in large organisations. This is why when we are trying to learn about leadership and purpose, we are much better off doing so in owner-managed enterprises, which could be as small as a one-person market trader than a large corporate multinational.

Communities are **rain forests of diversity and experience**, with people of all ages and abilities and a connectivity which is not dependent on quid-pro-quo or material relationships. Instead in a community, we have a micro-cosm of wider society and a chance to learn from one another without any mediation by data or calculations. We can share each other's stories and experiences, and during festival time, come to celebrate the joy of being, or fast together in a shared sense of self-discipline. No one is a CEO of a community, and leaders are never permanent, with volunteering as a norm rather than an exception. Communities help people to experience a world outside money and finance and to understand the power of giving and sharing. Students could be encouraged to experience community festivals and visit community centres to see what purposeful living can look and feel like.

'Belonging' to community can help retain and nourish the sense of purpose that is so critical to sustainable finance leadership. Belonging makes interdependence a lived experience, not a remote theory. It helps a leader to directly experience the impact of their actions on other human beings, which may be either positive or negative. Leaders stay grounded when they belong. Even where their impacts are adverse, if leaders can hear the criticisms from people whom they know and respect, they are more likely to trust them and listen to them more deeply. Hubris is checked when leaders feel a sense of duty and belonging. In contrast, a lack of belonging to community could mean that leaders are detached and do not listen or trust the people complaining about their actions and character. Communities can act as 'self-regulating' mechanisms for meaningful leadership and conduct, something which a course on purposeful leadership or even training over a period cannot provide.

PROTECTING PUBLIC INTEREST

As already explained, there are hardly any books or even research papers on what good purposeful finance leadership looks like, nor is finance leadership taught as a separate subject on a Master's degree in finance, which tends to be technical and universalist. The books that are there look at scandals like the collapse of Lehman Brothers or Enron or the 2008 Global Financial Crash and the roles of different leaders in enabling them – they expose bad leadership, usually after the damage is done. The hushed silence is truly baffling given how important it is for not just the firm they are leading, but more importantly the whole economy that is being affected by the financial institution. It also contrasts starkly with the thousands of books on good management leadership – despite accounting and finance being major professions in the world, the leadership question is avoided. Failures of financial institutions have profound system-wide consequences, as we have seen from decades of financial crises – this is why the leadership question is even more critical and urgent. It is really difficult to be greedy, responsible and ethical at the same time, and experts have not quite worked out the magic formula for doing so. It is possible that such research, which would have clear normative goals, would not sell in a world which is so positivistic, professionally secular and deeply materialistic.

We can speculate here as to why the leadership question is avoided in accounting and finance – because it would very quickly have to address the primary goal of money and profit and its sustainability. Belief would have to be discussed directly, rather than avoided by calculations and abstract assumptions about facts and evidence. Leaders would be required to engage with the fundamental nature and limits of money rather than avoid the question altogether. The leadership question is also avoided because these 'sciences' are presented in a very impersonal and technical way – so to even admit leadership as a theme would require the disciplines to engage with human beings and personal beliefs and psychology, which do not fit easily in the finance technocracy. Finance would also have to acknowledge the important influence of politics and power in its practice – something which it has abjectly separated and denied for decades, driven by its own 'scientific prejudices'.

John Christensen was born in Jersey – a beautiful island which also became a global tax and secrecy haven for elites from all over the world. Trained and qualified as an accountant (with Deloitte), who rose to become Chief Economist for the island, John had also gained a lot of experience in development economics prior to this role. However, when he saw what was happening on the island, and the illegal financial flows and tax avoidance and evasion, he decided to quit and set up the global Tax Justice Network[42] in 2001, a think tank which has transformed global awareness of tax avoidance and evasion. He took great personal risk to exercise this leadership, driven by values of fairness and equality, which are so rare in modern finance. When innovation is driven by public purpose, leaders do not need any lectures on purpose and instead should be invited by finance leaders to teach them a thing or two about how accounting can be truly purposeful.

Instead of keeping quiet and making money, John decided to take public finance seriously and give leadership to an area which had long been neglected and abused by professional enablers and elites. The economics of taxation is so simple – the state is an efficient low-cost provider of public services like transport, education, health and energy and utilities, law and policing. Hence for this to be sustainable, it is imperative that fair taxes are paid by one and all, and the rich corporate elites cannot escape this net. Here is finance leadership with a clear sense of meaning and purpose, even though John is not religious or spiritual. John's drive comes from social justice and equality, and a conscience to serve society and not exploit the ignorant or the illiterate. I was privileged to be on their advisory board. John's case shows that religious belief is not a requirement for purposeful leadership.

In 2021, the Tax Justice Network (TJN) was nominated for a Nobel Peace Prize, alongside the International Consortium of Investigative Journalists (ICIJ). The TJN is a very small team even today, but it has built a large network of relationships with non-governmental organisations, researchers and academics, public leaders and legislators and journalists and investigators. Nicholas Shaxson is a very important team member and driver, and he wrote two very influential books – Treasure Islands and the Finance Curse[43], which have transformed global understanding of the shady practices of financial institutions, markets and elites. The TJN relationship network, built patiently and with exceptional communication skills, has helped the TJN pull such a large global punch in a subject which can often be very complex for the general public to understand and engage with. They even have many political leaders and governments as allies in the fight for Tax Justice.

SOCIAL JUSTICE

In a similar way, Professor Lord Sikka has long been driven by the mission to promote equality and social justice in finance. He encouraged and inspired John Christensen and is a co-founder of the Tax Justice Network and is also non-religious. A professional accountant and academic, Lord Sikka pursued research which helped uncover the varieties of 'unspoken truths' about accounting and finance – from money laundering to financial secrecy and exposure of false narratives like free and efficient markets or neo-liberalism as the panacea to all economic ills. His research showed that the state is a key actor in finance, and it should use its powers to stop exploitation and expropriation. In one of his classic research papers[44], Lord Sikka exposed how the Big 4 accounting firms used political influence in the island of Jersey to create a new legal structure – LLP or Limited Liability Partnership – in order to maximise tax benefits and minimise legal responsibility for professional misconduct or audit failures. He also examined the hypocritical role of the UK in giving Jersey its shady powers and legislature to serve elite interests and encourage offshore secrecy. Whilst being an academic and intellectual, he continuously engaged with the public and the media and never saw a separation between study and activism, and to this day continues actively influencing regulatory and legislative processes of finance in the House of Lords.

For John and Prem, purpose is not a choice but a civic and public duty. The more one 'succeeds' in finance, the more responsible and accountable one should be. Any power should be treated with the highest sense of responsibility. I have learnt this from them over many years and seen how they operate in practice. Even though they are culturally different, Prem and John are key allies in speaking truth to power, without fear of the consequences. They also do this in a measured way, armed with evidence and sound research. They are both very good at building alliances with other organisations, like NGOs. One of the major early transformations they achieved was when they were working with development charities and convinced them that if corporations paid their fair taxes, there would be no need for development aid and countries would be locally empowered to pursue development and social welfare goals. NGOs like Oxfam then began to partner with them to campaign for tax reforms.

Intellectual leadership in finance also requires a public conscience and purpose. Throughout this book, we have seen the significant power of technocratic, materialistic and utilitarian economic ideas in the devastation of nature and society. This power has become hubristic and its leaders could benefit from a deeper sense of purpose and a sense of duty and accountability for their scientific ideas. The ethics of the researcher become important to the direction of the science and alliances – intellectuals need to feel a sense of rootedness to society, conscience and responsibility for its growing prejudices and inequalities. The two cannot be separated, and there is no such thing as an 'ethically neutral' or 'culturally neutral' finance. The TJN built important alliances with charities like Oxfam and Christian Aid and they also started training finance journalists about taxation and offshore secrecy and the impact this had on equality and social justice. They helped journalists break through the technocratic cloud to identify the hidden biases and injustices. They built and nurtured communities in their goal of transforming the public understanding of finance, where tax plays a central social equality role, but often has been misrepresented and maligned by experts and practitioners.

ACKNOWLEDGING MORAL, SOCIAL AND ENVIRONMENTAL LOSSES

The economic damage done by finance education and training when it avoids engaging with leadership culture, ethical principles and sustainable purpose cannot be understated. The separation from character and political power has a subconscious effect of turning leadership into a technical science rather than a humane craft. Furthermore, if what good leadership looks like is never discussed even in professional courses and exams, there is an implication that technical expertise is sufficient for becoming a good and effective leader. Equally damaging is the lack of dialogue on culture and values of the kind elaborated through the case studies in this book – this suppresses and diminishes the ethical resources students already have and can convert them into the 'religion' of selfish finance. Accounting calculations turn people into human resources rather than human spirits, and nature and society become tools for management spin rather than substantive compassion and care. It actively corrupts the leadership mind, making it cold and instrumental.

When such trainees come to occupy positions of decision-making and influence financial transactions and practices, they become increasingly unable to see meaning and purpose as it was never crafted into the science. One of the cases I studied extensively is the failure of HBOS bank, and the role of hubristic leadership in driving the bank into the ground. The regulatory banking licence gave leaders tremendous power and influence, but this needed to be exercised with the highest sense of responsibility and accountability. Instead, the accumulated losses, both direct and indirect, were immeasurable ($65 billion at one count). The wider damage to society can never be calculated. At root was a profound intellectual failure of meaning and purpose, combined with the arrogance of power and status by leaders who colluded to manage the bank on their own terms. They failed to understand the responsibility that came with their power and position, despite having 'superior' training and intellect.

Traditionally, the secular university has tried to proudly stay away from moralising as this would be seen as religious, and instead focused on positivism – trying to understand society as is, without imposing any moral filters or expectations. This distinction between positive and normative science has also been a major factor in our blindness to diversity and inclusion. Often, we have tried to universalise social science, when in reality, the sciences may be local and interwoven with cultures and belief systems which are native and therefore NOT universal. It is possible that within communities, we have a lot of purpose and responsibility, but not enough rational science or understanding. There may actually be a rationality and understanding, but it is woven with cultural beliefs and norms and also history and memory, which is not easy to understand or universalise. This may result in their dismissal as active hubs of finance and economic capital. However, this is a gross misunderstanding and misrepresentation, especially when we have seen throughout this book that finance has lost its sense of meaning and purpose. When communities have memory and history, it is possible that they are more likely to embrace responsibility and act with purpose – the history encourages them to preserve and protect culture.

Furthermore, the modern dilemmas of climate change and inequality force us to be moral and have a moral science which is responsible and accountable. The Anthropocene gives us widespread evidence of human immorality and its consequences. For leadership to be purposeful, morality has to be front and centre, although it need not be expressed in a domineering way, but through action, conduct and example rather than words or lip service. Creative narratives, stories and visits to businesses with students engaging with leaders can do more to educate and inspire in a purposeful way than mere analysis in the classroom. So little of that is done in finance, subtly giving the impression that a sophisticated knowledge system is enough to be a finance expert, even a leader. The distancing from the ground is a very real intellectual experience for most students – we should not be surprised when they then become purposeless and irresponsible.

The position of leadership gives select people an ability to make critical decisions and the power to impose those decisions on others. The real world is not singular but plural, not certain but uncertain. Real people and lives are affected by the decisions of finance leaders, and it is so important that the leaders have some sense of connection with these people and an understanding of the implications of the decisions on them. Power heightens the responsibility of finance professionals and leaders – not only do they have power from status, but they also have power with the resources they command and the ability to allocate those resources in certain directions and not in others – these choices have a direct impact on the lives of many.

HISTORY, MEMORY AND POLITICAL ECONOMY

Professor Janette Rutterford does not 'belong' to a faith community but has a lot of respect for people who do. Her training in finance was professional and working for Rothschilds gave her an experience of the world of banking. Through her four decades of experience of global teaching and training, she discovered that there is a diversity of practices and meanings for the same finance terminology in different parts of the world. For Rutterford, histories and institutional structures are different and cannot be ignored in studying finance practices, although they often are in contemporary finance textbooks. She found that in countries like France and Germany, there is more of a long-term relationship in finance, where Banks are happy to stand by struggling businesses, whereas in England, they do not care much and their concern is for enforcing their security and collecting their principal. However, she observed that by and large the theories and textbooks are standardised, mono-cultural and impersonal. Her research has shown that when women did get involved in investments in British history, they helped improve transparency and accountability in finance. Generally as compared to men, women are more cautious and take less risk. She also agreed that the absence of history in finance education means that context and memory have disappeared from finance. Prof Rutterford explained how for a long time, American finance theory and measurement were very narrow and parochial, with very little acknowledgment of international differences and global diverse cultures and portfolios.

Whilst large organisations may try to embrace global diversity of cultures and beliefs, they are also likely to struggle to assimilate and coordinate such diverse markets, products, services, employees and customers. The business literature does not like to admit ignorance or intellectual failure and also loves to sell solutions for problem solving to justify the need for expertise and training. Is it possible that for multinational corporations, there are also significant intellectual barriers to leadership, given the diversity of peoples and cultures they are working with? Can financial inclusion and respect truly be embraced within global corporations? These are open questions, and at the very least, purposeful leaders running such organisations should be humble and curious about learning different cultures and belief systems and listening to them rather than imposing their personal beliefs and values onto them. Where leaders have a good sense of purpose and self-belief, they are likely to also respect the cultures and beliefs of their employees, suppliers and customers. However, this cannot be guaranteed.

Shame, punishment and penalty have long been measures to discipline people, especially leaders who act selfishly and exploit or expropriate others, including nature and society. Sadly, the experience in the last four decades of financialisation is that leaders who have regressed in a variety of ways, rarely face any personal fines or punishment, and in many cases, they even get multi-million-dollar bonuses in spite of mismanagement and failure. What this means is that leaders do not see any fear or need for restraint in their selfish and purposeless practices. For example, the significant fraud in US mortgages prior to the 2008 crash not only led to widespread global financial and economic collapse, but also made millions homeless, ruining their personal and family health and security. Even though Lehman Brothers collapsed, its boss Dick Fuld did not have to repay any of the bonuses he had earned from the sale of such expropriative financial instruments, nor did he face prison[45]. The award-winning documentary 'Inside Job' revealed the breadth and depth of the cultural practices prevailing at the time, including the routine use of drugs and prostitution as a way of generating business. It also has a whole section on the intellectual capture of top finance academics in North America from universities like Harvard and Colombia to endorse egregious practices. The film revealed a systemic culture of greed and abuse, where networks and relationships were built on wider social and public expropriation for the benefit of financial leaders and institutions.

FLAWED INCENTIVES

Bad or adverse leadership is rewarded and encouraged in the financial system that we have inherited. This is not sustainable. It makes a mockery of all attempts to build and promote purposeful and ethical leadership – the power and political influence accumulated by selfish leaders can be used to overcome any shame or punishment. As an example even today, there is no random drug or alcohol testing in financial institutions despite the huge regulatory importance given to good culture. Addiction is normalised and allowed. At the pinnacle of finance, where decisions are made to allocate vast amounts of money to businesses and multi-national corporations, purposeful leadership is given rhetorical importance, even in the face of widespread experience of hubris and corruption. A principles-based approach to finance education avoids confronting these very serious and egregious practices by leaders who destroy good culture and prudent investment. It avoids looking at the networks of influence and capture which actively destroy purpose and ruin society. The science is presented in a politically neutral way when the reality is highly polarised and subversive.

The structure and incentives of financial institutions have a big influence on the kinds of leaders they attract and retain and on the way their purpose is defined and manifested. Purposeful leadership depends on the institutional structures and measurement systems prevailing, and over the last forty years in the West, we have seen this to be deeply problematic, especially for financial institutions which are often at the peak of the finance pyramid. There is a wide variety of institutions from retail banks to investment banks, market-makers and traders, hedge funds and private equity and fund managers and investors. We know from bitter historical experience that risks borne by specific institutions may have significant spill over and systemic impacts which can have wider economic and social ramifications. This makes it very critical that their management and governance are honest and take account of the public responsibilities that come from running these highly risky and powerful private institutions. Paradoxically, too big to fail banks have grown even bigger after the 2008 crash, due to mergers and consolidations, increasing the risk of failure to society. Size has led to growing power and become a dampener of purpose and conscience, with large banks and financial institutions becoming increasingly difficult to regulate morally and ethically. Too big to fail has become too big to jail too.

Where the incentive systems are such as to encourage greed and short-termism, and private as opposed to public interest, the ethical dangers are magnified, and sustainable purpose becomes a chimera. In such organisations, no ethical and conscientious leader could survive and flourish. The political and organisational structures would rule them out. The only solution seems to be to break up these institutions and to reconfigure our financial system such that there is close monitoring and regulation of leadership conduct and behaviour, including imprisonment for fraud and deceit. For such organisations, the culture and behaviour of the entire management board also need to be closely monitored, given the power and responsibility they occupy. It is likely that ethically minded leaders would not want to run or manage such organisations due to their size and structural challenges. Instead of being communities of caring and purposeful employees, these big financial institutions encourage individualism, bonus-seeking behaviour and bureaucracy. Public interest protection becomes remote and technocratic at best.

ROOTED, PLURAL AND INCLUSIVE WISDOM

The finance leaders I have interviewed for this research do not run such large and global financial institutions quoted on stock markets and with turnover in the billions. They are ambitious in a public interested way and contented in a financial way – profit and wealth creation are not the principal drivers of their actions and leadership – often purpose and meaning are their primary motive. They prefer owner-management rather than distant public ownership and are happy to use their own culture and conscience as a marker of responsibility and accountability. In fact, in the above examples of John Christensen and Prem Sikka, we see a deliberate priority given to protecting the public interest and the small man/woman, who may be financial illiterate and exploited by the system. In my estimation, they are unlikely to even want to run such organisations, as their culture and values make them intimate and personable, humane and soulful. I do not see them wanting to lead a large anonymous organisation with concentrated power derived from market capital and finance. Yet their leadership and character give us some really good examples of the kinds of people we WOULD want to lead such significant public financial institutions in a prudent, ethical and responsible way. Political manoeuvring and posturing are not what excites them, nor does power for its own sake. In fact, I would say when they find themselves in positions of power and influence, they shy away from publicity and self-promotion. Such leaders would rather serve the public than be in the media and public eye.

Reflecting on the interviews in this book and the links between culture and finance, I come to the conclusion that the core foundational assumptions of neo-classical economics and finance are both mono-cultural and deceitful at the same time. Individualism, materialism, profit and wealth maximisation, utilitarianism, rationalism and consumerism are foundational values which are taught to novice young undergraduates and professionals as if they are a science. This science has been embedded deeply in business education for four decades and grown in influence and reach, whilst at the same time hiding the greed values behind a technical façade few can penetrate. Often these young people end up becoming converted to this 'religion' and convinced by its universalism and righteousness. In this sense, they are counter-cultural and systemic, shaping the worldviews of future leaders of finance in a deeply unsustainable way. I do not use the word deceitful lightly. Caging these assumptions and their resulting theories as science is deeply damaging to the students and society more generally. The interviews in this book tell a much more different and diverse story of how success comes not from individualism and greed but from patience and relationships, and by honouring the trust that people place in the finance expert.

The findings also suggest that we need to do much more research on the private clubs and institution networks where contemporary finance leaders hang out, exchange inside information and potentially collude to undermine civic society, the state and its public institutions[46]. Every lunchtime and evening, pubs in the City of London are heaving with finance traders and professionals – what are they talking about, and what information are they exchanging? When Big 4 accountants KPMG in the UK decided to open its own private members club in Mayfair[47], it was a physical and commercial statement that elite networking is a core source of revenue, even when the firm is ostensibly a regulator of corporate accounting and taxation. Beancounters are very careful about their spending, and this must have been seen as a high return investment. These networks[48] need to be exposed and the ways in which the information and collusion are embedded ought to be revealed to show how fallacious many of the assumptions of free and competitive markets, with rational independent agents are. There ought to be evidence of market rigging and expropriation in the very heart of these secret networks and meetings, including tax avoidance and evasion on a giant scale. At the Glasgow COP26 convention in 2021, two-thirds of the delegates were linked to fossil fuel companies[49] – either executives or lobbyists, helping turn the whole event into a 'blah-blah-blah' failure of epic proportions at a time when the world desperately needs sustainable finance leadership. The same was repeated at Davos.

Business does not have to be large to be profitable. Profits do not have to be enormous for a business to be successful. Balance of profits and purpose can help sustain a business and grow the capital, organically over time. But how? First and foremost, it needs to be valued to be retained and conserved. Today we often hear stories of large start-up venture capital in the tech sector, but also large blow-ups as the promised growth or technology does not materialise. Is it possible that too much capital at start is also a problem? Could it be wasted rather than invested? These are difficult questions. One thing is for certain – scarce capital leads to frugality, especially when one comes from a culture of simplicity and prudence. Thrift requires dogged perseverance which purpose can give. A frugal culture can be very helpful for sustained success.

BIO-DIVERSITY TRANSFORMS FINANCE

The climate crisis is forcing us to look anew at finance. This book has shown the significant weaknesses of a mono-cultural, ideological and technocratic approach to finance. It has also exposed, through examples and case studies, the significant global diversity of cultural practices. These have hitherto been marginalised by the search for and imposition of a global unified 'culturally neutralising' finance. These stories and examples are only scratching the surface of the vast ocean of finance bio-diversity. The contemporary fashion of a blindness against faith has prevented us from seeing and acknowledging this diversity and its winning narratives and sustainable practices.

Given our urgent climate crisis, we have to work with all cultures and communities to enable global transformation, even where we disagree with their beliefs or traditions. To enable this, the first step is to acknowledge the global cultural diversity and the importance of culture in shaping finance practice, good or bad. Even the small market trader may have a globally significant story of finance practice, which large corporations need to learn from. Their practice is rooted in their local community and the need to serve them quality products at a fair price, seeing the customer eye-to-eye when completing the transaction.

There are so many parallels between financial ecocide and what plantations and agri-business have done to the land[50]. In the name of profit and wealth maximisation, they have destroyed our most elemental soil, water and air quality systems. By promoting economies of scale, technology and capital took over farming practices, removing labour and encouraging chemical farming, which has irreversibly damaged soil and water. The billions of animals killed every year by the meat industry have also been processed through factory techniques, rather than organic methods where they have a free and healthy quality of life. In turn, it has turned the land into feedlots, where focus is on growing cheap grain to feed the animals and fatten them as quickly as possible. From my schooling in Kenya, I remember the emphasis on 'cash crops' like coffee and pyrethrum, which came to dominate farming, making Kenyan farmers vulnerable to global commodities prices, as people could not eat coffee or pyrethrum when hungry. Even what is grown became impacted by market forces rather than nutritional needs. In fact, when we observe the environmental damage of modern agribusiness, we can see firsthand the violence on earth endorsed and promoted by finance theory. We could not get any more visible and direct evidence of the havoc caused by finance. This explains why there is so little research on climate change in finance – the findings would point the finger at itself as being the primary culprit.

If we study the science of a tree – it takes water and nutrients from the soil and absorbs sunlight to make the choicest fruits, which it gives to others for free, without eating a single one. On a hot day, it absorbs the heat and gives shade to others lest they suffer. It has no desire to expand, control and dominate – in fact, it does not even move from its spot, ensuring that its footprint on planet earth is light and non-polluting. It does not need any finance to grow – nature is enough. Lack of words means a silence and humility that is evidence for all to see and learn from. On stormy days, it moves with the wind, trying its best to be firm and resilient. It does not discriminate among the birds it invites or the people it feeds. Even its own consumption of water and nutrients is within limits, preventing gluttony and obesity. It is simple, purposeful and upright, contented with its own nature and inner spirit. One of the problems of modernity is that we have become obsessed with large organisations and globalisation and forgotten the price this creates for social and natural harmony. We then spend all our time trying to make these global organisations responsible, taxable and accountable, whilst they do their best to slip away from any regulation. Trees are our evidence-based teachers, if only we care to learn from them and respect them. We certainly should not be chopping them just for our own greed and selfishness.

There are thousands of cultures and rooted, purposeful ethical finance practices in the world which have not been discussed in this book. All I can do is apologise and hope you will be empowered to write your own article and book on the unique story of your community and its cultural practices. We hope the stories have provided readers from different backgrounds the deeper nuances of culture and diversity and their ability to uplift the lives of many, rather than enrich a chosen few. This book was never intended to be comprehensive – instead its focus was more to shift the research and teaching in a new moral direction, one which does not exclude culture or belief, and instead opens up dialogue and enquiry. We have shown what finance can look like if it is underpinned by morality, community and tradition.

INCLUSIVE AND PURPOSEFUL FINANCE THEORY

This book shows that finance knowledge could be vastly improved by being more grounded and rooted in people's practices and experiences, which include their diverse cultures, faiths, traditions and beliefs. The severance of culture from finance and imposition of an aggressive, selfish, individualist and materialist narrative and ideology as science has been deeply damaging for human society and contributed to the Anthropocene. This theory is simply unsustainable and needs to be reformed from the ground up. Neo-liberalism and neo-classical economics have been a direct attack on culture, traditions and history, and its free-market triumphalism has failed with significant global economic, social and environmental losses. The chapters, narratives and examples in this book have shown that culture and traditions can reframe political economy and our theories of finance. The current attempts by financial institutions and corporations to revive the importance of 'good culture' will abjectly fail if there is no engagement with the true and living nature of cultural bio-diversity in shaping sustainable economic practices. At best, such attempts will be cosmetic and therefore temporary and fragile. Even politics needs to reconnect with culture and morality if we are to reform economic practice.

Furthermore, this approach has considerable implications for pedagogy and methods of teaching, and the spreading of an American version of finance to the world needs to be stopped at its tracks. This book calls for a paradigm shift, which has been brewing for some time and cites a wide range of alternative finance stories and research which could help make this shift. Living ethics, and not just abstract philosophy, instead of being marginal or an after-thought should now be made central to a new inclusive finance theory. The role of cultures and communities in building a 'thick morality' different from the academic and philosophical, secular morality that prevails, is critical to this new shift. Ethical education needs to begin with experiences, beliefs and dialogue and not what Aristotle said thousands of years ago, but how people live and relate to finance every day.

Positivist, technical and market triumphalist finance has deliberately disconnected itself from history, tradition and experience. This too is unsustainable. This book has shown the range and depth of experience that many cultures and communities have accumulated over hundreds, even thousands of years. These need to be revived and brought directly into the classroom. The phrase 'wisdom' has been deleted from finance – we urgently need to revive it. Given that money is an age-old social construct, its past follies and wisdom are critical to a more equal and peaceful future, where finance is a servant to society, never its master. This is not a specialist subject in economic history, but central to a fuller, richer understanding of finance, one which should be the pedagogical responsibility of all finance academics teaching in a business school.

Leadership and its study have been equally deleted from finance, resulting in the vast ocean of damage that has not just local but global ramifications – think of the 2008 Global Financial Crash as an example. For a sustainable world, leadership theory and education, from a normative perspective and designed to build a fairer and nature-friendly society is a must in every finance degree. The character of the finance professional and leader, not a code of ethics, matters in the way finance is delivered. We need to improve soulfulness and reflexivity and bring stories and case studies into the classroom about how such leadership helps build sustainable businesses. Even taking students on a field trip to meet with finance leaders, whether it will be in the local market, or the Citizens Advice Bureau, or an ethical Bank, will make a big difference to how they learn and explore the personal duties (not choices) expected of a finance professional – it could energise them and stop them from madly rushing into investment banking. As an academy, we could use such methods to make sustainable finance cool and worthy of passion, adventure and fun too.

The overwhelming focus in business schools all over the world on corporate finance and financial markets, and that even the finance of large corporations and multinationals, has also been shown to be deeply partial, misleading and unrepresentative of the bio-diversity of finance practice. It is deliberately impersonal, and that is unsustainable. Bakan (2020) through careful empirical analysis, shows how hypocritical, misleading and divisive modern multinationals are in the face of today's climate and equality challenges. He calls for systemic reforms and exposes the bankruptcy of our celebration of big corporations in business studies. For culture to change, finance needs to be personalised and communities of finance need to be understood and analysed. Theories need to be revised to be much more culturally inclusive and respectful of the diversity of finance practice in the real world. The blindness to religion and its cultural influence is also an ignorance which needs to be overcome.

Smaller family-owned businesses have been shown to have a much more diverse, organic and often caring and trust-inducing approach to finance which is nowhere in the curriculum. Micro-finance, which is the finance of tiny local businesses, run by men or women, often in developing countries, is rarely in the MBA curriculum yet its practice affects millions of lives. Here again, these enterprises meet local needs and boost social capital, rather than deplete it as big business often does. The training and educational role necessary for micro-finance, and more generally the financial literacy needs of the poor and marginalised, could really empower students to come up with creative solutions and see the transformation of real lives if they get involved in field projects[51].

With small business finance, students can see raw finance and also the huge challenges small businesses face in accessing finance even when they have positive net present value projects. Creative solutions built by cultures and communities to support one another could help revive the cultural understanding of finance. Even student finance could come onto the syllabus, helping learners understand basic processes like planning, budgeting and saving, including loan repayments and return on educational investment. Hopefully, this will help them see that education is more than a paper certificate – if they engage directly with the learning, they can get much more bang for their buck and it could raise the quality of their mental health and well-being. Furthermore, when finance is personalised, its value becomes real, and the ethical dimensions help them understand the fundamental links between finance and sustainability.

As an example, Martin Lewis[52] gives the following simple consumer advice to everyone – "Do I need it? Can I afford it? How will I pay for it?" – it is questionable how many times this kind of advice is discussed in a finance class anywhere in the world. Discipline in consumption and saving leads to sustainable finance, not technical knowledge about stocks and shares or bond markets, and debt structuring of corporations. Gorging on debt can lead to waste and indiscipline. The basic needs of a person are food, housing, clothing and good health and wellbeing. A pension is needed for later life. There is no need to make life complex and unnecessarily burdened by high finance such that we become servants to wealth rather than people who understand the limits of wealth and the pleasures we get without having money.

The siloed disconnection between finance, gambling, debt and mental health is also very disturbing and unsustainable. There is vast evidence of the emptiness of materialism and the need for people to have experiences of belonging and connectedness[53]. Speculation and Gambling are often highly addictive, leading to other related intoxications and a frenzy of mental illness and social isolation. Many graduates are still attracted to the high stakes and competitive investment banking industry without understanding the cultural nuances and potential stress that comes with the pay packet. When finance theory celebrates materialism and speculation, is it 'causing' a mental health epidemic? Therefore, should we not take responsibility and leadership in showing the world what a purposeful finance looks like? Even university students often experience mental health problems as a result of debt, so this anxiety will affect the impact of our teaching. Sustainable purpose requires us to break this silo and discuss the links between finance and mental health in our classrooms. It also means we need to revise our theories to make them more inclusive of the personal and social consequences of materialism, whether at the individual level or at the corporate level. Moral and cultural detachment in finance theory is a core part of our sustainability problem.

A technocratic finance does not want to acknowledge the importance of culture and experience. There is an in-built paralysis of the mind and intellect, which is most disturbing and unsustainable. Culture is deemed to be subjective by nature and therefore irrelevant to the pursuit of universal objective science. The reality is that this universal science has brought widespread inequality, gambling, booms and busts and species extinction. This book has shown how much is lost when this is done. At a time when we desperately need ethical pioneers, we cannot afford to do damage to students' own communitarian and cultural experiences. A boy scout who comes to university can say a lot about a sharing and caring finance, if he is allowed to discuss his experiences of those camping adventures. So much can often be achieved with so little, if there is a determination, a team spirit and camaraderie which many communities already have. At times, zero finance can be better than a bank loan or an inheritance. We must discuss the nature and limits of money in the finance classroom, a subject which should be compulsory in Finance 101, yet is totally absent everywhere in the world.

The content of the finance syllabus is critical to the training of future generations. This book has opened the door to a variety of different possibilities centred around tradition, community, experience and purpose which need to be explored further and converted into course material. This does not mean technical aspects of finance should be excluded. Instead, they can build upon some of these core foundational values, and students can explore the strengths and limits of calculation in shaping a sustainable society. Imaginative new and diverse models of sustainable finance and purpose can emerge from such dialogues, giving learners much-needed empowerment, rather than the disempowerment that is so common in technical approaches to finance. The social and mental health consequence of gambling and speculation should also be brought into the classroom and also the 'swimming with sharks' culture of banking. Instead of education being top-down and disempowering, which so much of technical finance is today, it can be more interactive and engaging. Students could be asked to do sustainable finance research projects on a variety of themes, encouraging them to share what they have gathered from the field and their own family and cultural histories.

Over to you to continue this story ….If you share it with me, I could share it with the world.

Notes

1 Jackson & Parry, 2011.
2 Collinson and Tourish, 2015.
3 Pfeffer (2015) is a bestselling account of the false pretences and rhetoric of business leaders, especially in the western world. Fortunately for this book, we have interviewed leaders from Africa and Asia too and shown how different their perspectives have been.
4 Havel (1997) is a brilliant book on the politics of the possible.
5 Harrison (2010) and Harvey (2007).
6 Whyte and Wiegratz (2016) argue that a 'moral' economy of fraud was created by neoliberalism and its global export.
7 Harvey (2007).
8 Dar et al (2020).
9 See Shaxson (2012), Shaxson (2018) and Bullough (2018).
10 Zingales (2015).
11 See Collinson and Tourish (2015), Pfeffer (2015), Parker (2018a, b) and Dar et al (2020).
12 Sacks (1990) – the first BBC Reith Lecture, the Demoralisation of Discourse elaborates on such thinking very eloquently.
13 See Gladstein and Meadowcroft (2009).
14 Cocks (2020) is a comprehensive analysis of her life and influential legacy.
15 Beets (2015) details the growing influence of Rand's philosophy on cash-strapped Universities. There is little resistance to its ideological bias.
16 Diaz-Rainey et al (2017).
17 British Academy (2021).
18 Edmans (2020).
19 Kinley (2018) articulates this connection very well and calls Finance a 'Necessary Evil'.
20 Sacks (1990).
21 Sacks (2005) is a brilliant account of the richness of human diversity and belief in helping build a sustainable society.
22 Tyrie et al (2013) and Angelides (2011) strongly rebuke banking culture as a key contributor to the global financial crash, and this has provoked a new rhetoric on good culture. The UK Financial Reporting Council (2021) also recommends culture change as central to corporate governance and reform. It makes a small reference to equality and diversity, and no mention of faith.
23 Sacks (2003), Chapter 3.
24 See Boatright (1999), Hendry (2013), Santoro and Strauss (2013) and McPhail and Walters (2009).
25 Boyce (2008) exposes these dilemmas very well. Contemporary approaches to accounting ethics education make the situation worse, not better. Academics need to engage with students own' cultures and beliefs and deal with the structural factors which influence business finance and accounting which are beyond individual ethics or control, but often contribute to deeply unfair outcomes.
26 Gu and Neesham (2014) show that engaging business students with personal beliefs and identity lead to deeper ethical analysis and moral engagement.
27 See ICAEW (2020).
28 See McKenna (2019) about the KPMG US ethics exam teaching scandal, where partners were also involved.
29 See Beck (1992) for a comprehensive analysis of the perils of relying on scientific expertise alone.
30 See Mention (2019) for an evaluation of the future of fintech.
31 See Sikka (2015).
32 See Brooks et al (2019) and Brooks and Schopohl (2018).
33 See Gendron (2013) and Gendron and Smith-Lacroix (2013).
34 Khurana (2007).

35 Parker and Guthrie (2010).
36 AACSB – 'Our commitment to diversity, equity, inclusion and well-being', December 2021, www.aacsb.edu/diversity.
37 Edmans (2020).
38 Khosla was interviewed by Stanford graduates in 2015 – 'Failure does not matter. Success matters.' (YouTube).
39 See Chapter 18 by C.M. Norris in Bouckaert and Heuvel (2019).
40 Phipps (2012) has developed a conceptual framework on this and there are whole journals dedicated to spirituality in management (e.g. Journal of Management, Spirituality and Religion). Sedgmore (2021) develops a unique framework for spiritual leadership beyond patriarchy, which is holistic in its design and transformational in its capability.
41 Diaz-Rainey et al (2017).
42 Tax Justice Network (2015) is a good account of the critical importance of tax in a sustainable society. Website is www.taxjustice.net.
43 Shaxson (2012) and Shaxson (2018).
44 Sikka (2008a).
45 McDonald and Robinson (2009).
46 Hall (2009) focuses on investment banking elite networks in London and finds them to be very powerful, global and resilient, easily able to transform themselves to new scenarios and innovations. Glattfelder and Battiston (2019) find that corporate power networks are surprisingly resilient to booms and shocks, and command considerable influence. Vitali et al (2011) expose a core network of MNC's which are highly influential, and 75% of these are financial intermediaries, showing the might of finance and its influence.
47 Brooks (2018) begins with the story of this unique club and the fine foods and wines served at the table, no expense spared.
48 Bullough (2018) explains the concept of 'Moneyland' which is everywhere and nowhere for the networked plutocrats, who amass great wealth and fortunes free from political control or ethical conscience. Tett (2010) also describes many international meetings and conferences among elite financiers who spoke their own technocratic language.
49 503 lobbyists according to Global Witness press release of November 8, 2021.
50 Whyte (2020) and Ekins et al (1992).
51 It is embarrassing to note that in the UK, despite thousands of professors and lecturers in accounting and finance, the public education role of finance is fulfilled by Martin Lewis. Lewis is a social and media entrepreneur, who is not a qualified finance professional and began a website 'Money Saving Expert' which is now the go-to place for all kinds of personal financial information and advice. His advice is very professional, trustworthy and consumer oriented, exposing the tricks used by Banks and Institutions to coax them into selling poor products or exploiting them through hidden charges. The website is www.moneysavingexpert.com and he has also started a mental health charity exposing the deep connections between debt and mental health. The charity is trying to alleviate the harm to families ruined by debt.
52 www.moneysavingexpert.com.
53 See James (2007), Prasad (2012), Sweet et al (2013) and Gathergood (2012).

BIBLIOGRAPHY

AACSB. (2016) *A Collective Vision for Business Education*, Florida: AACSB, www.aacsb.edu.

Abbott A. (1988) *The System of Professions – An Essay on the Division of Expert Labour*, Chicago: University of Chicago Press.

Acemoglu D and Robinson J. (2012) *Why Nations Fail: The Origins of Power, Prosperity, and Poverty*, New York: Crown Business.

Addison S and Mueller F. (2015) The dark side of the profession – The Big 4 and tax avoidance, *Accounting, Auditing & Accountability Journal*, 28(2):1263–1290.

Adhariani D. (2020) The influence of the ASEAN economic community on the future of the management accounting profession, *Meditari Accountancy Research*, 28(4):587–611.

Admati A and Hellwig M. (2013) *The Bankers New Clothes*, Princeton: Princeton University Press.

Aggarwal R, Faccio M, Guedhami O and Kwok C. (2016) Culture and finance – An introduction, *Journal of Corporate Finance*, 41:466–474.

Akram T and Rashid S. Eds (2020) *Faith, Finance and Economy – Beliefs and Economic Well-Being*, London: Palgrave Macmillan, p 239.

Alpers E. and Goswami C. (2019) *Transregional Trade and Traders – Situating Gujarat in the Indian Ocean from the Early Times to 1900*, Oxford: Oxford University Press.

Angelides P. et al (2011) *The Financial Crisis Enquiry Report*, New York: Financial Crisis Inquiry Commission, p 633.

Annisette M. (2003) The colour of accountancy: Examining the salience of race in a professionalisation project, *Accounting, Organizations and Society*, 28(7–8):639–674.

Appiah KA. (2016) *Mistaken Identities*, BBC Reith Lectures, www.bbc.co.uk.

Armstrong K. (2006) *The Great Transformation: The World in the Time of Buddha, Socrates, Confucius and Jeremiah*, London: Atlantic Books.

Arnold P. (2009) Global financial crisis: The challenge to accounting research, *Accounting, Organisations and Society*, 34:803–809.

Arnold P. (2012) The political economy of financial harmonisation: The East Asian financial crisis and the rise of international accounting standards, *Accounting, Organisations & Society*, 37:361–381.

Aronowitz S. (2000) *The Knowledge Factory: Dismantling the Corporate University and Creating True Higher Learning*, Boston, MA: Beacon Press.

Augar P. (2005) *The Greed Merchants*, London: Penguin.

Augar P. (2019) *The Bank that Lived a Little – Barclays in the Age of the Very Free Market*, London: Penguin Books.

Avakian S and Roberts J. (2012) Whistleblowers in organisations: Prophets at work? *Journal of Business Ethics*, 110:71–84.

Azevedo M. (2019) Geo-economy and History, in Nnadozie E. and Jerome A. Eds, *African Economic Development,* Bingley: Emerald Publishing Limited, Chapter 4, pp 59–76.

Bakan J. (2004*) The Corporation: The Pathological Pursuit of Profit and Power*, New York: Free Press.

Bakan J. (2020) *The New Corporation – How "Good" Corporations Are Bad for Democracy*, New York: Knopf Doubleday, p 240.

Baláž V, Williams AM, Moravčíková K and Chrančoková M. (2021) What competences, which migrants? Tacit and explicit knowledge acquired via migration, *Journal of Ethnic and Migration Studies*, 47(8):1758–1774.

Banga A. (2017) *A Leader Listens*, Penguin-India.

Beattie V. (2014) Accounting narratives and the narrative turn in accounting research: Issues, theory, methodology, methods and a research framework, *British Accounting Review*, 46(2):111–134.

Beck U. (1992) *Risk Society: Towards a New Modernity*, London: Sage.

Beets S. (2015) BB&T, atlas shrugged, and the ethics of corporation influence on college curricula, *Journal of Academic Ethics*, 13:311–344.

Black J. (2014) Learning from regulatory disasters, *Policy Quarterly*, 10(3):3–11.

Blakeley G. (2019) *Stolen – How to Save the World from Financialisation*, London: Watkins Media Limited, p 316.

Boatright J. (1999) *Ethics in Finance*, Oxford: Blackwell.

Bouckaert S and Heuvel L. (2019) *Servant Leadership, Social Entrepreneurship and the Will to Serve*, London: Palgrave Macmillan.

Boyce G. (2008) The social relevance of ethics education in a globalising era – From individual dilemmas to systemic crises, *Critical Perspectives on Accounting*, 19: 255–290.

Boyer R. (2005) From shareholder value to CEO power: The paradox of the 1990's, *Competition and Change*, 9:7–47.

Brady Report (1988) *The October 1987 Market Break*, New York: Division of Market Regulation, United States Securities and Exchange Commission.

Brealey R, Myers S and Allen F. (2014) *Principles of Corporate Finance, 11th* Edition, New York: McGraw-Hill.

British Academy (2021) *Policy and Practice for Purposeful Business*, London: The British Academy, p 60.

British Business Bank. (2020) Alone, Together – Entrepreneurship and Diversity in the UK, Oliver Wyman and British Business Bank.

Brooks C and Schopohl L. (2018) Topics and trends in finance research: What is published, who publishes it and what gets cited? *The British Accounting Review*, 50(6):615–637.

Brooks C, Fenton E, Schopohl L. and Walker J. (2019) Why does research in finance have so little impact? *Critical Perspectives on Accounting*, 58:24–52.

Brooks R. (2014) *The Great Tax Robbery*, London: One World.

Brooks R. (2018) *Beancounters – The Triumph of Accountants and How They Broke Capitalism*, London: Atlantic Books.

Brown G. (2006) Speech at Mansion House, London, 22nd June.

Brunsson N. (2002) *The Organisation of Hypocrisy*, Copenhagen: Copenhagen Business School Press.

Bukovinsky DM. (2019) Handelsbanken – A radical business model transforms a conservative bank, *GBOE*, 39(1):14–20.

Bullough O. (2018) *Moneyland: Why Thieves and Crooks Now Rule the World and How to Take It Back*, London: Profile Books.

Butcher S. (2018) Maybe You Should Work for the CFA Institute? Executive Pay There Is Pretty Huge, efinancialcareers, 17ᵗʰ August, efinancialcareers.co.uk.

Carnegie G and Napier C. (2010) Traditional accountants and business professionals-portraying the accounting profession after Enron, *Accounting, Organisations & Society*, 35:360–376.

Carney M. (2021) *BBC Reith Lectures – How We Get What We Value*, www.bbc.co.uk.

CFA Institute. (2019) *Code of Ethics and Standards of Professional Conduct*, www.cfainstitute.org.

Chabrak N and Craig R. (2013) Student imaginings, cognitive dissonance and critical thinking, *Critical Perspectives on Accounting*, 24(2):91–104.

Chang H. (2011) *23 Things They Don't Tell You About Capitalism*, London: Penguin Books, p 286.

Cocks N. Ed. (2020) *Questioning Ayn Rand – Subjectivity, Political Economy and the Arts*, London: Palgrave Macmillan.

Coffee J. (2002) Understanding Enron: It's about the Gatekeepers, Stupid, *Columbia Law School*, Working Paper No. 207.

Coggan P. (2012) *Paper Promises – Money, Debt and the New World Order*, London: Penguin.

Cohan W. (2011) *Money and Power – How Goldman Sachs Came to Rule the World*, New York: Penguin.

Collier P and Kay J. (2020) *Greed Is Dead – Politics after Individualism'*, UK: London: Allen Lane.

Collinson D and Tourish D. (2015) Teaching leadership critically: New directions for leadership pedagogy, *Academy of Management Learning & Education*, 14(4):576–594.

Cooper D and Robson K. (2006) Accounting, professions and regulation: Locating sites of professionalism, *Accounting, Organisations and Society*, 31(4/5):415–444.

Cooper D, Everett J and Neu D. (2005) Financial scandals, accounting change and the role of accounting academics: A perspective from North America, *European Accounting Review*, 14(2): 373–382.

Covey S. (1989) *The Seven Habits of Highly Effective People*, Florence: Free Press.

Dalrymple W. (2019) *The Anarchy – The Relentless Rise of the East India Company*, London: Bloomsbury.

Daly B and Schuler D. (1998) Redefining a certified public accounting firm, *accounting, Organisations and Society*, 23(5/6):549–567.

Daly H and Cobb J. (1994) *For the Common Good – Redirecting the Economy Toward Community, Environment and a Sustainable Future*, 2nd Edition, Boston: Beacon Press.

Dar S, Liu H, Dy A and Brewis D. (2020) The business school is racist: Act up!, *Organisation*, 28(4):1–12.

Darcy K. (2010) Ethical leadership – The past, present and the future, *International Journal of Disclosure and Governance*, 7(3):198–212.

Das S. (2011) *Extreme Money – The Masters of the Universe and the Cult of Risk*, New York: Wiley.

Davies N. (2008) *Flat Earth News*, London: Chatto & Windus.

De Burgh H. Ed (2008) *Investigative Journalism*, London: Routledge.

Deegan C and Ward A. (2013) *Financial Accounting and Reporting – An International Approach*, London: McGraw-Hill.

Desai K. (2000) *A Pinnacle of Spirituality – The Inspirational Life of Shrimad Rajchandra*, Ahmedabad, India: Raj Saubhag Satsang Mandal.

Dewing I and Russell P.O. (2014) Whistleblowing, governance and regulation before the financial crisis: The case of HBOS, *Journal of Business Ethics*, 134:155–169.

Diaz-Rainey I, Robertson B and Wilson C. (2017) Stranded research? Leading finance journals are silent on climate change, *Climatic Change*, 143:243–260.

Dixson A. and Rousseau C. (2006) *Critical Race Theory in Education*, Oxford: Routledge.

Dodd N. (2014) *The Social Life of Money*, Princeton University Press.

Donaldson P. (1984) *Economics of the Real World*, 3rd Edition, London: Penguin.

Douglas M. (1987) *How Institutions Think*, London: Routledge and Kegan Paul.

Douglas M. (1992) *Risk and Blame*, London: Routledge.

Douglas M. and Wildavsky A. (1982) *Risk and Culture*, Berkeley, CA: University of California Press.

Dwyer R. (2018) Credit, debt, and inequality, *Annual Review of Sociology*, 44:237–261.

Eales B. (1994) *Financial Risk Management*, London: McGraw-Hill.

Economist. (2015) *Going Global – Secrets of the World's best business people*, 16th December, www.economist.com.

Edmans A. (2020) *Grow the Pie – How Great Companies Deliver Both Purpose and Profit*, Cambridge: Cambridge University Press.

Eeckhoudt L and Gollier C. (1995) *Risk - Evaluation, Management and Sharing*, Wheatsheaf, UK: Harvester.

Eisenstein C. (2021) *Money, Gift and Society in the Age of Transition*, Berkeley: North Atlantic Books.

Ekins P, Hillman M. and Hutchison R. (1992) *Wealth beyond Measure – An Atlas of New Economics*, London: Gaia Books.

Elkind P and McLean B. (2003) *The Smartest Guys in the Room – The Amazing Rise and Scandalous Fall of Enron*, London: Penguin Books.

Elkington J. (1999) *Cannibals with Forks – The Triple Bottom Line of 21st Century Business*, Oxford: Capstone.

Ellis E. (2018) *Anthropocene: A Very Short Introduction*, Vol. 1, Oxford: Oxford University Press.

Empson L. (2017) *Leading Professionals – Power, Politics and Prima Donnas*, Oxford: Oxford University Press.

Engelen E, Erturk I, Froud J, Johal S, Leaver A, Moran M and Williams K. (2012) Misrule of experts? The financial crisis as elite debacle, *Economy and Society*, 41(3):360–382.

Erturk I, Froud J, Johal S, Leaver A and Williams K. (2007) Against agency: A positional critique, *Economy and Society*, 36:51–77.

Erturk I, Froud J, Johal S, Leaver A and Williams K. (2008) *Financialisation at Work*, London: Routledge.

Ferguson C. (2010) *'Inside Job'*, Feature Documentary on the 2008 Crash, Director: Charles Ferguson, 108 minutes, USA.

Ferguson C. (2012) *Inside Job – The Financiers Who Pulled off the Heist of the Century*, London: One World.

Ferguson J, Collinson D, Power D and Stevenson L. (2009) Constructing meaning in the service of power: An analysis of the typical modes of ideology in accounting textbooks, *Critical Perspectives on Accounting*, 20(8):896–909.

Ferguson N. (2012) *The Ascent of Money – A Financial History of the World*, New York: Penguin.

Feyeraband P. (1975) *Against Method: Outline of an Anarchist Theory of Knowledge*, New York: New Left Books.

Financial Inclusion Commission. (2015) *Financial Inclusion – Improving the financial health of a nation*, Financial Inclusion Commission, UK.

Financial Reporting Council. (2018) Audit Culture Thematic Review, May 2018, UK.

Financial Reporting Council. (2021) *Creating Positive Culture – Opportunities and Challenges*, December, p 43.

Finel-Honigman I. (2010) *A Cultural History of Finance*, London: Routledge, p 338.

Fleming P and Jones M. (2012) *The End of Corporate Social Responsibility – Crisis and Critique*, London: Sage.

Folkman P, Froud J, Johal S and Williams K. (2007) Working for themselves? Capital market intermediaries and present day capitalism, *Business History*, 49:552–572.

Fortado L. (2015) Kweku Adoboli – A Rogue Traders Tale, *Financial Times*, October 22.

Frankfurter G and McGoun E. (2002). *From Individualism to the Individual – Ideology and Inquiry in Financial Economics*. Farnham: Ashgate Publishing, p 499.

Frankopan P. (2017) *The Silk Roads – A New History of the World*, London: Vintage.

Fraser I. (2015) *Shredded: Inside RBS – The Bank That Broke Britain*, Edinburgh: Birlinn.

Friedman B. (2021) *Religion and the Rise of Capitalism*, New York: Penguin Random House.

Froud J, Johal S, Leaver A and Williams K. (2006) *Financialisation and Strategy: Narrative and Numbers*, London: Routledge.

Gandhi MK. (1982) *An Autobiography – The Story of My Experiments with Truth*, London: Penguin Books.

Gathergood J. (2012) Debt and depression: Causal links and social norm effects, *The Economic Journal*, 122:1094–114.

Gendron Y and Smith-Lacroix J. (2013) The global financial crisis: Essay on the possibility of substantive change in the discipline of finance, *Critical Perspectives on Accounting*, 30:83–101.

Gendron Y. (2013) Accounting academia and the threat of the paying off mentality, *Critical Perspectives on Accounting*, 26:168–176.

Germain R. (2010) *Global Politics and Financial Governance*, London: Palgrave Macmillan.

Gladstein M and Meadowcroft J. (2009) *Ayn Rand*, Bloomsbury Academic.

Glattfelder J and Battiston S (2019) The architecture of power: patterns of disruption and stability in the global ownership network. Working Paper, *University of Zurich, Zürich, Switzerland*.

Goodhart C. (2010) How should we regulate the financial sector, *The Future of Finance*, LSE – www.futureoffinance.org.uk.

Goodman P. (2022) *Davos Man – How the Billionaires Devoured the World*, New York, NY: Harper Collins.

Goyal Y and Heine K. (2021) Why do informal markets remain informal: The role of tacit knowledge in an Indian footwear cluster, *Journal of Evolutionary Economics*, 31:639–659.

Graeber D. (2014) *Debt: The First 5000 Years*, Brooklyn: Melville House.

Gray J. (1998) *False Dawn – The Delusions of Global Capitalism*, London: Granta Books.

Gray R and Bebbington J. (2001) *Accounting for the Environment*, 2nd Edition, London: Sage Publications.

Gray R, Bebbington J and Gray S. (2010) *Social and Environmental Accounting*, London: Sage Publications, p 664.

Gray R. (1992) Accounting and environmentalism – An exploration of the challenge of gently accounting for accountability, transparency and sustainability, *Accounting, Organisations and Society*, 17(5):399–425.

Gray R. (2013) Back to basics – What do we mean by environmental (and social) accounting and what is it for? A reaction to Thornton, *Critical Perspectives on Accounting*, 24:459–468.

Gu J and Neesham C. (2014) Moral identity as leverage point in teaching business ethics, *Journal of Business Ethics*, 124:527–536.

Hall PA and Soskice D Eds (2001) *Varieties of Capitalism. The Institutional Foundations of Comparative Advantage*, Oxford: Oxford University Press.

Hall S. (2009) Financialised elites and the changing nature of finance capitalism: Investment bankers in London's financial district, *Competition & Change*, 13(2):173–189.

Hanlon G. (1994), *The Commercialisation of Accountancy*, London: Macmillan Press, p 265.

Harari Y. (2015) *Sapiens – A Brief History of Humankind*, New York: Vintage.

Hare RD. (1996) *Without Conscience: The Disturbing World of the Psychopaths Among Us*, New York: The Guilford Press.

Harney S and Dunne S. (2013) More than nothing? Accounting, business and management studies and the research audit, *Critical Perspectives on Accounting*, 24:338–349.

Harrison G. (2010) *Neo-liberal Africa – The Impact of Global Social Engineering*, London: Zed Books.

Harvey D. (2007) *A Brief History of Neo-Liberalism*, Oxford: Oxford University Press.

Havel V. (1997) *The Art of the Impossible – Politics as Morality in Practice*, New York: Knopf, p 273.

Hawken P. (1994) *The Ecology of Commerce: A Declaration of Sustainability*, London: Phoenix.

Heffernan M. (2011) *Wilful Blindness – Why We Ignore the Obvious at Our Peril*, New York: Walker & Co.

Hendry J. (2013) *Ethics and Finance: An Introduction*, Cambridge: Cambridge University Press.

Hertz N. (2001) *The Silent Takeover – Global Capitalism and The Death of Democracy*, London: William Heinemann.

Hillier DPSPS, Ross R, Westerfield J, Jaffe B and Jordan (2016) *Corporate Finance*, 3rd Edition, London: McGraw-Hill.

Hines RD. (1988) Financial accounting: In communicating reality, we construct reality, *Accounting, Organizations and Society*, 13(3):251–261.

Holland D and Albrecht C. (2013) The worldwide academic field of business ethics: Scholars perceptions of the most important issues, *Journal of Business Ethics*, 117: 777–788.

Hopper T. (2013) Making accounting degrees fit for a university, *Critical Perspectives on Accounting*, 24(2):127–135.

Hopwood A. (1998) Exploring the modern audit firm: An introduction, *Accounting, Organisations and Society*, 23(5/6):515–516.

Hopwood A. (2007) Whither accounting research? *The Accounting Review*, 82(5):1365–1374.

Hopwood A. (2008) Changing pressures on the research process: On trying to research in an age when curiosity in not enough, *European Accounting Review*, 17(1):87–96.

Hopwood A. (2009) Exploring the interface between accounting and finance, *Accounting, Organisations and Society*, 34:549–550.

Huhn M. (2014) You reap what you sow – How MBA programs undermine ethics, *Journal of Business Ethics*, 121:527–541.

Humphrey C, Loft A and Woods M. (2009) The global audit profession and the international financial architecture: Understanding regulatory relationships at a time of financial crisis, *Accounting, Organisations and Society*, 34(6/7):810–825.

Humphrey C. (2008) Auditing research: A review across the disciplinary divide, *Accounting, Auditing & Accountability Journal*, 21(2):170–203.

Hutton W. (2010) *Them and Us*, London: Little Brown.

ICAEW (2020) *ICAEW Code of Ethics*, London: ICAEW, p 204, www.icaew.com.

Innes A. (2021) Corporate State Capture: The degree to which the British state is porous to business interests is exceptional among established democracies, *LSE Politics and Policy blog*, April 16.

Jackson B and Parry K (2011) *A Very Short Fairly Interesting and Reasonably Cheap Book About Studying Leadership*, 2nd Edition, London: Sage.

James O. (2007) *Affluenza – How to Be Successful and Stay Sane*, Vermillion.

Jensen M and Meckling W. (1976) Theory of the firm: Managerial behaviour, agency costs and ownership structure, *Journal of Financial Economics*, 3:305–360.

Kamla R. (2015) Critical Muslim intellectuals thought: Possible contributions to the development of emancipatory accounting thought, *Critical Perspectives on Accounting*, 31:64–74.

Kandola B. (2018) *Racism at Work – The Danger of Indifference*, Oxford: Pearn Kandola Publishing.

Katona K. (2020) Is lack of morality an explanation for the economic and financial crisis? A catholic point of view, *Journal of International Advanced Economic Research*, 26:407–418.

Kay J. (2011) The map is not the territory – an essay on the state of economics, *Institute for New Economic Thinking*.

Kay J. (2015) *Other People's Money – Masters of the Universe or Servants of the People?* London: Profile Books.

Kellaway L. (2015) 'Hands Up if you can say what your company's values are', *Financial Times*, October 4.

Kets de Vries M. (2012) The Psychopath in the C Suite: Redefining the SOB, Insead Working Paper no. 119.

Khurana R. (2007) *From Higher Aims to Hired Hands: The Social Transformation of American Business Schools and the Unfulfilled Promise of Management as a Profession*, Princeton, NJ: Princeton University Press.

Kinley D. (2018) *Necessary Evil – How to Fix Finance by Saving Human Rights*, Oxford: Oxford University Press.

Komori N. (2015) Beyond the globalisation paradox: Towards the sustainability of diversity in accounting research, *Critical Perspectives on Accounting*, 26:141–156.

Korten DC. (1995) *When Corporations Rule the World*, London: Earthscan.

Kynaston D. (2011) *City of London – The History*, Chatto & Windus.

Lail B, MacGregor J, Marcum M and Stuebs M. (2017) Virtuous professionalism in accountants to avoid fraud and to restore financial reporting, *Journal of Business Ethics*, 140:687–704.

Lakshmi G. (2018) Gekko and black swans: Finance theory in UK undergraduate curricula, *Critical Perspectives on Accounting*, 52:35–47.

Latour B. (2014) *On Some of the Affects of Capitalism*, Copenhagen: Royal Academy.

Legrain P. (2007) *Immigrants – Your Country Needs Them*, Boston: Little Brown, p 374.

Lehman CR. (2005) Accounting and the public interest: All the world's a stage, *Accounting, Auditing and Accountability Journal*, 18(5):675–689.

Lehman CR. (2013) Knowing the unknowable and contested terrains in accounting, *Critical Perspectives on Accounting*, 24:136–144.

Lehman G and Mortensen C. (2021) Finance, nature and ontology, *Topoi*, 40:715–724.

Lewis A. (2020) *Counting Black and White Beans – Critical Race Theory in Accounting*, Bingley: Emerald Publishing.

Lewis M. (2008) *The Big Short*, London: Penguin Publishing.

Lewis M. (2011) *Boomerang – The Biggest Bust*, London: Penguin Books.

Lewis M. (2014) *Flash Boys – Cracking the Money Code*, London: Penguin Books.

Lewis M. (2016) Debt and Mental Illness are a Marriage made in Hell – This is How to Cope, *Daily Telegraph*, 5th April.

Lombardi L. (2016) Disempowerment And empowerment of accounting: An indigenous accounting context, *Accounting, Auditing, & Accountability*, 29(8):1320–1341.

Looft M. (2014) *Inspired Finance – The Role of Faith in Microfinance and International Economic Development*, London: Palgrave MacMillan.

Luyendijk J. (2015) *Swimming With Sharks: My Journey into the World of Bankers*, London: Guardian/Faber&Faber.

Mackenzie D. (2006) *An Engine, Not a Camera – How Financial Models Shape Markets*, Cambridge: MIT Press, p 377.

Manning P. (2013) Financial journalism, news sources and the banking crisis, *Journalism*, 14(2):173–189.

Marett P. (1988) *Meghji Pethraj Shah – His Life and Achievements*, Bharatiya Vidya Bhavan, www.meghraj.com.

Marques J. (2013) Understanding the strengths of gentleness – Soft skills leadership on the rise, *Journal of Business Ethics*, 116:163–71.

Mc Barnet D and Whelan C. (1992) International corporate finance and the challenge of creative compliance, in Fingleton J. Ed, *The Internationalisation of Capital Markets and the Regulatory Response*, London: Graham & Trotman, pp 129–42.

Mc Fall et al (2009a) Banking Crisis: Reforming Corporate Governance and the City, House of Commons Treasury Committee, HC 519.

Mc Fall et al (2009b) 'Banking Crisis: Regulation and Supervision', House of Commons, HC767.

McBarnet D and Whelan C. (1999) *Creative Accounting and the Cross-Eyed Javelin Thrower*, Oxford: Wiley.

McDonald L and Robinson P. (2009) *A Colossal Failure of Common Sense – The Incredible Inside Story of the Collapse of Lehman Brothers*, Princeton: Ebury Press.

McGoun E and Zielonka P. (2006) The platonic foundations of finance and the interpretation of finance models, *Journal of Behavioral Finance*, 7(1):43–57.

McGoun E. (1995) The history of risk measurement, *Critical Perspectives on Accounting*, 16:511–532.

McGoun E. (1997) Hyperreal finance, *Critical Perspectives on Accounting*, 18:97–122.

McKenna F. (2011) The Button Down Mafia: How the Public Accounting Firms Run a Racket on Investors and Thrive While Their Clients Fail, retheauditors.com.

McKenna F. (2019) The KPMG Cheating Scandal was much more Widespread than originally thought, *Market Watch*, June 18.

McKernan JF. (2011) Deconstruction and the responsibilities of the accounting academic, *Critical Perspectives on Accounting*, 22:698–713.

McLean B. (2017) How Wells Fargo's Cutthroat Corporate Culture Allegedly drove Bankers to Fraud, *Vanity Fair*, May 31, Summer Issue.

McManus (2014) Chinese walls' not the best solution for KPMG, *Financial Times*, March 3.

McPhail K and Walters D. (2009) *Accounting and Business Ethics – An Introduction*, London: Routledge.

McSweeney B. (2009) The roles of financial asset market failure denial and the economic crisis: Reflections on accounting and financial theories and practices, *Accounting, Organisations & Society*, 34:835–848.

Mea W and Sims R. (2019) Human dignity-centred business ethics – A conceptual framework for business leaders, *Journal of Business Ethics*, 160:53–69.

Mele D, Rosanas J and Fontrodona J. (2016) Ethics in finance and accounting – An introduction, *Journal of Business Ethics*, 140:609–613.

Mention A-L. (2019) The future of fintech, *Research-Technology Management*, 62(4):59–63.

Meyer E. (2015) *The Culture Map*, New York: Public Affairs.

Millo Y and MacKenzie D. (2009) The usefulness of inaccurate models: Towards an
understanding of the emergence of financial risk management, *Accounting, Organisations
and Society*, 34:638–653.

Minhat M and Dzolkarnaini Eds. (2021) *Ethical Discourse in Finance – Interdisciplinary and
Diverse Perspectives*, London: Palgrave Macmillan.

Mitchell A and Sikka P (2011), *The Pin-Stripe Mafia: How Accountancy Firms Destroy
Societies*, Basildon: Association for Accountancy & Business Affairs, p 72.

Molisa P. (2011) A spiritual reflection on emancipation and accounting, *Critical Perspectives
on Accounting*, 22:453–484.

Monbiot G. (2000) *The Corporate Takeover of Britain*, London: Macmillan.

Moore M. (2001) *Stupid White Men*, London: Penguin.

Moore P and Haworth M. (2015) *Crash, Bank, Wallop – The Memoirs of the HBOS
Whistleblower*, York: New Wilberforce Media, p 419.

Muradoglu G and Harvey N. (2012) Behavioural finance: The role of psychological
factors in financial decisions, *Review of Behavioral Finance*, 4(2):68–80.

Murphy R. (2015) *The Joy of Tax*, London: Transworld Publishers.

Murty KS and Vohra A. (1990) *Radhakrishnan: His Life and Ideas*, New York: SUNY Press.

Nadler C and Breuer W. (2019) Cultural finance as a research field – An evaluative
Survey, *Journal of Business Ethics*, 89:191–220.

Nielsen R. (2016) Action research as an ethics praxis method, *Journal of Business Ethics*,
135:419–428.

Nnadozie E and Jerome A. Eds (2019) *African Economic Development*, Bingley: Emerald
Publishing.

Oates G and Dias R. (2016) Including ethics in banking and finance programs – Teaching
'we shouldn't win at any cost, *Education + Training*, 58(1):94–111.

ODwyer M. and Edgecliff-Johnson A. (2021) Big 4 Accounting firms rush to join the
ESG bandwagon, *Financial Times*, August 30.

Oğuz F and Elif Şengün A. (2011) Mystery of the unknown: Revisiting tacit knowledge
in the organizational literature, *Journal of Knowledge Management*, 15(3):445–461.

Oswald M. (2017) *The Spiders Web: Britain's Second Empire*, You Tube, https://www.
youtube.com/watch?v=np_ylvc8Zj8 accessed 20/4/2020.

Palan R, Murphy R and Chavagneux C. (2010) *How Globalisation Really Works*, New
York: Cornell University Press, p 270.

Palma S. (2022) Tim Leissner's Testimony in 1MDB trial shines light on vast fraud,
Financial Times, March 15.

Parker L and Guthrie J. (2010) Business schools in an age of globalisation, *Accounting,
Auditing & Accountability Journal*, 23:5–13.

Parker L and Guthrie J. (2014) Addressing directions in interdisciplinary accounting
research, *Accounting, Auditing and Accountability Journal*, 27(8):1218–1226.

Parker L. (2008) Interpreting interpretive accounting research, *Critical Perspectives on
Accounting*, 19:909–914.

Parker L. (2011) University corporatisation – Driving redefinition, *Critical Perspectives on
Accounting*, 22:434–450.

Parker M. (2018a) *Shut Down the Business School*, London: Pluto.

Parker M. (2018b) Why we should bulldoze the business school, *Long read – The Guardian*,
www.guardian.co.uk.

Patel M. (2021) The Influence of Culture on Business Communities of India with Special Reference to Jain Community of Gujarat, in Bareja-Starzyńska A. and Akademia Nauk P. Ed, *Challenges of Interdisciplinary and Multidisciplinary Approach. New Horizons in Oriental Studies, Prace Orientalistyczne series*, Warsaw: Elipsa, pp 201–228.

PCES. (2014) Economics, Education and Unlearning, Post-Crash Economics Society, University of Manchester.

Perlman M. (1996) Jews and Contributions to Economics: A Bicentennial Review. In *The Character of Economic Thought, Economic Characters, and Economic Institutions*, Ann Arbor: University of Michigan Press, pp 307–317.

Perman R. (2012) *Hubris – How HBOS Wrecked the Best Bank in Britain,*, London: Birlinn, p 227.

Peston R. (2008*) Who Runs Britain? …And Who's to Blame for the Economic Mess We're in*, London: Hodder & Stoughton.

Petersen J. (1999) *Maps of Meaning – the Architecture of Belief*, London: Routledge.

Pettigrew A and Starkey K. (2016) The legitimacy and impact of business schools – Key issues and a research agenda, *Academy of Management Learning and Education*, 15(4):649–664.

Pfeffer J and Fong C. (2002) The end of business schools? Less success than meets the eye, *Academy of Management Learning and Education*, 1(1):78–95.

Pfeffer J and Fong C. (2004) The business school 'business' – Some lessons from the US experience, *Journal of Management Studies*, 41:1501–1520.

Pfeffer J. (2015) *Leadership BS: Fixing Workplaces and Careers One Truth at a Time*, New York: Harper Business.

Phipps KA. (2012) Spirituality and strategic leadership – The influence of spirituality on strategic decision-making, *Journal of Business Ethics*, 106(2):177–189.

Picciotto S. (2007) Constructing compliance: Game playing, tax law and the regulatory state, *Law & Policy*, 29(1):11–29.

Polman P and Winston A. (2021) *Net Positive – How Companies Can Thrive by Giving More Than They Take*, Boston: Harvard Business Review Press.

Pope F. (2015) *Laudato Si' – On Care for Our Common Home*, Vatican City: Vatican Press, p 179.

Poros M. (2011) *Modern Migrants – Gujarati Indian Networks in New York & London*, Redwood City: Stanford University Press, p 221.

Potter W. (2010) *Deadly Spin: An Insurance Company Insider Speaks Out on How Corporate PR Is Killing Health Care and Deceiving Americans*, London: Bloomsbury Press.

Power M. (2007) *Organised Uncertainty – Designing a World of Risk Management*, Oxford: Oxford University Press.

Power M. (2009) The risk management of nothing, *Accounting, Organisations and Society*, 34:849–855.

PRA (2015a) *The failure of HBOS plc*, A Report by the Financial Conduct Authority and the Prudential Regulatory Authority, UK; PRA and FCA, November 2015.

PRA (2015b) *Report into the FSA's enforcement actions following the failure of HBOS*, Andrew Green QC, Published by PRA and FCA, November 2015.

PRA (2015c) *Oral Evidence – Independent review of the report into the failure of HBOS*, House of Commons, Treasury Committee, HC654.

Prakash O. (2004) The Indian maritime merchant, 1500-1800, *Journal of the Economic and Social History of the Orient*, 47(3):435–457.

Prasad M. (2012) *The Land of too Much: American Abundance and the Paradox of Poverty*, Cambridge: Harvard University Press.

Prieg L and Greenham T. (2012) *Cooperative Banks – International Evidence*, London: New Economics Foundation, p 30.

Pruzan P and Mikkelsen K. (2007) *Leading With Wisdom – Spiritual-Based Leadership in Business*, London: Routledge.

Rajan R and Zingales L. (2003) *Saving Capitalism from the Capitalists*, New York: Crown Business.

Rajan R. (2019) *The Third Pillar – How Markets and the State Leave the Community Behind*, New York: Penguin Press.

Rebele J and Pierre ES. (2015) Stagnation in accounting education research, *Journal of Accounting Education*, 33:128–137.

Redding S. (1990) *The Spirit of Chinese Capitalism*, Berlin: De Gruyter.

Reinhard C and Rogoff K. (2011) *This Time Is Different – Eight Centuries of Financial Folly*, Princeton, NJ: Princeton University Press.

Rosenthal M. (1986) *The Character Factory – Baden Powell and the Origins of the Boy Scouts Movement*, New York: Collins Publishers.

Ross S, Westerfield R and Jordan B. (2012) *Fundamentals of Corporate Finance*, 9th Edition, New York: McGraw-Hill International.

Sacks J. (1990) *The Persistence of Faith*, BBC Reith Lectures, www.bbc.co.uk.

Sacks J. (2003) *The Dignity of Difference – How to Avoid the Clash of Civilisations*, London: Continuum Books.

Sacks J. (2010) *The Persistence of Faith: Religion, Morality and Society in a Secular Age (the BBC Reith Lectures)*, London: Continuum.

Said E. (1993) *BBC Reith Lectures 1993: Representations of the Intellectual*, London: British Broadcasting Corporation.

Said E. (1994) *Culture and Imperialism*, London: Vintage Books.

Sama L and Shoaf V. (2008) Ethical leadership for the professions – Fostering a moral community, *Journal of Business Ethics*, 78:39–46.

Sandel Michael J. (2012) *What Money Can't Buy: The Moral Limits of Markets*, London: Penguin.

Santoro M and Strauss R. (2013) *Wall Street Values*, New York: Cambridge University Press.

Sassen S. (2001) *The Global City – New York, London, Tokyo*, Princeton: Princeton University Press.

Sassen S. (2012), *Cities in a World Economy'*, 4th Edition, California: Pine Forge Press.

Saunders A and Cornett M. (2014) *Financial Institutions Management – A Risk Management Approach*, 8th Edition, New York: McGraw-Hill.

Sayer A. (2016) Moral economy, unearned income and legalized corruption, pp44–56, in Whyte and Wiegratz (2016) *op cit.*

Sedgmore L. (2021) *Goddess Luminary Leadership Wheel – A Post-Patriarchal Paradigm*, Winchester: John Hunt Publishing.

Seto-Pamies D and Papaoikonomou E. (2016) A multi-level perspective for the integration of ethics, corporate social responsibility and sustainability (ECSRS) in management education, *Journal of Business Ethics*, 136:523–538.

Shafak E. (2017) *The revolutionary power of diverse thought*, www.ted.com.

Shah A and Baker R. (2015) *Defining Financial Risk*, Working Paper, www.academia.edu.

Shah A and Rankin A. (2017) *Jainism and Ethical Finance*, London: Routledge.

Shah A and Sikka P. (2015) HBOS report does little to tackle systemic problems, *The Conversation*, 20th November.

Shah A. (1995) Creative accounting: Accounting policy choice – The case of financial instruments, *European Accounting Review*, 4(2):397–399.

Shah A. (1996a) Creative compliance in financial reporting, *Accounting, Organisations and Society*, 21(1):23–39.

Shah A. (1996b) Regulating derivatives: Operator error or system failure, *Journal of Financial Regulation and Compliance*, 4(1):17–35.

Shah A. (1996c) International bank regulation – Objectives and outcomes, *Journal of International Banking and Financial Law*, 11(6):255–258.

Shah A. (1996d) The credit rating of banks, *Journal of International Banking and Financial Law*, 11(8):361–365.

Shah A. (1996f) Why capital adequacy regulation for banks? *Journal of Financial Regulation and Compliance*, 4(3):278–291.

Shah A. (1997a) Analysing systemic risk in banking and financial markets, *Journal of Financial Regulation and Compliance*, 5(1):37–48.

Shah A. (1997b) Regulatory arbitrage through financial innovation, *Accounting, Auditing and Accountability Journal*, 10(1):85–104.

Shah A. (2007) *Celebrating Diversity – How to Enjoy, Respect and Benefit from Great Coloured Britain*, Rattlesden: Kevin Mayhew Publisher, p 163.

Shah A. (2012) *Boardroom Diversity – The Opportunity*, London: MAZARS.

Shah A. (2014) Drugs and the City: An open secret, so why no testing? www.theconversation.com.

Shah A. (2014) Financial literacy is shockingly low and the Academy must do more. The Conversation, www.theconversation.com.

Shah A. (2015a), The Chemistry of Audit Failure – A Case Study of KPMG, Working Paper, www.academia.edu.

Shah A. (2015b) Systemic Regulatory Arbitrage – A Case Study of KPMG, Working Paper, www.academia.edu.

Shah A. (2016) Q. What did Universities learn from the Financial Crash? A. Nothing', *The Guardian*, www.guardian.co.uk.

Shah A. (2018a) *The Politics of Risk, Audit and Regulation – A Case Study of HBOS*, London: Routledge.

Shah A. (2018b) *Reinventing Accounting and Finance Education – For a Caring, Inclusive and Sustainable Planet*, London: Routledge, p 105.

Shah A. (2020) *Aparigraha: Jain Theory and Practice of Finance*, www.academia.edu.

Shah A. (2022) Reform lessons from investigative journalism – Review essay of 'beancounters' by Richard Brooks, *British Accounting Review*, 54:101069.

Sharma B. (2019) *The Corner Shop – Shopkeepers, the Sharmas and the Making of Modern Britain*, London: Hodder & Stoughton.

Shaw E. (2012) New Labour's Faustian pact? *British Politics*, 7(3): 224–249.

Shaxson N. (2007) *Poisoned Wells: The Dirty Politics of African Oil*, New York: Palgrave Macmillan.

Shaxson N. (2012) *Treasure Islands – Tax Havens and the Men Who Stole the World*, London: Vintage Books, p 332.

Shaxson N. (2018) *The Finance Curse – How Global Finance is making us all Poorer*, New York: Grove Atlantic.

Shefrin H. (2000) *Beyond Greed and Fear: Understanding Behavioural Finance and the Psychology of Investing*, Boston: Harvard Business School Press.

Shephard K. (2015) *Higher Education for Sustainable Development*, London: Palgrave Macmillan.

Shiller RJ. (2012) *Finance and the Good Society*, Princeton: Princeton University Press.

Sikka P and Wilmott H. (1995) The power of 'Independence': Defending and extending the jurisdiction of accounting in the United Kingdom, *Accounting, Organisations and Society*, 20(6):547–581.

Sikka P, Filling S and Liew P. (2009) The audit crunch: Reforming auditing, *Managerial Auditing Journal*, 24(2):135–155.

Sikka P, Haslam C, Cooper C et al (2018) *Reforming the Auditing Industry*, London: Labour Party, p 169.

Sikka P, Wilmott H and Puxty T. (1995) The mountains are still there – Accounting academics and the bearings of intellectuals, *Accounting, Auditing & Accountability Journal*, 8(3):113–140.

Sikka P. (2008) Enterprise culture and accountancy firms: New masters of the universe, *Accounting, Auditing and Accountability Journal*, 21(2):268–295.

Sikka P. (2008a) Globalization and its discontents: Accounting firms buy limited liability partnership legislation in jersey, *Accounting, Auditing & Accountability Journal*, 21(3):398–426.

Sikka P. (2009) Financial crisis and the silence of the auditors, *Accounting, Organisations and Society*, 34:868–873.

Sikka P. (2015) The hand of accountancy and accounting firms in deepening income and wealth inequalities and the economic crisis: Some evidence, *Critical Perspectives on Accounting*, 30:46–62.

Sikombe S and Phiri M. (2019) Exploring tacit knowledge transfer and innovation capabilities within the buyer–supplier collaboration: A literature review, *Cogent Business & Management*, 6(1):23.

Simmel G. (1978) *The Philosophy of Money*, London: Routledge.

Simms A. (2007) *Tescopoly – How One Shop Came Out on Top and Why It Matters*, London: Constable & Robinson, p 372.

Soros G. (1998) *The Crisis of Global Capitalism*, Boston: Little Brown & Co.

Stein M. (2011) A Culture of Mania – A Psychoanalytic View of the Incubation of the 2008 Credit Crisis, In *Psychoanalytic Essays on Power and Vulnerability*, London: Routledge, pp 173–186.

Stiglitz JE. (2019) *People, Power and Profits: Progressive Capitalism for an Age of Discontent*, Bristol: Allen Lane.

Strange S. (1986) *Casino Capitalism*, Oxford: Basil Blackwell.

Subcommittee on Investigations. (2011) *Wall Street and the Financial Crisis: Anatomy of a Financial Collapse*, Washington, DC: Unites States Senate Permanent Committee on Investigations.

Sweet E, Nandi A, Adam EK and McDade TW. (2013) The high price of debt: Household financial debt and its impact on mental and physical health, *Social Science & Medicine*, 91:94–100.

Taibbi M. (2009) The Great American Bubble Machine, *Rolling Stone*, July 9.

Taibbi M. (2014) The Vampire Squid Strikes Again – The Mega Banks' Most Devious Scam Yet, *The Rolling Stone*, 12th February.

Tax Justice Network. (2015) *The Greatest Invention – Tax and the Campaign for a Just Society*, Margate: Commonwealth Publishing.

Tett G. (2010) *Fool's Gold – How unrestrained greed corrupted a dream, shattered global markets and unleashed a catastrophe*, London: Abacus Books, p 356.

Tett G. (2015) *The Silo Effect: The Peril of Expertise and the Promise of Breaking Down Barriers*, New York: Simon & Shuster.

Tett G. (2021) *Anthro-Vision: How Anthropology Can Explain Business and Life*, New York: Random House Business, p 304.

Thaler RH. (2013) *Misbehaving – The Making of Behavioural Economics*, New York: Norton & Co.

Tharoor S. (2016) *Inglorious Empire – What the British Did to India*, London: Penguin Books.

Thornburg S and Roberts R. (2008) Money, politics and the regulation of public accounting services: Evidence from the Sarbanes-Oxley Act of 2002, *Accounting, Organisations and Society*, 33(2–3):229–248.

Timberg T. (2014) *The Marwaris – From Jagat Seth to the Birlas*, Delhi: Penguin Random House India, p 184.

Toffler BL. (2003) *Final Accounting: Ambition, Greed and the Fall of Arthur Andersen*, New York: Broadway Books.

Tomasic R. (2011) The financial crisis and the haphazard pursuit of financial crime, *Journal of Financial Crime*, 18(1):7–31.

Tyrie et al (2013) *Changing Banking for Good*, House of Commons Treasury Committee Report HC175-11, London: Stationery Office.

Tyrie et al (2013a), 'An accident waiting to happen: The failure of HBOS', Parliamentary Commission on Banking Standards', Fourth Report of Session 2012-3, Volume I and Volume II, Published 4th April 2013, HC Paper 705.

Tyrie et al (2013b), Parliamentary Commission on Banking Standards Paper HC 175-III, House of Commons.

Ugoani J. (2014) Effect of tacit knowledge on business success among Igbo traders, *Management and Administrative Sciences Review*, 3(1):120–128.

Unerman J, Bebbington J and ODwyer B. (2007) *Sustainaibility Accounting and Accountability*, Oxfordshire: Routledge.

United Nations. (2015) *Sustainable Development Goals*, https://sdgs.un.org/goals.

Vitali S, Glattfelder JB and Battiston S. (2011) The network of global corporate control, *PLoS One*, 6(10):e25995.

Vollmer H, Mennicken A and Preda A. (2009) Tracking the numbers: Across accounting, finance, organisations and markets, *Accounting, Organisations and Society*, 34:619–637.

Way C. (2005) Political insecurity and the diffusion of financial market regulation, annals, *American Academy of Political and Social Science*, 598: 125–144.

Weintraub ER. (2014) MIT's openness to Jewish economists, *History of Political Economy*, 46:45–59.

West B. (2003) *Professionalism and Accounting Rules*, Oxford: Routledge.

Whyte D and Wiegratz J Eds. (2016) *Neoliberalism and the Moral Economy of Fraud*, London: Routledge.

Whyte D. (2020) *Ecocide – Kill the Corporation before It Kills Us*, Manchester: Manchester University Press, p 220.

Winder R. (2004) *Bloody Foreigners – The Story of Immigration to Britain*, London: Abacus Books, p 544.

Zeff S. (2003) How the US accounting profession got where it is today: Part 2, *Accounting Horizons*, 17(4):267–286.

Zingales L. (2015) Presidential address: Does finance benefit society, *Journal of Finance*, 70(4):1327–1363.

Zwan N. (2014) Making sense of financialisation, *Socio-Economic Review*, 12:99–129.

INDEX

Note: Page references with "n" denotes endnotes.